Motivating Your Secondary Class

Motivating Your Secondary Class

Maurice Galton
with
Susan Steward, Linda Hargreaves,
Charlotte Page and Tony Pell

Los Angeles | London | New Delhi
Singapore | Washington DC

First published 2009

SAGE Publications Ltd
1 Oliver's Yard
55 City Road
London EC1Y 1SP

SAGE Publications Inc.
2455 Teller Road
Thousand Oaks, California 91320

SAGE Publications India Pvt Ltd
B 1/I 1 Mohan Cooperative Industrial Area
Mathura Road
New Delhi 110 044

SAGE Publications Asia-Pacific Pte Ltd
33 Pekin Street #02-01
Far East Square
Singapore 048763

Library of Congress Control Number: 2008938529

British Library Cataloguing in Publication data

A catalogue record for this book is available from the British Library

ISBN 978-1-84787-259-3
ISBN 978-1-84787-260-9(pbk)

Typeset by C&M Digitals (P) Ltd, Chennai, India
Printed in Great Britain by the MPG Books Group
Printed on paper from sustainable resources

Contents

List of Figures

List of Tables

Introduction: Motivating Pupils in the Secondary Classroom

This book seeks to address issues that for the most part do not impact on the public debate about the success or otherwise of the nation's secondary schools. In a system where the quality of a school is mainly judged by its performance on national tests, little heed is paid to the older, more experienced teachers who argue that it is the current curriculum, and all that goes with it, that has a demotivating effect on pupils' willingness to learn, and that this situation has worsened over the last decade. Such strictures are generally viewed by critics of the present state system of schooling as excuses for poor teaching.

Rather than take the view that success in examinations and tests is sufficient motivation in itself, we would argue that in today's schools pupils, while recognizing that they need to do well academically in order to improve their life chances, nevertheless engage with the curriculum with little enthusiasm. This attitude to learning can have powerful negative effects on teachers, since when they attempt to get their pupils to use their new-found knowledge to extend their understanding of a topic, pupils are apt to ask, 'Is this on the syllabus? Do I need it to get the required grade?'. When the answer to both questions is 'No', then pupils often show little enthusiasm for undertaking further work. Anecdotal evidence from admission tutors at universities suggests that similar attitudes carry over into higher education.

Much of the research evidence on which these arguments are based has been carried out by the authors in studies undertaken in the Faculty of Education at the University of Cambridge. These include several studies of transfer and a major study of group work, the SPRinG (Social Pedagogic Research into Group Work) Project which was part of a national initiative designed to focus on aspects of contemporary pedagogy in English classrooms. We acknowledge the help of the Economic and Social Research Council (ESRC) who funded much of this research but we also drew on support from the then Department for Education and Skills (DfES), the National Union of Teachers (NUT) and Creative Partnerships for funding other studies which provided relevant data.

Although the book is conceived as whole, rather than as an edited volume, various members of the research team at Cambridge have taken responsibility for individual chapters. As such, whenever future writers refer to specific content from the book we would suggest that the appropriate author should be cited. Thus the first chapter by Tony Pell mounts the case for the alternative thesis that at secondary level in particular, the poor performance of English pupils relative to students in other comparable countries is a direct consequence of the limited vision provided by the current Key Stage 3 curriculum and the restrictions placed upon classroom practitioner by the pressure to 'teach for the tests' so as to do well in the league tables. Having established the urgent case for reform, the following three chapters look at some key factors that might bring about improvements in pupil motivation. In Chapter 2 we focus on the transfer of pupils from primary into secondary school arguing that these first impressions largely determine later attitudes. In Chapter 3 a case for the increased use of group work rather than whole-class instruction is put forward, not only on the grounds that pupils prefer to work collaboratively but also because there is evidence that when measures of attainment require pupils to demonstrate understanding and a capacity for problem solving rather than memorization, pupils do better in groups.

Chapter 4 looks at the aspect of communication, whether it takes place between pupils in groups or as part of class discussion with the teacher, and the links between talking and learning. Extended forms of discourse, so important in helping pupils to think critically, also have a major influence on motivation. This is because when the class engages in prolonged discussion it signifies a different relationship between the teacher and the pupils; one where both are co-learners, in contrast to the Government's preference for whole-class interactive teaching, delivered at pace, where the inference is that the teacher (because s/he is more knowledgeable) retains control of the learning. Chapter 5 then looks at the way in which various school cultures, particularly those of the core subject disciplines can either hinder or enhance cooperation in the classroom, while in Chapter 6 we examine case studies of teachers who have managed to resist the current trend and maintain high levels of pupil motivation. In the final chapter we look at the comprehensive school as an organization and suggest ways in which the system should change to make the teachers' task of sustaining pupil motivation easier. As an indication of what is possible, we look at the way that certain artists who work in schools set about the task of motivating pupils to renew their interest in learning.

We must acknowledge the help received from a number of colleagues who either collaborated with us on various research projects or provided wise advice. First, our gratitude goes to the late Jean Rudduck, who co-directed some of the transfer studies and also to the late Donald McIntyre whose observations and suggestions were always pointed and accurate. Both are sorely missed. We must thank John Gray and John MacBeath who were at various times co-directors of projects. Elsewhere, our appreciation goes to Peter Blatchford and Peter Kutnick who co-directed the SPRinG (Social Pedagogic Research into Group Work) Project. We must also acknowledge the crucial role played by Sally Roach, our secretary for several of these key projects. Not only did she sort out the idiosyncrasies of a manuscript where different members of the team were responsible for drafting various chapters, but acted as the all-important link between the researchers and the schools and proved an excellent sleuth when it came to ferreting out obscure references for the literature review.

Finally our thanks go to the schools and to the teachers who allowed us to sit in their classrooms and gave up time to collaborate with us on various aspects of the research. Their involvement and commitment demonstrate that the desire to improve the lives of their pupils is still the major reason why teachers are prepared to work such long hours and to subject themselves to such high levels of stress. Such teachers live for those 'magic moments' when 'the penny finally drops' and the pupil's puzzled countenance is replaced by a satisfied look of recognition. Sadly, because of the dominance of the present 'performance' culture in our schools such moments are not as frequent as they should be. If pupils are once more to learn to love learning for its own sake rather than for its economic potential, then we are going to need more of these magic moments and hopefully, this book can make a small contribution to bringing these about.

Maurice Galton

1

Is There a Crisis in the Lower Secondary School?

Tony Pell

This opening chapter presents evidence that Key Stage 3 schooling in England is under pressure despite the official view of increasing success and rising standards.

Attitudes in the three core subjects of English, mathematics and science are poor. International studies suggest that attainment and attitudes are both in decline. Motivation to school is much lower than motivation towards academic achievement, which questions the nature and delivery of the curriculum in the schools. While subject attitudes deteriorate over a typical year, attitudes to working in groups remain steady.

The decline in attitudes and performance in science is attributed to loss of specialist physics and chemistry teachers, the prevalence of a 'balanced' science and a target-driven test-oriented curriculum. Pupils now seem much more extroverted, which has implications for teaching strategy and the supply of physical scientists and engineers.

Classroom research with predominantly able and average ability pupils has identified four pupil types. Two of these are classified as 'anti-school'. In a sample of 39 classes, 13 classes had more than 50 per cent of pupils in this category. This finding alone begs serious questions about existing pedagogy.

All governments are fond of claiming that it is their reforms that have transformed the educational scene for the better, and the present Government is no exception to this rule. When, as in the present case, the main criterion for success is largely to be determined by a school's performance on public examinations some important questions emerge. Is it wise to judge schools on this basis? Are the measures used an accurate reflection of pupils' attainment? How far should one be more concerned with the student's general wellbeing where the World Health Organization's 2001–2 survey of *Health Behaviours in School–aged Children* (HBSC) shows that the decline among UK pupils is steeper than in most other countries. Is this decline exacerbated by the present 'performance culture'? If so what can schools do about it without falling foul of the inspectorate? These are some of the issues this book seeks to address. In this first chapter we look at several sources of evidence in an attempt to provide a more 'rounded' viewpoint than presented in 'official' government documents and reports.

In a survey of the professional lives of working secondary teachers, MacBeath and Galton (2004) found that the issue of greatest concern was poor pupil behaviour. An increasing amount of time is spent dealing with the behaviour problem, the sources of which the authors believe are to be found in today's challenging social context, the inability of many parents to cope and the nature of the curriculum. Behaviour problems, which are particularly acute in mathematics and science, apply a continuous pressure on teachers 'to maintain control'. As a consequence, the quality of teaching delivered and hence learning acquired suffers. Ofsted (2005) reports that the percentage of inspected, secondary schools failing to reach its 'good or better' behaviour criterion increased from 24 per cent in 1996–7 to 32 per cent in 2004–5. The most common form of pupil misbehaviour, according to Ofsted, is the low-level disruption of lessons, which hinders teaching and is a persistent stress factor. In recommending a flexible curriculum to deal with challenging behaviour, Ofsted finds that few schools attempt this with the Key Stage 3 strategy unlike at Key Stage 4. As the most recent study by Galton and MacBeath (2008) shows, teachers revisited three years on, feel that the disaffection problems among Key Stage 3 pupils are increasing.

A measure of disaffection with school is provided by the rate of truancy. The Government has been coordinating the regular 'truancy sweeps' conducted by around 90 per cent of Local Education Authorities in England. Children found at large in the community when they should have been attending school have been stopped and questioned. Data collected from these 'sweeps' are readily available from 2002 to 2006 (DCSF, 2008a). From the data, it is possible to calculate the percentage of children truanting from secondary school with no valid reason for absence. Figure 1.1 shows the year-on-year rise of secondary truanting. Given the demonstrated value of the 'sweeps', the Government's decision to end its coordinating role after publishing the data for 2006 would appear questionable.

It has been argued that schooling as currently presented to youngsters is so heavily constricted by the National Curriculum introduced in the late 1980s

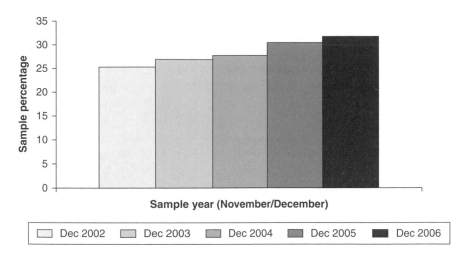

Figure 1.1 Secondary truancy rates as a percentage of 'sweep' sample over five years

and its associated testing programme (Standard Assessment Tasks or SATs) for all pupils at the ages of 7, 11 and 14 years, that teachers have found it necessary to adopt a minimalist approach to education not least because of the 'high-stakes' involved in the competitive 'league-table' world (Macbeath and Galton, 2004; Galton and MacBeath, 2008). In a 42-country international survey of pupil engagement for the OECD, Willms (2003) found that 15-year-old pupils in the UK reported higher classroom pressure levels than anywhere else apart from Iceland. A study for the World Health Organization (Currie et al., 2008) confirms these above-average pressures, which are particularly strong for girls.

Teachers themselves have suffered professionally within this pressurised environment. Teachers' ratings of their status in society over six, specific time-points has fallen alarmingly as is shown in Figure 1.2 (Hargreaves et al., 2007), although the fall has now 'bottomed out'. This 'status' research shows that teachers are possibly becoming more compliant with the changes required of them as three years after the initial survey of 2003 scores are not quite so negative (below 3.0 on a 5-point scale). Teachers' loss of autonomy in having to carry out mandated curricula, which has been called professional 'intensification', has contributed to many of the more creative teachers leaving the schools, which has only reinforced the difficulties of those remaining. By both directing curriculum content and assessing the cognitive outcomes, the Government has become the sole arbiter of attainment 'standards' which, unsurprisingly, have shown for the most part year-on-year improvements. Yet when external criteria are applied, international measures show a decline in the attainment levels of students relative to those from other countries, and in some instances the decline is not just relative but is in raw scores (Martin et al., 2004; OECD, 2007).

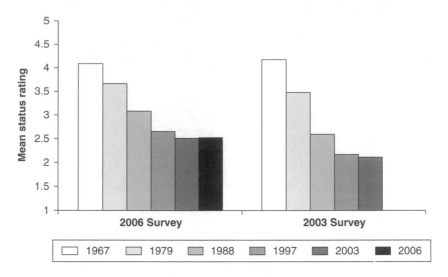

Figure 1.2   Decline in teacher status ratings from two surveys

Have the National Strategies resulted in improved performance?

For example, the Progress in International Reading Literacy Study (PIRLS) 2006 evaluation of reading comprehension (Mullis et al., 2007) lists 45 countries and provinces at the level of Grade 4 (Year 5 in England). England appears in 19th position on the list, although it is one of the five countries actually testing after five years schooling rather than four. Significantly fewer English pupils reached the PIRLS 'advanced international bench mark' in 2006 than did so in 2001 (respective figures are 15 and 20%). Similarly, the drop in the percentage of English pupils reaching the 'high international benchmark' in 2006 (48%) also declined significantly from 54 per cent in 2001. In 2006, England was one of the six countries, also including The Netherlands and Sweden, which recorded significant losses in reading comprehension achievement since 2001. The decline has affected girls as well as boys and is applicable to reading for information as well as literacy. So here is international evidence that reading comprehension 'standards' are most unlikely to be rising and at the very best are unchanged, taking into account sampling problems in England in the 2001 round (House of Commons, 2008b).

A second international reading study is PISA (Programme for International Student Assessment) 2006, which is part of a regular series conducted by the OECD (Bradshaw et al., 2007). After testing 15 year-olds from 57 countries, England was given a significant ranking of eighth. Girls scored higher than boys in all countries, but in England the gender gap was smaller than most. Earlier official PISA reports for 2000 and 2003 omitted data from the UK and England specifically, because of a failure to meet sampling requirements, but the Department for Education and Skills did report on the data collected in 2000 for England alone (Gill et al., 2002) and a later OECD Summary Report placed the UK and England in seventh place in the list of 27 OECD countries with a score of 523 (standard error 3.0) for reading literacy (OECD, 2004a). Using the same reading tests in 2003, the score for the UK is deduced to be 512 (standard error 3.7; OECD, 2004b), which is a significant fall. By 2006, scores had dropped considerably again to 496 for England and 495 for the UK placing England/UK in 13th place in the list of 29 OECD countries (Bradshaw et al., 2007). Here, then, this time from the secondary stage, is news of falling reading literacy and of England losing ground to other countries.

If we look at what is available as evidence within England, the problem to which we return time and time again is that the same authority that is responsible for the curriculum and its development is also responsible for its evaluation, so it is in the interests of this authority to show itself in the best light possible. Thus, Key Stage 3 results for English do not show up the same falling 'standards' for reading at the international level but rather the reverse. For example, the recently published *Getting Back on Track* (DCSF, 2007) refers to the progressive improvement in Key Stage 3 English since 1997 with what is a 30 per cent increase in those achieving Level 5. This is not to say that government policy makers are complacent. *Getting Back on Track* looked at the 5 per cent of pupils who either do not progress from the nationally defined standard in English at Key Stage 2, which is Level 4, and fail to reach the standard (Level 5) at Key Stage 3, or having achieved Level 5 or 6 at Key Stage 2 fall back to Level 4 at Key Stage 3. The recommendations address the key areas of reading and punctuation, with check lists for both pupils and teachers including the opportunity to discuss their reading with others and letting their peers review their punctuation. It is recommended that these activities should be interesting and enjoyable.

Turning to attainment in mathematics, the PISA 2000 study of learning and achievement of 15 year-olds showed England occupying eighth place in the list of 27 OECD countries with a score of 529 (standard error 2.9; OECD, 2004a). By 2006 the raw score had dropped to 495 (standard error 2.5) with 18 other countries recording significantly higher mean scores (Bradshaw et al., 2007). Boys did better than girls and the overall spread of marks was less than in science, for example. The difficulties experienced in the UK in meeting the sample requirements for these international studies once more means that there are no PISA mathematics scores available in 2003 for an intermediate comparison.

In the second international study, the Trends in International Mathematics and Science Study (TIMSS) evaluation of achievement in mathematics across 49 countries at Grade 8 (Year 9 in England) (Mullis et al., 2004, 2005) shows England in 18th equal place in 2003. This puts England behind most of the countries of the Pacific Rim. The performance of boys and girls is identical this time in being above the international average. English pupils, like those in Australasia and Scandinavia, tend to be better at mathematical reasoning than mathematical knowledge. Comparing achievement in 2003 with TIMSS

1995 and TIMSS 1999 shows no change, which is typical of most other countries over this period. An important point, almost always overlooked when looking at the TIMSS tables, is that England together with Scotland and New Zealand are virtually alone in starting formal schooling at 5 years, while more than 90 per cent of the participating countires have a starting date one year later (Joncas, 2008). This means that puplis from England have had an extra year's schooling when taking the TIMSS tests. This effect might be expected to be greatest with the youngest pupils and contributes to a seventh-place position in the TIMSS Grade 4 maths table in the recently published data for 2007 (Mullis et al., 2008). The placing of England in seventh position in the latest TIMSS Grade 8 mathematics table has led to some excitement in government circles and the media (Mansell, 2008b), however the placings rely on scores with sizeable standard errors, so statistically the scores of 2007 do not differ significantly from those of 2003.

So the international results, taken together, at the best interpretation point to little change and to a fall in mathematics performance at the worst. But again the government statistics for England and Wales tend to convey upwards progression at Key Stage 3 (Year 9) as the years go by. For example, *Getting Back on Track* (DCSF, 2007) draws attention to the official improvement in the proportion of the age group achieving Level 5 in mathematics from 60 per cent in 1997 to 77 per cent in 2006.

In terms of science attainment, the TIMSS studies show that English Year 9 students compare favourably with other countries, where student have one year less schooling. Attainment is stable, even if attitudes to science are dropping. Science scores for English students are high enough to occupy seventh place in the list of countries in 2003, seventh in 1999 and eighth in 1995. The most recently published figures are for 2007 (Martin et al., 2008) and appear to give England a comfortable rating of fifth, just behind four countries of the Pacific Rim. Taking into account the error in the scores, however, England becomes one of six countries where the statistical overlap places the countries equally in a shared band from places 5 to 10.

Science attainment measured by PISA 2006 showed seven countries with significantly higher scores than the UK/England (Bradshaw et al., 2007; OECD, 2007). The spread of achievement of UK science students, though, is particularly large, with only New Zealand and Israel showing a wider range. As in most other countries, boys are better than girls at explaining phenomena in scientific terms. In terms of overall raw scores in 2006, the UK occupies 14th place, having fallen from 4th in 2000 (Gill et al., 2002), and has now been overtaken by Canada, New Zealand, Australia and Germany. Technical problems with the UK sampling in 2003 caused PISA to omit UK data from international comparisons for that survey (OECD, 2004b) but even so there is still evidence that UK performance has been falling since 2000.

Just as in mathematics, the findings from the two international surveys are mutually supportive in science only in so far as ruling out rising achievement levels. The differences in the results from the two surveys appear to lie in the nature of the test questions. Those of the PISA survey require a high level of reading comprehension, while those of TIMSS more obviously and directly test knowledge, understanding and the application of scientific concepts and principles. Given that PISA has reported a significant fall in reading comprehension for UK/English pupils, the discrepancy between the two international studies might be explained by the reading comprehension in 2006 being less likely to unravel the intricacies of the questions despite the level of scientific understanding remaining unchanged.

The view on science attainment from within England and Wales in the *Getting Back on Track* Report (DCSF, 2007) is unsurprisingly much more positive with data presented to illustrate an apparently clear improvement at Key Stage 3 with the 59 per cent achieving the National Curriculum defined Level 5 in 1998 becoming 72 per cent in 2006. Nevertheless, the report does reveal that science creates more problems for 'failing' students than do either English or mathematics. Not only do a greater proportion of Key Stage 3 students (as many as 7%) find that they are still marooned at Level 4, but a further 1 per cent actually go back one or more levels from those achieved at Key Stage 2 to subside to Level 4 at Key Stage 3. These 'failing' or slow-learning pupils, characteristically, liked being active, learning through practical experiments and working in groups. In reality, these pupils spent most of the lesson time copying from textbooks or the blackboard. They have poor reading comprehension and, needless to say, find the subject hard. Among the recommendations of this report are the need to provide more investigatory practical work and to provide learning in groups and pairs, where the pupils can discuss ideas and understanding and demonstrate their scientific skills.

There is psychological evidence from research that the cognitive levels at which English pupils operate today have declined over the last 30 years. Using Science Reasoning Tasks developed in the 1970s (Shayer and Adey, 1981), Shayer (2008) has recently shown that a sample of 800 English 14 year-olds have the higher-level cognitive thinking skills of the 12 year-olds of 1976. Shayer atributes this decline to the introduction of the National Curriculum testing and target setting; passive multi-channel TV viewing, and especially for boys, much less time spent playing with gadgets and other mechanisms. Shayer's latest study follows an earlier one (Shayer, 2006) that found that the cognitive abilities of 11 year-olds in handling the physics of mass, weight and density has shown a general decline since 1975 with present-day youngsters up to three years behind those of 30 years ago. Indirect evidence to support Shayer's findings comes from the failed attempt of the Assessment and Qualifications Alliance (AQA), the UK's biggest examinations board, to maintain standards in science, which was resisted by the government's examinations regulation department, Ofqual (Mansell, 2008a). To add further weight to the hypothesis of a decline in levels of intellectual achievement, the Royal Society of Chemistry (RSC) has pointed to the lack of rigour in science testing, teaching to the test and a dramatic decline in school standards for the failure of today's 16 year-olds when faced with exam papers from 40 years ago (RSC, 2008a). The RSC suggests that the illusion of rising standards in England resulted from easier tests and better examination preparation (RSC, 2008b).

The evidence of rising achievement levels of pupils in England, which is questioned by the findings from PISA and TIMSS and the recent research evidence, rests upon the reliability and especially the validity of the Government's Standard Assessment Tasks (SATs). The impact of these tests of English, mathematics and science in England has been recently thoroughly reviewed by a House of Commons Committee (House of Commons, 2008a). The Report Summary, in pointing out the negative effect of 'teaching to the test', refers to the type of English, mathematics and science now being taught in the schools as being not necessarily synonymous with education but rather a prerequisite of what can be conventionally tested. Thus, achievement of prescribed targets might not be indicative of a deep understanding and wide breadth of learning in these subjects. A particular point is made about the research evidence for the superficiality of learning at Key Stage 2 (House of Commons, 2008a). This would seem to explain why SATs' scores can 'drive up standards' at the time of testing while conceptual, subject mastery at a deeper level proceeds in the opposite direction. This hypothesis has been supported at Key Stage 3 by Fairbrother (2008), who has shown that the science SATs do not test at the higher cognitive levels at all, thus weakening the base for later studies as well as 'giving a poor image of science'. Yet in a Government report the Office for Standards in Education (Ofsted, 2008) continues to support the claim of rising achievement in science at Key Stage 3. The House of Commons Committee Report, in calling for substantial reform in the testing system, goes on to say that the present multiple purpose use of SATs for both individual pupil and 'system' evaluation leads to some pupils being unprepared for employment and higher education, which is a powerful indictment of recent changes from our elected representatives. The rhetoric employed by the Goverment in defending its SATs testing programme now appears to have been exposed by its sudden reversal in policy, which will see the end of compulsory testing of 14 year-olds at Key Stage 3 although teacher assessments will continued (DCSF, 2008b).

In the remainder of this chapter, therefore, the case will be made that despite the centrally driven changes in the curriculum of the last decade or two in England, which include Numeracy, Literacy and Key Stage 3 strategies among others, not only has attainment in the core subjects remained static or, in the worse interpretation, has fallen, but that the education it offers to Key Stage 3 pupils is failing to arrest declines in motivation and in attitudes, especially in the important core subjects of mathematics and science. Evidence will be drawn from recent attitudinal and motivational research carried out at the University of Cambridge, and from the deliberated findings of the Royal Society and a Select Committee of the House of Lords. The evidence will show how the personalities and motivational styles of English pupils have apparently altered in the last 30 years or so. Classrooms now contain far more extroverts than in days gone by. Pupils today seem to be more motivated by external factors such as getting good marks and getting a good job, and the concept of 'intrinsic motivation', that is, of wanting to know and understand for its own sake has virtually disappeared. In addition, by using a technique known as 'cluster analysis', we have begun to identify a range of stereotypical pupils who respond and achieve in characteristic ways to the learning on offer.

Collecting pupil data on motivation, personality and subject attitudes

Questionnaires can be used to gather information about attitudes. This technique has been used widely to monitor how students feel about their school subjects, their motivation and their personality. At Cambridge, two recent projects (Galton et al., 2003; Pell et al., 2007) have produced a wealth of information from the Key Stage 3 years. Typical questionnaires used in these projects appear in Appendix A. Data were collected from samples of several hundred to several thousand pupils. After statistical analysis, various factors were identified such as *liking mathematics* and *enjoyment of school*. Scores were then computed for each of these attitudes and dispositions and, referring to the response scales, average scores were expressed as a percentage of the maximum possible obtainable score, which might vary from 0 to 100 per cent. A score of 50 per cent represents a neutral attitude. Above 50 per cent the attitude or disposition is positive: below 50 per cent it is negative. Outcomes from the research are reported as charts for maximum clarity, but this approach does not readily present the random errors that are always present in measures of this kind. Just because one bar in a chart is taller than another one does not necessarily mean the two bars indicate different scores! When this difficulty is likely to arise, the commentary in the text will refer to the differences as being *significant* or not, as the case may be.

Measuring motivation in the classroom

The concept of motivation is somewhat dependent on one's starting point and, in terms of schooling, on the current context. For instance from theories of behaviour, motivation is seen as *intrinsic* to the act of learning, where satisfaction is gained from within the study itself. Ernest Rutherford's motivation to push back the boundaries of physics in the early 20th century, for example, was so powerful that he was contemptuous of other scientific disciplines and, according to Wikipedia (2008) reportedly once said that 'in science, there is only physics; all the rest is stamp collecting'. Alternatively, motivation is seen as *extrinsic*, which is a response to certain external demands such as learning to secure a specific job. In pursuing a task, *achievement* motivation is a drive for success by reaching a goal, which for some pupils might be further enhanced by *fear of failure* motivation if the goal is not reached.

A student's perception of his or her ability will thus determine the form of motivation to learning in a given situation. Students who feel that they can achieve through their own efforts will be displaying high levels of *mastery* motivation. These students will not be concerned about their progress in relation to others. Conversely, students who conceptualize their ability as fixed, use other more able students as reference points and become enveloped by thoughts of failure and develop task-avoidance strategies including *learned helplessness* and strong teacher dependence. Others with low mastery motivation will reject the values of school learning to varying degrees, becoming 'oppositionals' (Hargreaves, 1982) or the 'dossers and shirkers' of

Rudduck et al. (1996) and will see the other more successful learners as 'boffins'. The direction in which a learner will proceed in school will be governed to a degree by innate ability and motivation qualified by personality. Anxious students are particularly 'at risk' from fear of failure in a competitive, target-driven culture (Covington, 1992) and the more extroverted can well retreat to the 'security' of a peer-group culture which derides success as part, if not the whole, of the school experience (Marsh, 1989).

The current emphasis on performance in schools in the form of target setting, Standard Assessment Tasks and school performance 'league tables', all tend to inhibit the growth of mastery motivation and discourage intrinsic motivation. Where outcomes are rigidly prescribed, and where freedom to explore alternative approaches in seeking solutions to problems is severely restricted as a result, intrinsic motivation is not going to flourish (Brophy, 1999).

Pell et al. (2007) investigated the nature of motivation in the present-day classrooms of the lower secondary school. Questionnaires were assembled using items from existing instruments measuring *intrinsic-extrinsic* motivation and *mastery* motivation, supplemented by items arising from student interviews with the target groups of Years 7 to 9. These questionnaires were further tried out with other samples of student before being administered in a 'before and after' (pre-test/post-test) study over two school years. On the final administration, several additional 'anti-school' items were added. The actual items decided upon appear in Appendix A.

Two forms of motivation

An initial analysis of these questionnaires showed no sharp division into intrinsic and extrinsic motivation, but instead tended to distinguish classroom environments as being either *learning* or *performance* oriented (Watkins, 2003). The two motivation factors which appeared were (a) *achievement mastery* and (b) *academic satisfaction*. The former was measured by a scale of 5 items such as:

- Item 3. I am pretty confident in doing the tasks I am set.
- Item 5. I try to learn as much as I can.

Academic satisfaction motivation places the emphasis on performance and the satisfaction derived from doing outstandingly well. It is measured by a scale of 5 items such as:

- Item 4. I do my best to get the highest level in SATs.
- Item 10. I feel proud when I get good marks.

Academic satisfaction expresses a self-image very much in keeping with today's school climate. The full scales appear in Appendix A.

The two new scales, which showed stability when readministered after a short time period of a few weeks, show a transition from the classical *intrinsic-extrinsic* motivation to the drive to personal achievement (*mastery*) through

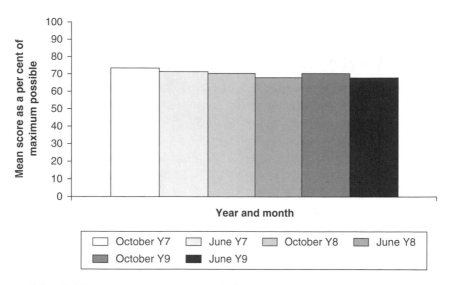

Figure 1.3   Achievement mastery motivation: Year 7 to Year 9

effort in the classroom and the need to get (*academic*) satisfaction by reaching external standards (pleasing parents and getting to university). While *academic satisfaction* is a form of *extrinsic* motivation, *achievement mastery* has shifted the *intrinsic* focus from the nature of the learned material to the prescribed task. According to this hypothesis, whether or not one finds a subject interesting has little or no effect on progress or achieving one's goals.

The pupil's view of ability determines the depth of *achievement mastery* motivation (Dweck, 1986). Only pupils with a strong belief in their own competence will be highly motivated. Such pupils will believe that hard work and extra effort will allow them to succeed. Contrast this with low-mastery motivation pupils, who see ability as fixed, which they can do little to alter, and who see the strong performance-oriented classroom of today with its regular assessment and target setting as a threat to their self-esteem. These pupils will seek support from their like-minded peer group and form the core of Hargreaves' 'oppositionals'.

Motivation in the lower and middle secondary years

Figure 1.3 shows *achievement mastery* motivation scores at the beginning and end of the school year for Years 7 through to 9. There are no differences between the boys' and girls' scores and these are not shown. Mean scores fall significantly with age.

Although mean scores drop significantly at the transition to Year 8, when comparing Figure 1.3 with the later subject attitude charts, it is clear that *achievement mastery* motivation holds up extremely well in the secondary school, while subject attitudes tend to be neutral to poor. This supports the hypothesis that subject attitudes are subsidiary to the stronger driving force of

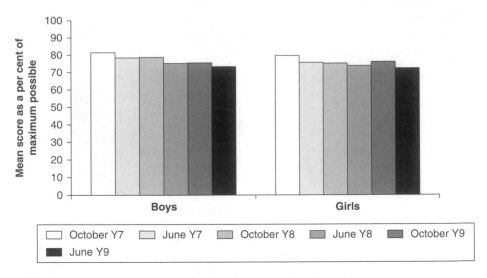

Figure 1.4   Academic satisfaction motivation: Year 7 to Year 9

mastery motivation. Our research at Cambridge shows that the correlation between attainment and *achievement mastery* motivation increases during the school year, especially for girls, suggesting that a motivation gap between the more and less able widens as the school year progresses.

Figure 1.4 shows *academic satisfaction* motivation scores at the beginning and end of the school year for Years 7 through to 9. For each age group, the boys' scores are significantly higher than the girls'. Mean scores fall significantly with age, but again, scores are very high compared to those for subject attitudes. Unlike *achievement mastery* motivation, being proud of what one is succeeding in at school is not restricted to the most able so the correlation of *academic satisfaction* motivation with attainment is very weak.

At the start of Year 7 the correlation between the two forms of motivation is 0.72 for boys and 0.70 for girls. By the end of Year 9, the correlation has dropped to 0.56 for boys and 0.63 for girls. This slight weakening of the association between the two forms of motivation as students move through the secondary school points to either *academic satisfaction* being achieved with lower levels of *achievement mastery* or high *achievement mastery* pupils showing less *academic satisfaction*. One interpretation of this is that the lower achievement mastery motivated pupils are becoming more reconciled with their position and are taking some satisfaction in what they are succeeding in. In the context of the general decline in motivation referred to in the opening part of this chapter, this interpretation is more doubtful than a second possibility. This is that the higher achievement mastery motivation pupils are becoming less enamoured by the extrinsic rewards that are part of academic satisfaction motivation. The second hypothesis fits more easily with the perception that academic success at school is of lessening significance by the end of Year 9 as the pupils attempt to come to terms with adolescence.

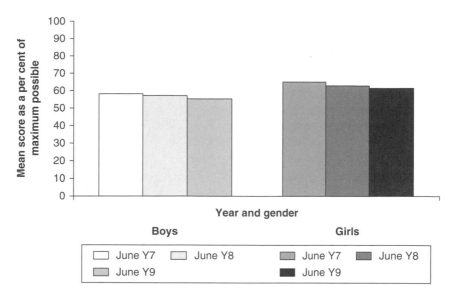

Figure 1.5 Pro-school motivation: Year 7 to Year 9

Motivation towards school

The evidence presented in the Introduction is that standards of behaviour in secondary schools are deteriorating. Supporting evidence comes from the measurement of attitudes to school by such studies as the ORACLE research into transfer into Year 7 over the period 1997–2004 (Galton et al.,1999a, 2003; Hargreaves and Galton 2002) and from the later secondary years by Berliner (2004), who reports that only 27 per cent of a sample of 1000 secondary pupils rated their overall school experience positively. Both of these studies found disturbing evidence that the higher attaining pupils might have the less positive attitudes about their experiences. Internationally, the outlook is not too good either. The recent World Health Organization study (Currie et al., 2008) places both boys and girls in England below average on their respective ranked scales of 41 countries, when asked whether school was well liked.

The negative effect of low motivation towards school was detected in the initial pre-testing in the Cambridge study of group work, which will be discussed in greater detail in Chapter 3. The 6 items for this scale arose from pupil interviews and the work of Rogers (1994) and Rudduck et al. (1996). The strongest items are:

- Item 11. I am often in trouble at school
- Item 13. I don't do much homework.

The scoring on this scale was arranged so that the final score was a measure of a pro-school attitude. The full scale appears in Appendix A.

Figure 1.5 shows the percentage scores on the scale. Girls are significantly more positive about school than are the boys. Mean scores appear to decrease with age,

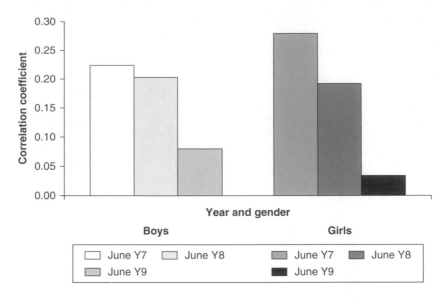

Figure 1.6   Correlation of pro-school motivation with attainment: Year 7 to Year 9

that is, older students become less positive about school, but in statistical terms the differences are not significant. What is of interest is that *motivation towards school* is less pronounced than either *achievement mastery* or *academic satisfaction* motivation. It is as if the students have to some degree separated their need for cognitive development from the institution that is charged with providing it.

Pro-school motivation correlates at around 0.5 with the other two forms, but the pro-school raw scores are much lower. In the Cambridge research, 22.9 per cent of 857 Years 7 to 9 pupils were classed as having negative attitudes to school (scoring below the mid-point of the scale). The proportions having negative *achievement mastery* and *academic satisfaction* motivation were just 6.4 and 4.2 per cent respectively. Of the 196 students with negative attitudes to school, 68.9 per cent had positive *achievement mastery* motivation and 81.6 per cent had positive *academic satisfaction* motivation.

Figure 1.6 shows that the correlation between pro-school motivation and teacher estimates of attainment decrease for both boys and girls as they get older. The correlations become insignificant in Year 9. This implies that the more able pupils become less positive towards school as they move up through the lower secondary school. However, this finding does need to be treated with caution because the teacher estimates of the pupils' ability may not always be accurate.

Subject attitudes in the lower secondary years: attitudes to English

Combining the results of both the transfer and group work projects, Figure 1.7 shows school attitudes to English for year groups from Year 6 to Year 9. Key items on the *Liking English* scale, which appears in full in Appendix A, are:

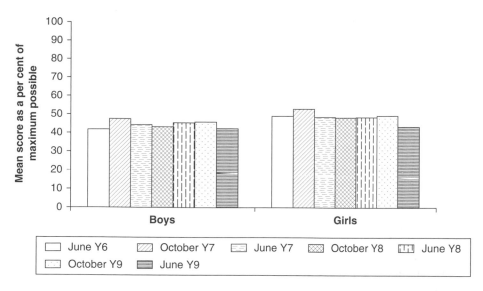

Figure 1.7 Liking English: Year 6 to Year 9

- Item 11. I always look forward to English lessons.
- Item 13. Learning English makes me think better.

Girls' attitudes are seen to be always more positive than boys'. The typical girl pupil just manages to display a positive liking for English after transfer to secondary school in Year 7, otherwise attitudes hover just below the neutral level (50% of the maximum possible). The average boy's liking of English remains in the negative half of the chart, although transfer to secondary school cause a slight positive surge, which is soon dissipated. By the end of Year 9, girls' attitude scores have subsided to the level of the boys, although over the three-year period the change in attitude in English is relatively small when compared with the changes in attitudes to maths and to science.

It is difficult to put the trends in attitudes to English in the wider context of the recent development of the National Curriculum and its associated changes or in the context of other international languages. The two major international studies of attainment, the PIRLS reading literacy evaluation (Mullis et al., 2007) and the PISA reading studies (Gill et al., 2002; Bradshaw et al., 2007), did make some secondary measures of attitudes to reading and reading literacy. The PIRLS study of primary pupils used four reading statements scored on a 4-point agreement/disagreement scale. Statements included 'I would be happy if someone gave me a book as a present' and 'I enjoy reading'. Pupils were then effectively assigned to positive, neutral or negative categories. Over all 40 countries and five Canadian provinces, the 2006 data show 49 per cent of pupils with positive and 8 per cent with negative attitudes. The corresponding figures for England are 40 and 15 per cent. Not only are English pupils' attitudes below the international average, England is one of the five countries where both the percentages have changed for the worse since 2001. When asked to rate their own reading ability, pupils in England were less confident than the average 'international' pupil. After drawing attention to the relationship of attitudes to reading and reading comprehension achievement, the authors of the PIRLS report (Mullis et al., 2007: 140) comment that this is a worrying trend: 'It may be a matter for concern that a greater number of participants had decreased percentages of students at the high (positive attitude) level, including ... England'.

For 15 year-olds, the PISA 2001 international study (OECD, 2004a) places the UK equal 19th and below average on a list of 27 OECD countries ranked according to reading engagement, which is a composite measure of attitude to reading, reading widely and reading for pleasure. There have been no other PISA evaluations of reading attitudes since 2001, but the results from PIRLS 2006 for the primary pupils suggest that the secondary situation is unlikely to have improved.

Our attitude results shows that English is hardly rated a popular subject by boys, with the mean score never even reaching a neutral level for Year 6 to Year 9 pupils. The attitudes of the girls are slightly more positive and actually cross the neutral line briefly upon transfer to secondary school in the Autumn term of Year 7. Even if the international evidence on attitudes is somewhat piecemeal it is reasonable to assume that attitudes to English in this country are not outstandingly high. Adding the evidence from Figure 1.7, which shows a progressive fall in attitude scores with age, questions need to be addressed about the nature of English being taught in our schools and what might be done to make it more enjoyable and interesting. At the very least, enjoying the subject more is worthwhile intrinsically, but more importantly, greater enjoyment leads to greater motivation to learn and to improved achievement as PIRLS and others have pointed out.

Subject attitudes in the lower secondary years: attitudes to mathematics

Again, by combining the results of several of the Cambridge projects, Figure 1.8 shows school attitudes to mathematics for year groups from Year 6 to Year 9. Key items on the *Liking mathematics* scale, which appears in full in Appendix A, are:

- Item 1. I like maths more than any other school subject.
- Item 3. I like doing maths projects.

There is plenty of evidence that mathematics has a polarizing effect on people. In its worst manifestation, this appears as a fear and dislike of the subject (Cockcroft, 1982). Mature adults training to be primary teachers, have reported being frightened and terrified by mathematics and according to Haylock (2001: 3) 'several recalled having nightmares' about the subject.

In comparison with English, one would expect pupils' attitudes to be even more negative and drop more rapidly as school experience lengthens.

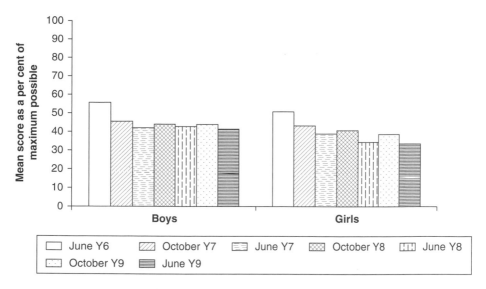

Figure 1.8 Liking mathematics: Year 6 to Year 9

Figure 1.8 shows this supposition is correct, but the sudden dip at transfer from primary to secondary school is perhaps surprising. The average boy or girl at the end of primary school in Year 6 seems to have a slight positive affection for mathematics, but a month after transfer attitudes show a sharp drop.

What is it about secondary mathematics in Year 7 that can cause such an abrupt change? Is it, as the next chapter dealing with transfer will argue, because the subject content and its teaching in the secondary school is very similar to the Year 6 curriculum in the primary school so pupils become bored? *Getting Back on Track* (DCSF, 2007) identifies the lack of discussion in pairs and groups and lack of enjoyment as two of the characteristics of the 2 per cent of Key Stage 3 pupils who become stuck at Level 4 in maths in the secondary school. But how true is it of the pupils in general that more pair or group work would improve outcomes in Year 7?

The TIMSS 2003 study (Mullis et al., 2004) reports that English pupils are much less likely to spend time on maths homework during the week. If such time is taken as a measure of motivation towards maths, then English students might be well below the international average on attitudes. Later the TIMSS 2003 report looks specifically at attitudes to reveal that the proportion of English Year 9 pupils in the highest 'liking/valuing maths' category fell significantly below the international average in 2003. Indeed, since 1995, the percentage of English pupils disagreeing with the statement, 'I enjoy learning mathematics' has increased from 20 to 47 per cent in comparison with a relatively static international level of 34 per cent. A similar disenchantment is recorded by English Year 5 pupils from 16 to 30 per cent. The latest TIMSS study of 2007 (Mullis et al., 2008) shows the deterioration in 'liking' mathematics even more starkly. In the 2007 Report, England occupies 35th position out of 59 countries on the Year 9 list. The English pupils show the largest fall of all the countries from the testing of 1999 and 1995. Despite this, boys in England have the highest self-confidence in learning mathematics of all the boys from the other countries. Perhaps this asks questions about the rigour of the current mathematics curriculum?

For mathematics, teachers' subject expertise does not seem to be such a strong factor as it can be, for example, in science. The National Foundation for Educational Research reports that around 24 per cent of secondary maths teachers are non-specialists, but, as the Mathematical Association has argued, it is the *way* mathematics is being taught rather than degree of subject knowledge possessed by teachers that is the main problem. According to the representatives of the Association, giving evidence to a House of Lords committee, 'the present system has elevated "teaching to the test" to a position that now biases all classroom activity towards the goals of maximum test results and achieving the governmental prescribed "standards"' (House of Lords, 2006: 157). Ofsted appears to support this view in lamenting the poor ability of students above Key Stage 3 level to apply the mathematical knowledge that is essential for further study (House of Commons, 2008a: 45).

Subject attitudes in the lower secondary years: attitudes to science

The combined attitudes to science results of several of the Cambridge projects are shown in Figure 1.9 for year groups from Year 6 to 9. Key items on the *Liking science* scale, which appears in full in Appendix A, are:

• Item 1. I like science more than any other school subject.
• Item 3. I should like to be given a science kit as a present.

In recent years governments, of whatever persuasion, have attached particular importance to the attainment and attitudes in science of our young people, because of the role of technology in our society and the need for national economic goals to be established on a vibrant and extensive bedrock of scientific manpower. The fact that all was not that it should be in science education was the rationale for an extensive enquiry under Professor Fred Dainton (1968) during the 1960s, which identified a 'swing away from science' in the schools. In the intervening years, success in arresting the 'swing away' has proved elusive. Despite the introduction of a core 'general science' into the curriculum for all from the primary school, the output from the school system of scientifically literate specialists has seen the closure of many university physics and chemistry departments. In those that remain and in the departments of engineering, typified by Mechanical Engineering at Imperial College, London, such is the poor quality of even the highest-grade students arriving from the schools that three-year degree courses are being expanded to four years to allow a first year to repair and supplement the learning from the schools (Paton, 2008).

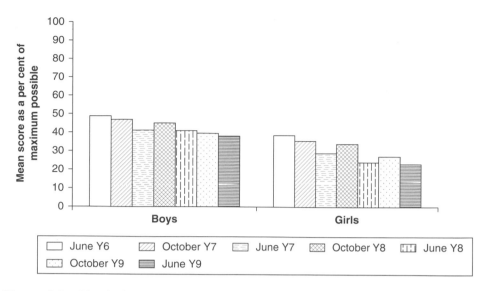

Figure 1.9   The decline in liking science: Year 6 to Year 9

The data from the various Cambridge studies show a worrying picture (Figure 1.9). At no time during a school life from the end of Year 6 to the end of Year 9 is the average 'liking science' score able to struggle out of the negative domain and even become neutral. The situation for the girls is particularly sad, especially as there has been so much research in this area and many initiatives undertaken (Kelly, 1981, 1987; Kelly et al., 1987; Opportunity '2000', 1996).

Internationally, the TIMSS evaluation of achievement and attitudes in the sciences across 47 countries in 2003 (Martin et al., 2004) shows that for most countries, attitudes improved significantly from 1995 to 2003, with students equivalent to Year 9 in England almost doubling their rating on the enjoyment of science item. In 1995, 23 per cent of all students 'agreed a lot' that they enjoyed science. By 2003, this figure had increased to 44 per cent. Over the same period, the attitudes of students in England in this category has remained static at around 27.5 per cent, while the percentage of English students disagreeing that they liked science increased from 18 to 32 per cent. Over all countries, the average per cent 'disagreement' decreased from 28 in 1995 to 23 in 2003, so an international observer might well be asking, 'What has been happening in Year 9 science education in England since 1995 to make it less popular?' The Commentary on the 2003 TIMSS results for England by the DfES (Ruddock et al., 2004) is of little help here as it doesn't comment on the longer-term trend. The latest TIMSS Report of 2007 (Martin et al., 2008) shows that the doubts raised are fully supported by the latest data. England shares bottom place with Denmark on the 36-country list of 'liking' science for countries that teach the subject without division. England tops the 'disliking' science list with the Netherlands. The rating of 'liking' science has deteriorated since 1995 by more than for any other of the 36 countries. Unlike mathematics in 2007, self-confidence in learning science is well below the international average (28th out of 36), and there is no significant difference in the ratings of boys and girls.

The PISA survey of 57 countries in 2006 focused on science, and unlike other studies in the series, was able to monitor, indirectly, pupils attitudes to science. Bradshaw et al. (2007: 40) point out that when English 15-year-old pupils in the UK classification are compared with those of other OECD countries

> students [*in England*] were in general similar in their attitude to learning science, and more positive in their enjoyment of doing science problems, they appear to be more negative about enjoyment of science for its own sake. They find science less fun and report less enjoyment of reading about it, compared with the average response in other OECD countries.

The PISA survey concludes that although English pupils acknowledge the importance of science in today's world, the majority do not see science as something of personal value in their future lives.

Both international studies detect lower enjoyment levels in UK/English pupils. The attitude measures of the TIMSS study were the more quantitative in terms of response categories to a specific item over a time period, while the PISA results were inferred from responses to more general science questions on a single occasion. The conclusion from the two studies is that attitudes to science in England/UK decline over time and are less positive than those of the average student in the other OECD countries.

The decline in attitudes to science

There are various hypotheses that can be put forward to explain the steep decline in attitudes to science. The first of these is centred on the nature of the subject in a 'one size fits all' curriculum. The second is the capability of the teachers to make the subject material they have been directed to teach both relevant and interesting so that the teacher's enthusiasm for the subject can be conveyed to the pupils.

Most continental European countries teach separate subject sciences in Grade 8 (Year 9) while Australasia, the Far East and the USA, for the most part, integrate the sciences as is the case in England (Martin et al., 2004). The National Foundation for Educational Research (NFER) estimate that 44 per cent of all secondary science teachers in England are biologists, 25 per cent chemists and 19 per cent physicists (House of Lords, 2006). In some schools, there are no physicists or chemists. Given that the physicists and chemists are most likely to be teaching in the upper school at GCSE or A-level, it is reasonable to assume that pupil attitudes to the 'general' science of the Key Stage 3 years arise in science classes taught by biologists, who might be lacking confidence in the knowledge and rules of the physical sciences, and who are unable to show that enthusiasm and excitement in putting over what they know and *feel*.

Arguably, the bias in the teaching force towards biology is responsible for the intriguing finding from PISA 2006, that English/UK students express a particularly strong interest in human biology when compared with other OECD students. The PISA survey reports achievement in the three science content areas of Earth and Space, Living Systems and Physical Systems. For English/UK science students' mastery is strongest towards Living Systems, while The Netherlands leads in Physical Systems and the USA in Earth and Space.

The need for good-quality science and mathematics education in our schools has been acknowledged in a recent report by The Royal Society (2007). The present state of science teaching in schools has itself been the subject of an enquiry conducted by the Select Committee on Science and Technology of the House of Lords (2006). The Royal Society Report makes the point that the knowledge and understanding gained from learning and enjoying mathematics and science prepares students for the demands of life in the modern world and allows them to 'discover the rich heritage from centuries of global experimentation and adventure' (Royal Society, 2007: 13). The role of the teacher of science/mathematics is seen as particularly critical because parents tend to be able to offer less support in these subject areas than in others. The best teachers will show a ready enthusiasm for their subject in passing on their own knowledge and passion for learning, leading to many students making life-changing decisions.

The Royal Society Report then addresses the role and requirements for subject specialism in the secondary school, for which there is a long-standing history (Hirst, 1968; Musgrove, 1968). From the point of view of science in particular, it is somewhat ironic that the evolution of a 'science for all' in the National Curriculum of the 1980s led to the 'marginalizing' of the separate disciplines of physics, chemistry and biology (Royal Society, 2007) in favour of general science, or as renamed in some professional science education circles, 'balanced' science (ASE, 1979). This was despite psychological evidence that, while sharing a common organizational structures of inductive thought, experimentation and deduction, the three traditional disciplines required different cognitive learning profiles (Shayer and Adey, 1981).

The Government's inspectorate has also highlighted the links between specialist subject knowledge, teaching and students' enthusiasm and imagination, interest and attainment (Ofsted, 1998). Nevertheless, the biggest growth area in initial teacher training for the sciences today is in general or 'combined' science. In terms of advertised science teaching posts, 80 per cent of all posts in England in 2006–7 were for 'combined' science (Royal Society, 2007). The Royal Society report points out that it is not clear whether the prevalence of 'combined' science in recruitment is because it is intrinsically attractive or because it is a practical requirement of the National Curriculum in most schools. The Royal Society Report also makes the recommendation that post-graduate teacher training in the separate sciences is needed wherever universities have strong reputations in the sciences. Meanwhile, many science teachers have shown a preference for the Independent sector, where they are more likely to be able to teach their specialist science subject (Oversby, 2006; NUT, 2006), and Kinchin (2004) has questioned whether science teachers still maintain their enthusiasm and pride in the job that they had prior to the coming of the National Curriculum. The Confederation of British Industry is quite specific in locating today's shortage of graduates in physical science and engineering to too few studying the three sciences; too few specialist physics and chemistry teachers and too little time spent doing experiments (House of Commons, 2008b).

The importance of making separate subject sciences available is now officially acknowledged by the Government. Future policy now includes the stated entitlement that all pupils reaching Level 6 at Key Stage 3 should be allowed to study science as separate disciplines (DfES, 2006: 3). This move has been welcomed by both the House of Lords and the Royal Society (House of Lords, 2006; Royal Society, 2007). Reading between the lines of the House of Lords Report, there seems to be a general criticism of Government policy, which has instituted too many curriculum changes, too rapidly and without proper piloting and evaluation (House of Lords, 2007).

This last comment brings the discussion back to Government's implementation strategy for the National Curriculum and in particular the key role it has assigned to the Standard Assessment Tasks (SATs). At the beginning of this chapter, the negative influence of SATs on science attainment was pointed out. The professional association of science teachers, the Association for Science Education (ASE) is also clearly of the opinion that the SATs and their associated targets impact on the enjoyment of learning science (House of Commons, 2008a).

Peer relationships

Our work at Cambridge has involved investigating how pupils related to each other in the secondary classroom. The social behaviour undercurrents in school have been well documented elsewhere and it is from the work of Coopersmith (1967) Covington (1992), Rudduck et al. (1996) Marsh (1989) and Rudduck (2003) that we were able to build up a wide range of possible questionnaire items that described the interactions of the pupils with their peers. These items were supplemented and revised in the feedback from visits to classrooms. A trial or pilot use of the questionnaire identified 10 relevant items, which were shown to be statistically valid and which when used subsequently in the main study, clearly split into two sub-sets. One set were seen to be measuring the degree of passivity towards *active participation* in classroom activities, while the second set referred to the *anti-boffin sub-culture* of denigration of academic success.

A high-scoring *active participant* is keen to participate in discussion and debate. The *active participation* scale consisted of 3 items:

- Item 3. I like to make my point of view.
- Item 4. I have lots of ideas to share with others.
- Item 7. I keep quiet about my ideas (reversed scored).

The two key items on the *anti-boffin sub-culture* scale are:

- Item 1. If I don't like working with someone, I won't work with them.
- Item 5. It's cool not to be too smart.

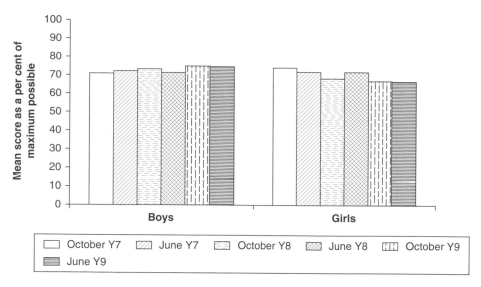

Figure 1.10 Active participation: Year 7 to Year 9

This scale reflects an anti-school, social sub-culture among secondary pupils giving rise to what Rudduck et al. (1996) describe as the 'dossers and shirkers' and what Hargreaves (1982) termed 'oppositional'. Scores on the *anti-boffin sub-culture* correlate negatively at around 0.3 with *motivation to school* as might be expected.

As Figure 1.10 shows, *active participation* scores are high, with the boys' ratings being significantly more than the girls'. Scores at the end of the year are the same as at the beginning. Boys' scores tend to remain unchanged from Year 7 to 9, but girls' scores drop significantly. In Year 7, the more able boys and girls tend to rate themselves high on active participation but this distinction disappears as the students get older.

Figure 1.11 shows *anti-boffin sub-culture* scores for boys and girls. The boys' mean score is significantly higher than the girls', as might be expected. Scores tend to remain unchanged over the course of the year. Girls' scores do not alter significantly from Year 7 through to Year 9, but boys seem to become more 'oppositional' as Year 7 progresses but then mend their ways somewhat in Years 8 and 9. Averaging over all three Years 7 to 9, for a sample of 393 boys, 55 per cent scored above the neutral mark on this scale in October and 47 per cent remained above in June. The corresponding figures for 387 girls are 45 and 39 per cent. These proportions of relatively disaffected students are substantial and must limit the quality of learning in many classrooms. When *anti-boffin sub-culture* scores are correlated with teacher estimates of attainment, we found a consistent negative association at around 0.25 for the three age groups. This means that, unsurprisingly, pupils who exhibit disaffection with school and who identify with an anti-learning counter-culture, are likely to be poor achievers.

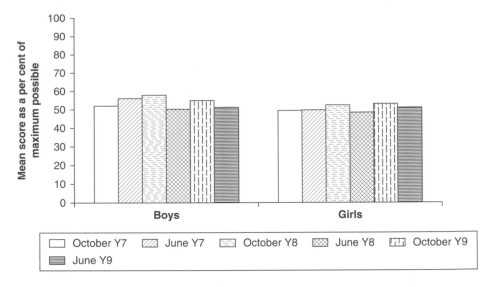

Figure 1.11   Anti-boffin sub-culture: Year 7 to Year 9

Hargreaves (1982) argues that these alienated pupils are supremely indifferent to most school lessons, but regard the school day as an excellent opportunity for social interaction with friends. This socialization takes place against a background 'noise' of lessons which the participants occasionally 'switch [in] on'. This creates a strong anti-school counter-culture among these 'oppositionals', which is marked by strong peer loyalty. Rudduck's extensive classroom research into pupil behaviour (Rudduck et al., 1996; Rudduck, 2003) has shown how friendship can, nevertheless, be an important source of learning support for many Key Stage 3 pupils. Rudduck distinguishes between the social and academic friendship patterns of pupils. With increasing maturity and independence, pupils are able to use their friends in different ways to achieve their goals. Not all youngsters who have joined the anti-school, anti-learning culture, wish to remain part of it for ever. Rudduck sees Years 8 and 9, in particular, the Years where 'nothing much is happening', as fertile ground for the growth of this school counter-culture.

Personality in the lower secondary years: measuring personality in the classroom

In England the Junior Eysenck Personality Questionnaire (JEPQ; Eysenck and Eysenck, 1975) has typically been used to measure personality factors such as extroversion and anxiety. Given the elapse of time since the instrument was first constructed, for the Cambridge projects it was revalidated by combining items from the original JEPQ, which still seemed relevant in the 21st century, with those from the anxiety dimension of other, self-esteem questionnaires of Coopersmith (1967) Lawrence (1981) and Marsh (1989). Additional items were added based on the comments from interviews with today's Key Stage 3 pupils. Pilot testing showed up the two factors of anxiety and extroversion with a similar, slight negative correlation to that found by Eysenck 40 years ago. However, there were problems with a number of Eysenck's extroversion items in that the Key Stage 3 pupils resolutely refused to associate these with others that were otherwise clearly strong extroversion indicators.

The analysis showed how easy it is for some terminology to go out of fashion so that piloting of even well tried and well respected measuring instruments is always advisable. In this present case anxiety is measured by 9 items of the type:

- Item 2.   Do you always feel under pressure?
- Item 6.   Do you find it hard to sleep at night because you are worrying about things?

After pilot testing, just 6 extroversion items remained of the type:

- Item 8.   Can you let yourself go and enjoy yourself a lot at a lively party?

This particular item came from Eysenck's JEPQ. Eysenck was particularly keen on using an item such as going to parties as a measure of extroversion. However, another two of the JEPQ extroversion items were clearly not interpreted by the pupils as Eysenck had intended. These were:

- Item 5.   Would you like parachute jumping?
- Item 14.   Would you call yourself happy-go-lucky?

Item 5 was another Eysenck favourite, while the term 'happy-go-lucky' in Item 14 confused today's pupils. In the event, the computed extroversion scores relied on just 4 items which are listed in Appendix A.

Unlike the other sections of the questionnaire, where a 5-point scale was used, the items measuring personality were answered by either 'Yes' or 'No' in keeping with the procedure used by Eysenck and Coopersmith. Despite the relatively truncated scales the reliabilities comfortably exceeded the 0.7 figure usually used as the minimum criterion for judging the internal consistency of the measure.

Changes in pupils' anxiety

When used with a sample of about 450 pupils in Years 7 to 9 (Pell et al., 2007), anxiety was found to remain relatively stable over the school year, although by the end of the Summer Term a small but significant gender gap had opened up with the girls slightly more anxious (Figure 1.12). The 50 per cent line in the figure separates 'being anxious and worried' (above 50%) from being 'calm and stable' (below 50%). On the whole, these pupils in the lower secondary school are stable rather than anxious.

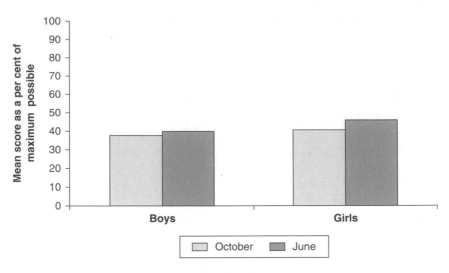

Figure 1.12   Change in anxiety over the school year

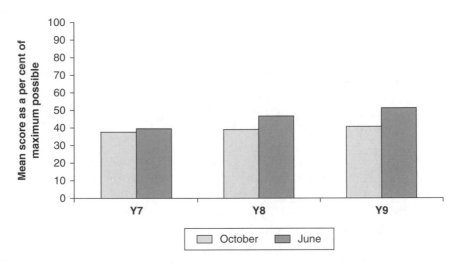

Figure 1.13   Change in girls' anxiety over the school year: Year 7 to Year 9

When anxiety scores are analysed by year group, boys' scores tend to remain steady, but, as Figure 1.13 shows, girls' scores increase with age and by the end of Year 9 have just entered the 'anxious-worrying' domain. During Year 7 girls' scores are steady, but in both Years 8 and 9 girls' scores increase significantly over the school year. The overall increase in girls' anxiety scores is in keeping with Eysenck's original research findings (Eysenck and Eysenck, 1969). Rudduck (2003) refers to the strong intensity of girls' friendship attachments during this period of school life. An interesting feature of Figure 1.13 is that the long holiday from school in the summer appears to allow for some emotional 'recovery'.

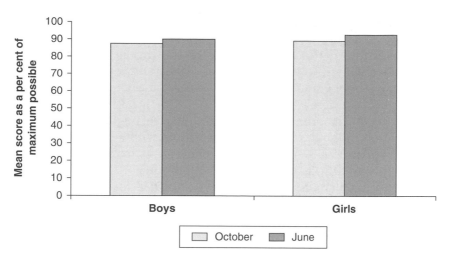

Figure 1.14   Change in extroversion over the school year

Changes in extroversion among lower secondary school pupils

Figure 1.14 shows the extroversion scores for the pupils. The most striking feature is the extremely high values for both boys and girls. As the 50 per cent line represents the cross-over from introversion (being 'bookish' and happy to learn by oneself) to extroversion (being sociable and outward-going), these high mean scores suggest classrooms of today probably present difficulties that were not present during Eysenck's active research time. One must be conditional here, because the extroversion scale, though based upon Eysenck's work, differs in detail. The Eysenck JEPQ (Eysenck and Eysenck, 1975) presents extroversion scores for boys and girls at Key Stage 3 age of around 75 per cent. The anxiety scores are typically 50 to 55 per cent, so there has been little change in the anxiety levels of pupils over the 30 years or so. If the extroversion measure we used at Cambridge is comparable to the earlier Eysenck one, then teachers today are faced with more voluble and less compliant pupils than in days gone by. This does not necessarily mean that classrooms have become more disruptive because of the higher extroversion levels since pupil anxiety remains steady. It is the anxious, unstable extraverts whose personality tends to push them into disruptive and anti-school behaviour (Fontana, 1977). The results of the Cambridge research point to a possible increase in the amount of relatively benign, stable extrovert pupil behaviour, which as Fontana remarks, can contribute to a cheerful and cooperative classroom. However, this leads to three possible consequences.

First, if extroversion levels overall have increased, there will likely be an increase in the proportion of the anti-school, neurotic extroverts in the classes. As teachers are fully aware, any increase in the number of this type of pupil is not good news. Second, if Key Stage 3 pupils are becoming classified in personality terms as stable extroverts, what are the implications for teaching and learning? Earlier personality research in the 1970s identified stable extroversion as the key to success in the primary schools. As pupils mature intellectually, the prerequisite personality disposition for success in the secondary school gradually shifts towards introversion (Eysenck, 1972). A possible implication here is that majority of Key Stage 3 pupils today respond to their classrooms as primary children did 30 years ago. Thus an approach based mainly on individualized working within a whole-class framework may not be appropriate for pupils whose predominant extrovert personality is associated with an affinity for group work (Fontana, 1977). If, as the earlier studies suggest, an element of introversion is needed for academic success in the secondary school, does Figure 1.14 indicate that the criteria for this success should be redefined whereby pupils would perhaps be judged by the breadth rather than the depth of their knowledge with the achievement of a Baccalaureate taking precedence over three 'gold standard' Advanced Levels?

Third, further maturation in the secondary school and in higher education leads to career choices where introverts can succeed even if they are anxious (Entwistle, 1973). There is strong evidence that pure scientists, especially those of physics and chemistry, as well as engineers tend to be introverted (Eysenck, 1972; Entwistle, 1973; Entwistle and Wilson, 1977; Fontana, 1977). A decline in the proportion of introverts in Key Stage 3 classrooms is therefore a possible predictor of the difficulties facing those policy makers seeking to increase the supply of professional scientists and technologists over the next decade.

Despite the high extroversion scores of Figure 1.14 in both October and June, it is possible to detect a small but significant increase in girls' scores over the school year pointing to some classrooms where girls retain a robust extroversion at least equal to that of the boys. There is no variation of extroversion scores over the three Key Stage 3 year-groups, supporting the idea that the high proportion of extroverted pupils is a stable feature. The Cambridge personality study was unable to follow the same pupil from Year 7 through to Year 9, so it is uncertain whether high extroversion scores remain steady for *individual pupils* throughout the Key Stage 3 years, but if they do, this could reflect a significant shift in sociological demographics as children grow up in a community where juvenile–adult attitudes are becoming more highly polarized (Mayer, 2008) and family life shows increasing signs of breaking down (Resolution, 2008).

Attitudes to working in groups in the lower secondary school

Part of the Cambridge research addressed attitudes to the use of group work in the Key Stage 3 years (Pell et al., 2007). The research required pupils' attitudes to be monitored both before and after a teaching sequence in one of the three core subjects, which made use of working in groups to achieve the learning objectives. Already in this chapter, the lack of group work has been cited as a contributory factor in the Government's *Getting Back on Track* report for the failure of some Key Stage 3 pupils who are failing to make progress in mathematics and

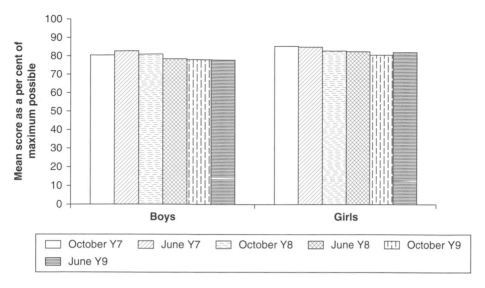

Figure 1.15 Attitudes to cooperative group working: Year 7 to Year 9

science (DCSF, 2007). The evaluation of new Key Stage 3 curricula by Stoll et al. (2003) report that 90 per cent of Year 8 pupils surveyed expressed a preference for working in groups compared to whole-class teaching. As we have shown previously, the typical personality profile of today's Key Stage 3 pupils suggests a preference for belonging to socially interacting groups.

To measure pupils' feeling about working in groups, the Cambridge researchers piloted three specific scales, which were to investigate (a) *cooperative working*, (b) *liking group work*, and (c) *the quality of the group working environment*.

Attitudes to cooperative working

Five items remained on this scale after piloting a range of statements from the literature and pupil interview responses. Key items of the scale, which appears in full in Appendix A are:

- Item 4. If we don't all agree, we should look for common ground.
- Item 13. We should all have a say in the decisions made.

Figure 1.15 shows the mean scores at the pre-test in October and the post-test in June.

Mean scores are significantly higher for the girls. Comparing end-of-year June testing with October testing for all age groups shows no significant attitude falls, indeed for Year 7 boys scores show a significant rise. The more able pupils in Year 7, according to their teachers' ratings, record higher scores. For the other age groups, attitude scores are not related to ability. Thus pupils in the anti-school, anti-learning sub-groups appear to value working together as well as their generally more able peers.

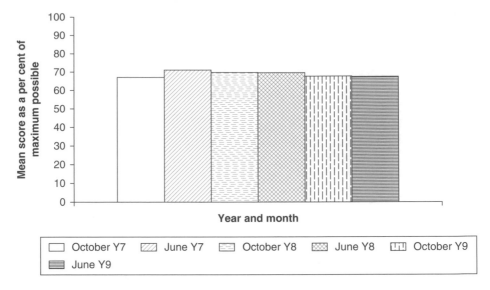

Figure 1.16   Liking group work: Year 7 to year 9

Liking group work

A substantial number of items measuring *liking group work* remained after piloting statements from the literature and pupil interview responses. Just 5 items were selected to keep the length of the scale reasonable for administration in the main research study. The scale appears in Appendix A. Key items are:

- Item 2.   Learning is more interesting in groups.
- Item 5.   Groups encourage you to work hard.

The pre-test and post-test scores at the beginning and end of the school year show no significant gender differences so Figure 1.16 compares the changes in 'liking' across the year groups for all pupils.

Year 7 pupils actually achieve a significant gain in *liking group work* over the year. The Year 8 and 9 pupils' scores remain steady. When teacher estimates of pupil attainment are taken into account, able boys score significantly below other boys on the scale, with the gap widening over the school year. Able girls, although initially less positive than other girls about group work in October of Year 7, reach parity with other pupils by June but fall back again in Year 9.

Quality of group-working environment

Again more items were generated from the literature and student interviews than were needed in the questionnaire and, after piloting, only the 6 items that gave the highest internal consistency of an *attitude to the group-working environment* were selected. The scale appears in Appendix A. Key items on this scale are:

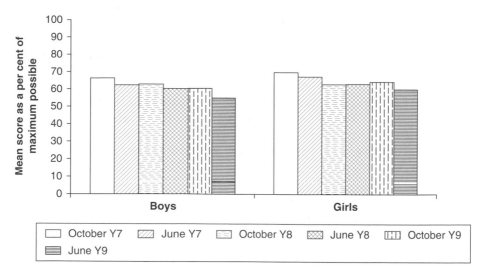

Figure 1.17   Quality of the group-working environment: Year 7 to year 9

- Item 2.   We take turns in talking.
- Item 5.   There is interrupting or cutting off. (scores reversed)

Although, *liking group work* scores remain remarkably steady over the school year, which is against the common trend of subject attitudes' fall-off, Figure 1.17 shows that *the quality of group working* appears to decline in the same period, because the pupils' rating of their experiences in groups drops significantly by June. The fall is the same for groups in English, mathematics and science, and is shown by both boys and girls. Boys' scores tend to fall more than the girls', although this does not necessarily mean that scores fall in every class. In seven of 38 classes studied mean scores were actually higher in the June test, pointing to a strong teacher effect.

Teachers' ratings of pupil ability suggest the decline in the quality of group working is greatest among able boys in science classes. These pupils' ratings in the June post-test show particularly noticeable and significant drops.

Group working in the lower secondary school: a summary

The rationale for group working in the secondary school has tended to be pragmatic rather than being based on psychological evidence. According to Blatchford et al. (2001) the rationale for grouping in both primary and secondary schools appears to be dominated by issues of classroom organization rather than pedagogy or possible benefits to students. For instance, Stoll et al. (2003) found that teachers would often set up groups in science based on the numbers of items of equipment available and in English on the amount of written resources.

The value of group work for addressing some of the quantitative losses in attitude and attainment at Key Stage 3 will be discussed in the following chapters of this book. At this point already though, there is justification for an expanded role for group work in that there is strong research evidence that students do not think they get enough of this form of teaching approach. In the Cambridge research mean '*liking group work*' attitude scores were around 70 per cent and did not fall over the school year, unlike subject attitudes, and mean *attitudes to cooperative learning* were over 80 per cent and also remained steady. This positive disposition towards working cooperatively together is maintained despite a fall in the quality of what takes place inside the groups.

Pupil stereotypes inside the secondary classroom

So far in this chapter, mean scores and correlations have been used to draw certain inferences which emerge from attainment and attitudinal data collected from students in various national and international contexts. Such an approach gives a valuable broad picture. Over time, positive and negative trends can be picked out and, if necessary, macroscopic policy changes can be introduced. In this way, if a case can be made for a greater use of group working at Key Stage 3 to arrest attitude decline, for example, then future national programmes would be expected to reflect this approach. In reality, the broad picture of the average student is an over-simplification. Looking at the characters who make up a typical class, how many fit the profile of the average as illustrated by the charts of this chapter? There will be some who react positively to group discussions, others will do the opposite. There will be some who are pro-school and introverted. There will be others who are anti-school and extroverted. For some of these *types* of pupil, correlation coefficients for ability and attitudes will be positive, for other types the correlations will be negative, while for other there will be no correlations at all. This complexity has led some researchers to withdraw from any attempts to quantify what is happening in classrooms.

Statisticians have attempted to deal with this problem by means of the technique of *cluster analysis*. This produces a profile of each student in terms of their attitude, motivation and attainment scores, and indeed any other measures which are reliably available. *Cluster analysis* puts the students into specific types, in each of which the students have relatively similar scores on each of the different variables such as *attainment, academic satisfaction motivation, anxiety* and so on. Each type though differs significantly from all the others on the mean scores for most of the variables. Granted that a class of 30 pupils comprises 30 different individuals, there will be sufficient similarity in test scores, and by implication in behaviour, for these 30 students to be separated into, say, five or six groups, each group having broadly similar characteristics.

In our research at Cambridge, full data from 818 pupils in the classes of 44 Key Stage 3 teachers of English, mathematics and science in 22 schools of two education authorities were cluster analysed to identify the student types.

Table 1.1 Characteristics of the four pupil types

| Scale | Mean Scale Scores | | | | Change over the year for all pupils |
	Type 1 (N = 264)	Type 2 (N = 338)	Type 3 (N = 153)	Type 4 (N = 163)	
Cooperative group working	L –	H+	L –	H+	Nil
Liking group work		H+	L		Sig. rise
Group work quality	L –	H+	L –		Sig. fall
Anxiety		L –	H+	L+	Sig. rise
Extroversion	H+	H+	L –	L –	Sig. rise
Active participation	L –	H+	L –		Nil
'Anti-boffin' sub-culture	H+	L –	H+	L	Sig. fall
Liking mathematics	L –	H+	L –		Sig. fall
Liking English	L –	L	L –	H+	Sig. fall
Liking science	L –	H		H+	Sig. fall
Achievement mastery motivation	L –	H+	L –	H+	Sig. fall
Academic satisfaction motivation	L –	H+	L –	H+	Sig. fall
Pro-school motivation˙	L	H	L	H	
Percentage of boys	45.5	49.4	58.5	52.1	
Teacher's attainment estimate in October	L	H	L		

L = significantly below other mean cluster scores
H = significantly above other mean cluster scores
+ = significant residual gain since pre-test
– = significant residual loss since pre-test
˙ No pre-test scores available

Table 1.1 shows the characteristics of the four main types that the analysis could pick out. Thirty-five pupils were impossible to 'classify' because of their uniqueness. Should there have been sufficient time and resources available these unique pupils could have been followed up as individual 'case studies'. The letters L and H are used in the table to denote whether the scale score in the June post-test was statistically significantly lower or higher than scores in the other clusters. The final column indicates the October to June change for all 818 pupils on each scale, so the positive (+) or negative (–) signs indicate whether the June score was an improvement or a deterioration of the October one. For example, for *liking mathematics*, attitude scores fall significantly for all pupils, but for Type 2s the post-test scores are above average and do not fall by as much, possibly even increasing over the year.

Type 1 pupils, forming 32.3 per cent of the total sample, are below average in attainment and motivation but exhibit a strong streak of extroversion. Their subject attitudes in the October pre-test are the least positive of the four types. Over the course of the year their attitudes to all three subjects continue to deteriorate. These pupils express strong *anti-boffin sub-culture* characteristics and these feelings increase during the school year. At the end of the school year, scores on the *pro-school* scale are significantly lower than those of the other pupils. They present mixed attitudes to group work. While not opposed to being in groups they appear to attach little value to working cooperatively, the inference being that they like the groups for social rather than academic reasons. They report that the quality of activity within the group declines over the year, and for the most part these pupils choose to adopt a passive approach, being content to let other group members perform the required tasks or actively contribute to the discussion. The highest achieving Type 1s are likely to be those who are not as negative about the classroom learning culture, and who are of a stable personality disposition. Type 1 pupils have been referred to as *dossers* or *shirkers* by Rudduck (2003). As Hargreaves (1982) has commented, this type of pupil subverts traditional school culture so that hostility to teacher and school gives the feeling of status and dignity.

Type 2 pupils form the largest cluster and are *active collaborators*. Their estimated attainment levels are above average; they are highly motivated, and their positive attitudes towards cooperative learning in groups increase over the course of the year. They tend to have a preference for mathematics and science rather than English and for the most part are confident pupils (low on anxiety and high on extroversion) and this disposition improves over the course of the year. They have sound attitudes to school and increasingly positive ones to classroom learning as measured directly by *pro-school motivation* and inversely by *anti-boffin sub-culture*.

Type 3 pupils form the smallest cluster. Having some of the characteristics of Type 1s, they differ in personality terms being *anxious introverts*. This means a lack of confidence in comparison with the extroverted *shirkers* of Type 1. Rather than being part of a social mix within a class, Type 3s are *struggling loners*, who do not wish to get involved. Like the *shirkers* they are among the less able; display anti-learning *(anti-boffin sub-culture)* characteristics, anti-school tendencies and are poorly motivated. The World Health Organization survey (Currie et al., 2008) intriguingly reports that peer support ratings for 13 and 15 year-olds in England are in the bottom three of the list of 41 countries. This suggests that the Cambridge research might well have underestimated the proportion of Type 3s in our classes. Attitudes to science for Type 3s are not as negative as are those towards English and mathematics, possibly because of the subject's practical aspects, and the higher achievers in science tend to be much less anti-school.

Type 4 pupils demonstrate the classical personality characteristics of learners who traditionally have done well in secondary education and above, especially in the physical sciences (Eysenck, 1972; Entwistle, 1973; Entwistle and Wilson, 1977; Fontana, 1977). These are the *stable introverts*. Motivation scores are high both towards personal achievement and to school. Type 4s are supportive of cooperative learning but are less prepared to become involved in the cut and thrust of group-work discussions. They have a preference for English as a subject compared to the other types, and this positive effect must be very strong, given that the average attitudes to English were the highest of the three subjects initially for all the pupils. Type 4s can be found at all ability levels, but in mathematics and science, the higher achievers tend to be particularly cool towards working in groups. Type 4s are not dissimilar to the *quiet collaborators* first identified in earlier studies of primary pupils (Galton et al. 1980).

Given that each classroom is likely to contain more than one type of pupil, and an 'average' mixed-ability class of 30 could comprise 10 Type 1 *shirkers*,

12 Type 2 *active collaborators*, 2 Type 3 *struggling loners* and 6 Type 4 classical learning *quiet collaborators*, the task facing the teacher is laid out for all to see. In 31 of the 39 classes studied, the relative proportions of the student types did not differ significantly from this typical profile. In an ideal world, classrooms are populated with Type 4 students and a sprinkling of their more sociable and extroverted cousins, the Type 2s, yet of eight classes with significantly different Type profiles, four were dominated by the 'anti-school', more difficult to teach Type 1s and 3s. In all, 13 of the 39 classes had more than 50 per cent of their class members drawn from the anti-school, anti-learning Types 1 and 3.

Conclusion

It is interesting to compare Hargreaves's (1982) subjective view of four pupil types in the secondary classroom of 30 years ago with the outcomes from the Cambridge study of today. Hargreaves's 'oppositionals' (similar to our Type 1s) remain and make up about one-third of the Cambridge sample, although the criteria used by the two studies are not identical. Teachers rated around 85 per cent of the Cambridge sample as being of average ability or above, which is supported by the depth of intensity in motivation towards personal success shown by most of the pupils. What this most recent research suggests is that the delivery of the present largely prescribed curriculum within the institution of the school is highly problematic since clearly 'one size' cannot fit the needs of all these varying types of pupil.

Curriculum delivery is undoubtedly being affected by the imposition of Standard Assessment Tasks and the Government's target culture. 'Teaching to the test' appears to be distorting the learning taking place across the core curriculum so it is possible for internal 'standards' in England to have risen over the last decade, while internationally achievement has for the most part dropped. It is of some interest that another Government department, that of the Police Service, which is also 'target driven', is now questioning the direction in which it has been compelled to move (Hope, 2008). Teachers must live in hope that there will be a change in direction in the schools that will restore them a measure of professional autonomy.

In this chapter a case has been made that pupils' feelings, personal adjustment to society and attitudes should be of more than a passing concern in a school system focused on attainment. The evidence presented in the previous pages has shown that current attitudes to the core subjects of English, mathematics and science at Key Stage 3 are poor and are continuing to decline over time. The international studies cited support this assessment that attitudes have deteriorated. Motivation towards school and to learning is only moderate, and in any class with a range of ability there are likely to be problems for teachers as a result. In the Cambridge study Type 2s (*active collaborators*) and Type 4s (*quite collaborators*) are readily identified with those pupils classified by Hargreaves (1982) as being 'committed to school values' in so far as they seem to be relatively comfortable in the surroundings of the school. The distinction between these two types may be to some degree artificial, being a consequence of the design of the Cambridge study, which was looking into the effect of group work. The pupils with a 'positive disposition to school' were consequently split according to their support for this style of learning. Types 2 and 4 comprise just over 60 per cent of the Cambridge sample, which suggests that around 40 per cent of average and above-average ability pupils are becoming alienated by school over the Key Stage 3 years. When pupils of below-average ability are brought into this discussion, it is not unreasonable to speculate that more than half of today's pupils are currently disaffected with the school experience. There is therefore a need for some radical thinking, not only about current classroom practice (the subject of much of the remaining chapters) but about the structure of secondary schooling itself. We end this chapter therefore with several questions.

 Questions for discussion

1   Would it be valuable if schools were to assess the attitudes and motivation of their pupils as well as monitoring attainment? Quick checks might be done at the start and end of the school year using attitude items like those in Appendix A.

2   Given the prominence given by Government to the personalized learning agenda, how valuable is it to identify different types of pupil, as in the Cambridge studies so that the curriculum can be tailored to their different needs as reflected in these profiles?

3   A constant criticism of present policy is that there have been too many initiatives, many of which have not been adequately trialed. In what ways can schools have a greater say in policy formulation so that the impact at classroom level is better understood?

After 20 years of prescription and change driven by the 'education-3' political mantra, the excessive reform agenda of recent years has arguably little to show for all the effort expended. Particularly serious is the decline in pupils' intrinsic motivation resulting in poor attitudes to subjects such as science and mathematics. The following chapters will explore further the research into what exactly is happening in Key Stage 3 classrooms and the possibilities for bringing about change in pupils' present dispositions to learning. We will begin by looking at the initial reactions of pupils when they make the move from primary to secondary school.

2

Initial Encounters: Moving to Secondary School

Maurice Galton

In this chapter we look at the impact on pupils when they first arrive at secondary school. Transfer is often described as an anxious time but it is perhaps more accurate to say that most pupils generally feel excitement tinged with a touch of apprehension. In the following pages we look at what schools are doing to make transfer a satisfactory experience for most pupils and suggest some areas where new initiatives may be required.

It would seem only reasonable to assume that the pupils' first impressions will have a part to play in deciding the way they will cope with their start at secondary school. Some newcomers will seek to immerse themselves fully in the playground activities, seeking to ingratiate themselves with both more senior students as well as the leaders among their own peers. Others, of a more reserved nature, will perhaps look for like-minded pupils and seek to join the computer or chess club where they can take refuge during lunchtimes and breaks. Because these earlier experiences can have an impact on a pupils' academic performance, causing dips in progress, this process of transfer (often also termed *transition*) from primary to secondary school has therefore been given considerable attention by recent governments. For example, one of the aims of the National Curriculum under the then Conservative Government of Mrs Thatcher, was to improve the continuity between the primary and secondary curriculum, while in the early stages of New Labour's term in office, schools were required to write into their development plans specific proposals to improve transfer arrangements. This was followed up by the award of Beacon Status to two authorities, Suffolk and North Lincolnshire, who were charged with improving the quality of the transfer process in other parts of the education system.

Transition as a continuous process

Two main theories have dominated the debate about transfer. The first of these might be described as a 'matching' theory whereby it is argued that transfer works best when the school environment fits the young adolescents' perceived psychological needs and dispositions. In the United States this *stage–environment fit* theory was first proposed by Eccles et al. (1984). According to these researchers, a poor fit resulted in dips in both pupils' attitudes and also their attainment. Key elements in the young adolescent developmental stage, according to Eccles and colleagues was a desire to be free to make their own decisions about where to go, what to do and whom to do it with. This was coupled with what might be termed 'goal aspirations' or the stirrings within an individual of what he or she would like to do with their lives on reaching adulthood. These researchers contrasted the ways in which primary (or in the United States, elementary schools) contrived to create an environment in the senior part of the school which supported these developmental characteristics so that the pupils were encouraged to take more responsibility for their own learning and for the organization of some aspects of the classroom, whereas at secondary school pupils reported more competition, less freedom to make their own decisions (for example they were told where to sit) and work that consisted mostly of teacher-dominated classroom discourse where learning was very much controlled by the teacher.

Indeed, there has been some work in the United States suggesting that there is a link between the capacity of pupils to identify poor matching school environments and the onset of puberty. Miller (1986) for example, compared parental reports of their children's development and used this to investigate the 'match' between pupils' *ideal* view of their freedom to make decisions in school and the *actual* reality. Pupils' beliefs about decision making were assessed at the beginning of the final elementary school year and then again towards the end of the spring term. Girls, who showed signs of early development, were more likely to recognize that the actual allowed amount of decision making was less than their ideal, so that the person–environment fit was poorer for these pupils. Boys who reached puberty earlier detected little difference but this, it was suggested, was partly because it was more difficult for parents to decide the rate of pubertal development in their male offspring.

Although not developed as a specific theory, these ideas about person–environment matching were very popular in the United Kingdom during the 1970s and in the early 1980s, partly because they supported the notion of a three-tier system in which middle schools acted as a transition between the primary and secondary ethos (Hargreaves and Tickle, 1980). Some Local Authorities found the concept of a middle school very attractive because it enabled them to convert to comprehensive education using the existing school buildings. Thus it was argued that there was a key period in the development of pupils as they moved from childhood to adolescence requiring a special kind of school (Schools Council, 1972) but whether this period took place from the ages of 8 to 12, 9 to 13, or 10 to 14 seemed to depend largely on the number and size of the available schools in the particular Local Authority.

The notion of a 'person–environment fit' suggests an approach based on gradual change to match the developmental changes taking place within the individual. This leads to an emphasis on continuity at transfer, particularly curriculum continuity, including both subject matter and teaching methods (Gorwood, 1986). Indeed, some schools went further in their desire to make the secondary transfer school appear more like primary by isolating Year 7 so that, as far as possible, the form teacher took most lessons, children were provided with a separate playground to keep them away from the dangers of mixing with their older peers and increased use of various pedagogic strategies such as group work was encouraged. Research by Youngman (1978) and Youngman and Lunser (1977) tended to suggest, however, that such dramatic organizational adjustments were not necessarily cost effective. Their research showed that pupils' reactions to the move to secondary school varied considerably and that for many pupils the effects were transitory and lasted only for a relatively short period. Such findings were supported by other research in Northern Ireland (Spelman, 1979) and in Scotland (Dutch and McCall, 1974). The first of the Oracle (Observational Research and Classroom Learning) evaluations of primary schools between 1975 and 1980 also took up the question of transfer and found mixed reactions among pupils in one school which adopted the policy of separating Year 7 from the remainder of the year groups. Pupils in this school told interviewers that they regularly risked breaking out of their own playground to mingle with older peers because it was 'more fun' and because 'they wanted to test themselves'. Testing could involve joining in impromptu games and generally learning to survive in situations where they were in hostile crowds. As in the earlier studies dips in attitudes and attainment were relatively small for most pupils over the course of the first year in secondary school and the different environments (three-tier versus two-tier systems; protected Year 7 versus no differentiation) appeared to make very little difference to pupils' attitudes. For most pupils the trauma of transfer (slight apprehension mingled with anticipated excitement) had been forgotten by the middle of the first term. In only about 12 per cent of pupils were the dips sustained and relatively serious (Galton and Willocks, 1983).

Transfer as a status passage

An alternative approach to the problems of transfer, which offers a different perspective on the above research findings, borrows from anthropology and makes use of the concept of 'status passage' (Measor and Woods, 1984). In most societies the move from childhood to adolescence, or indeed any change in status such as getting married, involves a number of special rites which are designed to initiate an individual into their new status. Accompanying this change in status there is likely to be a certain amount of folklore which includes myths about what happens during the induction process. Transfer when viewed in this light, bears many of the hallmarks of a status passage. Going to big school marks a point in time when 'grown ups' such as parents and teachers, no longer see pupils as children but as 'young adults'. Initiation into the big school involves a series of rituals to do with new subjects, moving to teachers in different parts of the building rather than spending time in a single classroom and learning how to cope with different organizational arrangements, such as mastering the procedure for selecting one's lunch from a cafeteria style self-service menu. Accompanying this change in status are certain myths such as *'the royal flush'* whereby new pupils are alleged to have their heads held down the lavatory bowl while another pupil pulls the chain. These myths appear to be global.

As Measor and Woods (1984) point out, the view of the transfer process as a status passage is at odds with the previous notion that the main tasks of the primary and secondary school is to ensure that there is as much continuity as possible. These authors point out that if the process of transfer was so managed that the changes before and after the move to the big school were minimal, then pupils would have little evidence to suggest a change in status. In this approach, therefore, the desire for continuity needs to be balanced by an element of discontinuity which recognizes the need in pupils for some 'outward signs' that they are successfully managing the change from childhood to young adolescence. The anxiety, or more properly the apprehension, mingled with excitement, which arises during the transfer process is therefore largely a result of this continuity–discontinuity mix. This can be seen in the way that pupils talk about their hopes and fears during the last few weeks of primary school. They worry about losing existing friends but are looking forward to making new ones. They are looking forward to doing new subjects but worry whether they can cope with the work. In the same way they look forward to meeting and having more teachers but are concerned about whether some teachers will be too strict. In this version of events transfer is full of these kinds of dilemmas. Transfer schools need continually to review their approach to transition to take into account changing trends in primary and secondary education so that the continuity–discontinuity balance changes according to the circumstances pertaining in the feeder schools.

In practice, during the 1970s and 80s, the person–environment match that saw primary schools as centres of exciting innovations and secondary schools as dull, formal and hidebound by tradition, was often the subject of myth. The Oracle research (Galton et al., 1980) demonstrated that, in practice, primary classes were not hubs of creativity in which children discovered things for themselves, nor did pupils work for a large part of the time cooperatively in groups and nor were these schools places where pupils participated in the decision making about how the class and the curriculum was to be organized. Other studies, notably that of Mortimore et al. (1988) and Alexander et al. (1989) confirmed that this was the case so that although classroom organization differed between the primary and secondary school, the forms of instruction were very similar. In primary schools children sat in groups but worked alone whereas at the secondary level they more often sat in rows but again worked alone, and direct instruction was the norm in both kinds of establishment. In one way, therefore, there was continuity of pedagogy in that pupils experienced much the same teaching, albeit within different structures (mixed ability versus bands; single/pair seating versus groups etc.). Viewing the process of transfer as a status passage would suggest that one of the reasons for the persistent decline in attitudes, referred to in the first chapter, comes about because pupils expect to be taught in different ways after transfer but this rarely turns out to be the case, particularly in the core subjects of mathematics and science where the decline in attitude is steepest.

However, notwithstanding this argument, the introduction of the National Curriculum was specifically designed to improve continuity according to the then Secretary of State for Education, Kenneth Baker (1993). A repeat of the original Oracle study mainly using the same primary and secondary school as in the late 1970s, however, showed that there were a number of significant changes which had taken place with regard to the administration of the transfer process and that schools had moved to eliminate some of the immediate anxieties which earlier studies of transfer had highlighted. Some of these changes were less the result of fresh thinking about transfer and had more to do with the changed circumstances of schools, particularly the decline in the power of the Local Education Authorities and the 'market forces' approach to education with its emphasis on parental choice, which had been the flagship of the Conservative administration (Tomlinson, 2005).

Induction days: 1970s to the present

Thus in the late 1970s when the first Oracle transfer study was carried out the choice of secondary school was largely determined by the Local Authority, who allocated pupils to the school catchment area in which they resided. For the most part, therefore, secondary schools gave little thought as to how to accommodate parents' and pupil wishes so that a 'take it or leave it' attitude tended to dominate. Thus in most cases in the original study children visited the school for one morning only. There they were addressed by the Year 7 tutor, given a conducted tour of the school and then packed back to their primary feeder schools before lunch. A Parents' Evening would be arranged towards the end of the Summer Term prior to transfer but its main purpose would be to instruct the audience on the rules of the school and the clothing policy, particularly the required items for PE and various sports (Galton and Willcocks, 1983; Delamont and Galton, 1986).

By the 1990s however all this had changed. Most schools had Liaison Committees where issues of transfer were considered. Unlike the 1970s these arrangements were less hierarchical in that the chairperson tended to rotate between the primary and secondary headteachers. In an effort to gain as many new pupils as possible several Parents' Meetings now took place and this involved opportunities to visit classrooms and see pupils (brought in especially for the evening) engaged in various curriculum activities. In some cases the transfer school's facilities were available for use by the primary schools, particularly science laboratories, drama studios and ICT suites. But as suggested earlier, the reasons behind these moves often appeared to have less to do with the actual transfer process and were more concerned to encourage pupils' parents and pupils to choose the particular school so that its numbers could be boosted and its finances increased. Hence these contacts were often supplemented by regular newsletters and other documents, designed to inform potential clients of the advantages of bringing their child to the particular institution.

The major change, however, was in the treatment of pupils prior to transfer. Now almost every local authority organized a Transfer Day during the late Summer Term when all children whose parents had opted to send them to a particular school spent a whole Induction Day on the premises. In most schools the Induction Day followed a similar pattern. Pupils were initially divided into their tutor and form groups and spent some time getting to know each other through a series of ice-breaker activities. There would be an assembly at which the school Principal would welcome the new pupils followed by a conducted tour of the school. Whereas the tour in the 1970s was often superficial with the volunteer pupil briefly stopping outside a room to say, 'This is where you do French', or 'This where you queue for snacks', these latter tours were generally conducted by the form tutors with frequent pauses to allow question-and-answer sessions. In most schools the tour was followed by an early lunch to avoid the queues when the main body of pupils finished morning sessions. In between and during the afternoon there were various lessons, a mix of core and other subjects. These lessons were generally made as exciting as possible so that, for example, in Science there would be plenty of explosions and lots of smoke accompanied by strange smells. The final session would usually consist of questions and answers about any remaining issues that the pupils might have. Sometimes these were conducted by the Year 7 Coordinator but more often space was allowed for the visiting primary intake to question existing Year 7 pupils. At some point during the day there would be an early introduction into the school routines and rules, generally during a tutor meeting with the pupils.

Interviews with the pupils (Hargreaves and Galton, 2002) found that the response to these activities was generally positive. Pupils found that their immediate anxieties were dealt with. These usually consisted of whether they would make new friends and get on with pupils from other primary schools, getting to see what the new teachers were like and working out practical arrangements such as how one paid for lunch, what one did in break time and where to put one's bag. The conclusion of the Oracle Replication Transfer Study was that, in respect to these activities designed to improve social adjustment, little more could be done. Indeed, to do more would be perhaps to tip the scales too far away from the direction of maintaining some degree of discontinuity; in this case slight apprehension on the parts of the pupils so that they would continue during the summer vacation to see the move to the new school as a significant change in their status.

Transfer and pupils with special needs

One important change concerned the efforts made on behalf of children with special educational needs. In most secondary schools, the SENCO now played an important part in the arrangements preceding transfer. They visited the various primary schools to identify pupils at risk, and made arrangements for these children to visit the secondary school separately from the remaining intake so that they had a longer period to adjust. Yet as other studies (MacBeath and Galton, 2006) have shown this increased liaison often has little to do with the learning needs of these special pupils and has more to do with administration; making sure that there are enough learning support assistants for the numbers of children with learning difficulties who are expected to come to the school in the following year.

The situation with regard to special needs has been exacerbated by the decision made by the New Labour Government to switch to a policy of almost total inclusion. In the publication, *Removing the Barriers for Achievement* (DfES, 2004a) it was argued that placing more children in mainstream and creating closer links with outside children's services would result in improved expectations and that educational disadvantage would thereby be reduced. In practice, this has not happened in most schools. While, according to Tomlinson (2005), pressures by knowledgeable middle-class parents for specialist segregated facilities within some schools have concentrated precious resources on more 'contemporary' highly publicized disabilities, such as Autism, ADHD and Dyslexia, this has often been at the cost of providing adequate support for pupils with lesser levels of special educational need, a conclusion also reached by the Audit Commission (2002).

The intention of the New Labour Government had been to place educational provision of the disabled members of the community within the framework of the equal rights legislation and as such inclusion has generally been welcomed by teachers. Some critics did argue, however, that the initiative was driven, in part, by the Treasury's enthusiasm for the savings that might result in reducing the number of special schools. In practice, as MacBeath and Galton (2006) have documented, schools lack the necessary expertise, funding and resources to make inclusion work effectively. In Year 6 the pressure to do well in the league tables has meant that the special needs children only get the teacher's attention on rare occasions. In one school visited the two Year 6 classes were divided in February into three groups. The first group, *the certain level 4s* were taught by one teacher, the next group, *the borderline level 4s* were taught by the other teacher while what were described as the *no hopers* were assigned to an untrained classroom assistant.

After transfer the situation rarely improved. SENCOs were often too busy to support teachers who said they felt insufficiently skilled to tackle the various types of learning disorder that they encountered. Most of the SENCOs' time was taken up with administrative tasks and in meetings with other welfare agencies and parents. The favoured solution was therefore to allocate such children to a Learning Support Assistant (LSA), often someone with a maximum of two days attendance, on a special needs course (MacBeath and Galton, 2006).

Wedell (2005) has argued that the *velcro-ing* of LSAs to pupils in this way is a form of within-class segregation and suggests that there is little likelihood of a change in the circumstances of these special needs pupils while the 'standards agenda' continues to drive the reforms and the assumption that improvements are best achieved through whole-class teaching is maintained. This view, perhaps surprisingly, has been supported by Ofsted (2004) who, despite their continued enthusiasm for whole-class teaching, have commented that the inflexibility of school and classroom organization are sometimes 'handicaps to effective developments' in pursuit of inclusive policies. The National Workload Reform, particularly the introduction of time for teachers to carry out planning, preparation and assessment tasks (PPA time) has led to a massive increase in the numbers of unqualified staff. There are now 115,000 teaching assistants according to Frean (2007). This works out at two unqualified staff for every three teachers. Many, with responsibility for children with special needs are now required to plan, teach and assess these pupils' work (Galton and MacBeath, 2008). The following description appears to be typical of what now takes place:

> My primary role is working with a child who has a statement for 15 hours. A lot of the lessons she doesn't need one-to-one support so I work with the gold group which is the lower-ability group. When any writing is involved I tend to work with that group of children. I also do the reading schemes for those. (TA, 7 years' experience)

There is a lack of systematic research concerning the impact of transfer on this group of children but insofar that changes to the transfer procedures have taken place since the 1980s it would seem that they have mainly concentrated on the administrative and the social aspects of transfer. The quality of the educational provision has received little attention.

Bridging Units as an aid to curriculum continuity

Following the fall of the Conservative government, New Labour continued to take the view that the continuing dips in attainment and the persistent decline in attitudes were primarily caused by a lack of curriculum continuity. One particular strategy for overcoming this problem was to develop what have become known as 'Bridging Units'. These consisted of a series of exercises, mainly in English, mathematics and sometimes science, which pupils started in the last few weeks of their primary school. The books with the pupils' work then moved with the pupils to the secondary school and further exercises and worksheets were continued during the first month in Year 7. The aim of the Bridging Unit was to enable teachers to gain insights to the capabilities of the primary children and to build on these as part of the work which was continued in the secondary in the first weeks after transfer. The first of these units, developed by the Qualification and Curriculum Authority (QCA) met with a mixed success. An evaluation as part of a government-sponsored study (Galton et al., 2003) found that these Bridging Units were received with mixed feelings by both primary and secondary teachers. This was particularly true of the mathematics units. Teachers at primary level said that throughout the year the need to devote each morning to literacy and numeracy activities meant that the rest of the curriculum was squeezed so that children missed out on things like art, drama and PE. There was also little time available to do extended investigations based around certain topics. Generally primary teachers tended to use the time after the National Curriculum statutory tests in May to do more imaginative and creative activities that the children had missed out on during the early part of the year. Consequently, there was a certain degree of resentment at having to devote more time to the core subjects, particularly since the topics chosen by the QCA for mathematics included fractions, a topic which was 'done to death' already during Year 6 as part of the National Curriculum. Where primary teachers did do the units, therefore, they tended not to follow their logical order but to pick and choose from various sections which they thought would be more interesting to the pupils. This made a mockery of the idea of continuity.

For the secondary teachers there were also problems. To begin with, not all transfer schools had distinct catchment areas because under the current system now operating pupils might feed into Year 7 from around 10 or 15 primary schools. While the main proportion of Year 7 pupils would come from perhaps three or four main feeder schools others might contribute as few as half a dozen pupils. Given these few numbers it was likely that liaison with some primary schools would be poor and that pupils might arrive for the first term after the move to secondary school having not done any of the Bridging Units. This presented problems to the teachers, who then had to have some pupils doing the work that others had already done in the main feeder primary schools. This situation could be further exacerbated in some inner-city secondary schools in larger conurbations where there were high rates of pupil mobility and where the Year 7 intake was often distributed across a large number of primary schools.

Moreover there appeared to be uncertainties among secondary teachers as to the purpose of the Units. Many teachers saw them as yet another element in the process of social adjustment by giving them work with which they would have been familiar from primary school, thus providing an easy introduction into academic life in the secondary school. Where this view prevailed certain consequences followed. For a start, teachers spent less effort in reviewing the previous work done before transfer, since they did not see the curriculum continuity issue as of vital importance. This in turn produced indifference on the part of the pupils who thought that the teachers were not interested in the work and therefore did not take the initial task set at secondary level seriously. More importantly, because teachers did not see that the purpose was to promote curriculum continuity they tended to see the Units as a finite piece of work, including the pupils' efforts in the primary school, and therefore did not associate what was undertaken with what was to follow subsequently. As one pupil interviewed by Galton et al. (2003) responded in relation to a science Bridging Unit, 'Once we'd finished it the teacher put on his white coat and we did the Bunsen burner'.

There was also another interesting result which reflects on the continuity versus discontinuity issue and supports the view of transfer as a status passage. One mathematics teacher reported to Galton et al. (2003) that she completed the Bridging Unit during the first three weeks of the new autumn term. At that point the pupils needed new mathematics books and she gave these out with instructions to her Year 7 set to cover them with paper and write on the front, 'Year 7, Set 2 Maths Book'. She recounted that immediately she spoke these words the class cheered loudly. The implication here is fairly clear. The pupils had associated the work done in the Bridging Unit with work they did in the primary school. It was only when they received their Year 7 maths book that their new status was confirmed and the cheers may have been ones of either relief at finally emerging from their primary school status, or anticipation at the new challenges which they assumed they would face now that they were going to do 'Year 7 work'.

Sharing pedagogy across transfer

Schools have also attempted to become more aware of each other's teaching approaches. In the 1970s there were the occasional attempts by secondary teachers to visit primary schools and to observe lessons. By the new millennium these visits had become something of a regular occurrence and, moreover, some of these exchanges were two-way so that primary teachers were also able to come and see what was taking place in Year 7 classes. These reciprocal visits have been well received by teachers who during interview often spoke of the interesting things that were going on in the primary school compared to the rather restricted approaches used at Year 7 and Year 8. However, the research based on observation seems to challenge these claims. In Figure 2.1 the overall teacher–pupil interactions recorded during the Oracle Replication (Hargreaves and Galton, 2002) are shown. In the Oracle approach interactions are divided into different types of questions, different types of statements, silent interactions (mainly when teachers are listening to pupils report or explain or read) and periods where there are no interactions because teachers are housekeeping (giving out books) or monitoring what is happening. As the figure shows, the patterns are almost identical in both the Year 6 and the Year 7 classes. Classroom talk is dominated by teachers making statements.

Figure 2.2 shows a breakdown of class questions. In the Oracle observation schedule: these can be either to do with seeking facts, obtaining a single

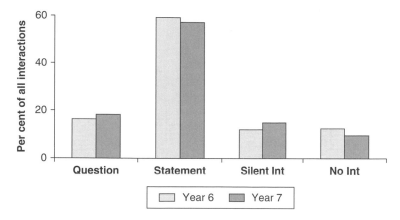

Figure 2.1   Percentage of interactions: pre and post transfer

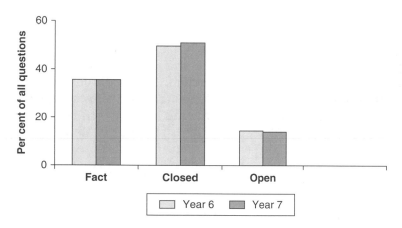

Figure 2.2   Percentage of questions before and after transfer

answer (closed), or more challenging in that they allow for possible alternative answers (open). These latter so called challenging questions were intended to be a central feature in New Labour's push for 'interactive whole-class teaching'. At both primary and secondary level the proportions of the different type of questions are the same, with open questions constituting the smallest percentage overall at around 5 per cent of the total number.

In Figure 2.3, where the proportions of statements used are analyzed, there are some minor variations (in the order of 5%) between Year 6 and Year 7. Secondary teachers make more factual statements and give more directions overall while primary teachers appear to be concerned more often with routine. This is fairly easily explained in terms of the classroom situation where a primary teacher will have what has been called 'periods of evaporated time' when the class or a group of children in a class switch from one curriculum area to another. These switches often require pupils to change

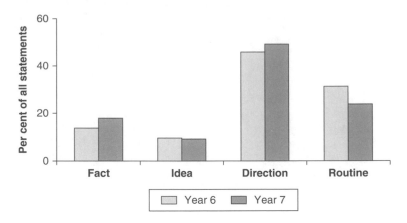

Figure 2.3   Percentage of statements before and after transfer

places or move in and out of groups and teachers to collect in old and hand out new books or to return homework. In relation to making statements of ideas, again associated with problem solving, exploration and higher order thinking, Year 6 and Year 7 classes show both the lowest percentage and also equal amounts of activity. Overall, therefore, despite the claims of teachers who visit each other's classroom that there are major differences in the ways that pupils are taught, the patterns of interaction suggest that the classroom pedagogy in both Year 6 and Year 7 classes is remarkably similar.

How then to account for the fact that the perceptions of teachers differ from this research evidence? Two factors provide possible explanations. The first of these concerns the period in the year when these exchange visits tended to take place. Typically, when teachers were questioned about timing they said that the visits took place in June and July. This was because it was convenient for the secondary teachers since they had more free time, having 'got rid of Year 11 classes', while the primary teachers were concerned that the visits should not take place until after they 'had finished with the SATS'. But as has been seen in the account of the use of Bridging Units, the period after the National Curriculum tests is just the time when teachers in primary schools are likely to engage in more creative problem-solving activities. Thus what the secondary teachers see on these visits is not typical of what takes place during the rest of the year when, as other studies have shown, there is a considerable amount of coaching and direct instruction (Alexander, 2004: Smith et al., 2004).

A second factor which may explain the discrepancy is that the visits of teachers tend to be largely unstructured. It may be, for example, that when the teachers see pupils in the primary school sitting in the groups they make the assumption that they are cooperating whereas the research evidence (Kutnick et al., 2002) suggests that often this may not be the case. Indeed more recent studies have suggested that there has been a reversal in trends in primary schools towards even more direct teaching. Commenting on a series of studies stretching from 1976 to 2005 Galton (2007) has shown that while the amount of questioning in primary classes has risen the actual proportion between open and closed questions has remained at the ratio of 80 to 20 per cent in favour of the closed type. Looking at the pattern of statements, those concerned with facts remained roughly the same at around 15 per cent between 1976 and when they were again observed in 1996. By 2005 however they had doubled to around 30 per cent. Statements of ideas had hardly changed nor had giving directions, with the latter category accounting for roughly around 50 per cent of all teacher statement interactions. The increase in statements of facts had come about by the corresponding fall in the number of routine statements. In another study by Webb and Vulliamy (2006) 18 out of the 45 primary classrooms visited now had desks or tables arranged in rows. While therefore the patterns of questioning seemed to have remained stable in primary classes the shift to whole-class pedagogy seems to have promoted a dominance of teaching as transmission. A similar conclusion was reached by Smith et al. (2004) whose analysis suggests that teacher questioning is now conducted at a rapid pace using predictable sequences of teacher-led recitation. Smith and colleagues conclude from analysis of the data that much of the teaching in the primary classroom, like that in the first year of the secondary school, was interrogative and directive in nature.

Thus the wheel appears to have come full circle in that the changes mandated by governments have promoted a high degree of continuity in the pedagogy used by teachers in primary Year 6 and secondary Year 7. However, whereas the starting point of those concerned in the 1970s was to make secondary teaching more like primary teaching (albeit as we have seen primary teaching was not as exciting as was often claimed) legislators have now succeeded in making primary teaching much more like typical secondary teaching with the consequences that the dips in attainment, attitude and motivation continue because pupils expect things to be more interesting and varied, when they move to the secondary school and quickly find out that things are not so different. One pupil when interviewed towards the end of the first term after transfer reported that in mathematics, 'It's the same here [*as at primary school*] but more complex ... We just do bigger numbers'.

Becoming a professional pupil

Another area affecting transfer concerns the pupils' capacity to develop as *independent learners*. On Induction Day many headteachers will often develop this theme in their opening address but from what follows during the remainder of the day it would seem that a more accurate description of what the school requires is for pupils to become *independent managers*. There are usually constant references about bringing the right books and equipment on a particular day, of not leaving all the weekend homework to the Sunday evening, of having the correct dinner money and of finding the shortest routes around the school so that one arrives on time for lessons. Little is said about the kinds of adjustments that pupils will need to make in learning how to operate independently of teachers and in building up meta-cognitive understanding of the strategies which are best used in different subjects to develop their knowledge and skills. Some researchers have described this process as 'learning to be a professional pupil' (Lahelma and Gordon, 1997). At secondary schools pupils must learn to cope with different teachers, all of whom may have different standards and different requirements. They must not only learn how to manage a complex timetable, but also learn various strategic shortcuts for solving problems in science or mathematics, for interpreting emotional responses in literature and art and for making judgements about the validity of the evidence in history and the social sciences. In this sense they must learn to think as scientists, writers, historians and artists and in so doing must come to understand the nature of the disciplines in which they are engaged, although the standardized approach of the various strategies with their three-part lesson format may have restricted the nature of these intellectual demands.

Some schools have approached this problem by developing a *post-induction* programme. These were conceived initially by secondary schools whose intake came from a large number of feeder primary schools, some of whom, because they supplied only a few potential entrants, did not participate in the summer Induction Day, nor were visited by the transfer school staff. Post-induction was therefore seen as an additional settling in period. In some schools, however, the process has been taken further and extends over the first term with the aim of giving the new students the skills they require to cope with different subjects and different teaching approaches. These post-induction arrangements are generally organized around form tutors. Initially they will consist of orientation activities designed to familiarize the new pupils with the school. In one school, for example, pupils were presented with a virtual image of the school layout on the computer and were asked to find and plot the shortest way from, say, their form room to the science lab or to the dining area without infringing the one-way traffic system. Other sessions concerned trust exercises and identification of learning styles but there was also work in study skills and strategies to help thinking such as using concept maps.

One of the main problems associated with this kind of activity however is that the skills that pupils acquire are not always integrated into subject lessons so there is little transfer of learning. In the example given earlier, the Mathematics and Science departments opted out of the scheme on the grounds of pressure to cover the Key Stage 3 curriculum. In one session the observer saw children use various techniques to help them summarize paragraphs so that when they were sent to find sources from the library or from the Internet they did not copy the extracts but selected the important points from the material. In the exercise that was observed they were given a passage and then asked to present the salient points in a one-minute presentation to the remainder of the form group. However, from interviews with these pupils it emerged that they were never asked to do a similar exercise in History, English or in any other subject area during the course of the following week. There was therefore very little transfer of learning and pupils tended to see the activity as another attempt to provide a gentle introduction into secondary education rather than

Table 2.1   Five Transfer Bridges (1997–present)

Transfer Bridges	Practice 1977	Practice in 1997	Practice now
1. Administrative (designed to smooth the process of transfer)	Occasional meetings of headteachers Transfer of pupil records, Pre-transfer tests	Headteachers meet regularly Fewer records exchanged Visits to Y6 classes by Y7 coordinator and Senco)	As in 1997 but with computerized data transfer Some subject specialists now also visit primary feeders
2. Social/User Friendly (measures to ease pupils' anxieties)	Brief visit to transfer school followed by parent evening	Summer Induction days Several parent evenings Use of transfer school facilities (ICT, PE, drama)	As in 1997 but more pupil exchanges Buddy schemes E-mail exchange More reliance on pupil voice
3. Curriculum (seeking to maintain continuity and progression)	No activity	Bridging Units (QCA) Summer School (gifted in Art/drama; less able in maths and literacy)	More use of locally constructed Bridging Units Fewer summer schools Using Y7 as a motivating year (more active curriculum etc.)
4. Teaching and Learning	No activity	Little activity	More two-way teacher exchanges involving peer observation sometimes structured
5. Managing Learning (helping pupils become 'professional learners')	No activity	Little activity	Some post-induction programmes but mostly excluding core subjects

as a key element in the way they were expected to learn over the course of their time at the school.

Recent transfer initiatives

Table 2.1 summarizes the main changes observed during the last 10 years using what has become known as the *five bridges of transfer*. It can be seen that in the administrative sphere there is greater use of computers for data transfer and packages such as SIMS (School Information Management System) are now more widely available. In the social awareness area there is increasing use of email and the Internet to link primary and secondary pupils so that before transfer it is possible for those in primary school to quiz their peers in the secondary school concerning their anxieties. Some schools organize pupil exchanges so that when the Year 7 coordinator goes to a primary school he or she takes Year 7 pupils with them to answer the Year 6 pupils' questions. Some schools have adopted a buddying system whereby on arrival at the secondary school the new Year 7 pupils is allocated a particular individual who will help and support him during the year. More often these buddies are taken from Year 9 whereas, since one of the main complaints of Year 7 pupils is that they resent reverting after transfer to the most junior status, the use of the current Year 7 in relation to the Year 6 intake would at least give them a certain degree of responsibility for which they appear to yearn. If this kind of system was developed then the buddying system could go right through the school so that new Year 7 pupils retained their buddy in Year 8 and Year 9.

Perhaps the biggest change has been in the use of Bridging Units as a means of improving curriculum continuity. There is little evidence that the Units that replaced the QCA's units as part of the Key Stage 3 strategy have been taken up by a large number of schools. Instead the preference seems to be for schools to develop their own Units. This has several advantages compared to the weaknesses of the QCA Units which were discussed earlier in the chapter. First, such Units are more likely to provide a meaningful context so that the pupils can study recognizable topics with which they are familiar and which hopefully are of interest to them. Investigating the canals in a Midland town, the characteristics of a coastal region in a school on the Norfolk/Suffolk border, solving a murder mystery entitled, *Who Killed the Chef*? based on a famous city hotel which had been the subject of a TV programme are all such examples. In the latter case pupils in the primary school used microscopes to identify materials found at the murder scene in order to deduce from the evidence the most likely guilty person. On coming to the secondary school they were introduced to the idea of chromatography and on retesting various samples were able to arrive at a new suspect. It is noticeable that in all of these examples schools have tended to use an integrated approach which combines some work in science with different forms of writing and some mathematics calculations. This has the advantage that pupils do not have to do too many units thus making them feel, as in the earlier example, that they are still doing primary school work. Such an approach will only work however, if there is active cooperation between the various departments within the secondary school and it is not just part of an induction programme handled by the form tutors.

Whatever decision is taken about the form or the number of Bridging Units, the second and perhaps most important advantage of having a locally produced product is that it improves the quality of the communication between primary and secondary teachers. A decision to develop one's own Units means that there will be discussions not only around the actual curriculum content but also the pedagogy to be used in order to deliver the materials. For example, in one particular school pyramid where not all children attending the secondary school did the Bridging Unit, those producing it decided to include group activity. This solved the problem of what to do about pupils who had not taken part at primary level since within the groups children who had done the earlier part of the unit could tutor those that hadn't. A further advantage stems from the finding that because teachers are involved in the planning and have ownership of the Units there tends to be fewer problems concerning commitment. The primary teachers no longer resent having to do the Units after the national tests because they can incorporate activities which they would have done in the post-SAT period and secondary teachers can plan the work so that they are not simply one-off topics but can extend into future existing work, thus giving a degree of control over curriculum back to teachers.

As Table 2.2 shows, apart from work on peer observation there has been little additional activity in respect of teaching and learning or in developing the idea of helping children to become professional pupils. In the current context, with the continued emphasis on performance, there is surely a need to introduce an element of discontinuity so pupils can discover that being in the secondary school presents different kinds of intellectual challenges to those experienced in the Year 6 primary class. A number of schools have begun to address this problem given the decision of the Government to allow more experimentation at the Key Stage 3 stage. Whereas the recommendation has been to shorten the stage into Year 7 and 8 so that the preparation for GCSE can begin in Year 9 other more adventurous schools have sought to confine the Key Stage 3 work to Years 8 and 9 while devising a Year 7 programme which is specifically designed to re-engage pupils in learning. For example, one school has divided their faculties in the lower secondary school into various specialist areas such as Sports Science, Performing Arts, Design and Technology. Throughout Year 7 the emphasis is on practical activities with the core subjects, Mathematics and English, integrated in part into this work. More concentrated direct instruction in these subjects and also in science then takes place in Year 8 and 9. This school argues that there has been an observable change in children's motivation as a result of this shift of emphasis in the make-up of the curriculum and its associated pedagogy which contrasts sharply with the children's experience in their final year at primary school.

The push elsewhere to reduce Key Stage 3 to Years 7 and 8 and to begin GCSE in Year 9 seems to emerge from the finding in Galton et al. (2003) that Year 8 pupils saw this a 'fallow year'. However, the strong evidence which has emerged as to the pressure that Year 6 children (as well as teachers) feel under by the need to do well in the National Tests would suggest that to condense the Key Stage 3 stage in this way would only add to these pressures and do little to reduce the dips in attainment or to improve motivation and attitude. Pupils come to secondary school excited by the possibilities and demotivated by the experiences of their final year at primary school. Creating some discontinuity in the way that the curriculum is organized and taught in Year 7 so that it really does represent 'a fresh start' would seem the more appropriate option.

Other schools have adopted a different approach. In some, a small team of teachers work together to redesign their approach to the curriculum so that the emphasis is on 'learning to learn' rather than on 'learning to perform'. There are reduced amounts of direct teaching and increased use in the amounts of cooperative and collaborative group work of which more will be said in the next chapter. The principles behind assessment for learning are used to provide feedback and to set targets. The teachers from the primary feeder schools are invited into these lessons in order to comment and evaluate changes in their former pupils' learning patterns. Again this arrangement is designed to promote a degree of discontinuity in the existing system.

Dealing with the attainment dip

Some schools have sought to deal with the problem of those children who come to secondary school having already failed to perform satisfactorily in the Key Stage 2 National Tests. These are among the pupils whose academic performance dips during the first year after transfer. In one case special classes of no more than 20 pupils were created for all children who failed to score Level 4 in English and mathematics. This was done partly by employing an extra teacher but also increasing the numbers in the other Year 7 classes. Typically, this gave rise to four classes of 20 and four classes of 32 pupils. Pupils in the reduced class size were taught in a special area with the mornings devoted entirely to literacy and numeracy but integrated into other humanities work. This increase in time had consequences for the number of periods in the other subjects; most were reduced by half compared to the other Year 7 classes. For example French received only one period a week and Science two compared to the normal two and four sessions respectively. Initially, for the pupils in the reduced size Year 7 classes an experienced primary trained teacher was employed to act as the group leader. She developed an integrated form of curriculum which was delivered mainly through practical activity using a cooperative approach based on group and pair work. Other teachers received training in this approach in the summer term prior to the start of the programme.

In the two years in which an evaluation was carried out by staff from the local University, over 95 per cent of pupils gained at least one level and nearly 40 per cent at least two during their time in Year 7. More importantly these pupils, when they joined their peers in Year 8 in normal-sized classes were able to compete with them for places in higher sets in both French and Science (two subjects where they had received less teaching). But the main change in the children appeared to be the attribution that they gave for failure and success in their learning. On coming to these reduced classes children explained their presence largely in terms of their lack of ability, 'I didn't do very well in primary school. I wasn't good at maths, I only got a Level 2'.

At the end of Year 7, however, when asked how they would cope in the bigger classes when they went to Year 8 they replied, 'We're going to have to work harder'. This final response represents quite a remarkable change in attribution to that elicited previously. Whereas at the beginning of Year 7 pupils thought that failure to do well in primary school was due to a lack of ability on their part, by the end of the year avoiding future failure now depended on one's own efforts rather than some innate intellectual trait. This positive change in self-image also caused these pupils to re-evaluate the reasons why they did badly at primary school. Initially, they had seen their failure as largely of their own making, but now these pupils had something to say about the quality of the teaching arguing that, 'Teachers didn't explain things in the same way that they did in Year 7. If you didn't understand something then they'd explain it and if you still didn't understand it explain it again in another way until you understood'.

There has subsequently, however, been a disappointing sequel to this success story. In the following year after the evaluation the mathematics department pressed for the reintroduction of separate subject teaching in these smaller classes. The motive for this change was a positive one; they wanted to place some of these pupils who had caught up into the higher Year 8 sets and felt that for this to work successfully the Year 7 syllabus should have been fully covered. But the result of this decision, in some respects, has appeared to be counter-productive in that the number of incidents of serious misbehaviour has increased (with some pupils being excluded) and teachers have reported that pupils appear less motivated now that some of the practical activities have had to be replaced by drill and practice exercises from the text book when preparing pupils for the end of Year 7 examination which is used to construct the Year 8 sets. Using the Year 7 text also posed some problems for certain teachers whose specialisms were in humanities and arts.

Listening to the pupil voice

Perhaps the key lesson to emerge from the earlier example is that as well as taking research evidence into account when reviewing transfer arrangements it is equally important to find ways of listening to the pupils' authentic voices about their initial encounters in the secondary school. Creating opportunities for pupils to express their views about the way that their school functions has become almost a prescribed feature of the recent government initiative on *personalized learning* (DfES, 2004b) but as Rudduck and Flutter (2004) argue, much of what currently takes place can be branded as 'tokenism' and rarely engages with issues of teaching and learning. It is of course somewhat easier for a trained outsider to engage in conversation with pupils about their classroom experiences, since both sides have little to lose from the encounter. With a teacher from the same school there can be feelings of betrayal when listening to students talking critically about a colleague, while pupils are never quite sure whether their criticisms will be taken seriously or whether there may be a price to pay in future for expressing such views. It is also difficult to break away from the typical question-and-answer sequences which characterizes so much classroom discourse and to allow genuine dialogic debate. However, discussions about the transfer process can overcome some of these problems by seeking the assistance of the primary staff who taught some of the pupils previously and asking them to conduct interviews.

When pupils were interviewed in a recent, as yet unpublished study of three transfer schools in an East Midland's town, it was clear that by the end of the first half of the Autumn Term they had formed very clear ideas about subjects that they liked and disliked. Art for girls and then PE for boys got the most positive mentions then History. It was noticeable that in most cases what the pupils emphasized was taking part in activities rather than engaging in what they termed, 'desk work'. They particularly disliked the amount of writing (mainly note taking) required:

> I used to hate Art at primary but here it's unbelievable. You've got so much information, lots of equipment and so much that you can do.

> I like athletics, sprinting, hurdles and things. I now go to a real gym on a Friday night, go on the treadmills and stuff.

> History is fun. We make things like modern roundhouse out of straw and I tried it at home also.

Note also that in two of these examples there appears to be a shift in motivation towards more intrinsic levels, in that things pupils did at school they continued with at home in their leisure time. This is a very different situation from the negative responses usually received to the following question on the motivation questionnaire: 'Is there anything you do at school that interests you sufficiently to continue to do it at home?'

The least liked subjects were mathematics (the highest number of negative mentions) followed by science and then languages:

> We write more in maths than we do in English. She writes on the board and then says, 'Here you go, open your books and do questions 1, 2 and 3'. So we just write.

> We hardly do any practical. If we do it then it don't last long and then we have to write up the experiment from the board.

> We couldn't understand our teacher's French then we had a supply and couldn't understand her English so we just copy from the book.

Here, the emphasis is on the lack of activity and the large amount of writing which also replicates the Year 6 curriculum which they experienced in the previous year.

Perhaps the greatest current initial concerns are to do with bullying. Here is an amalgam of what children have said to us during recent interviews:

> The older years act as if you're really tiny.

> Year 8 pick on you because they're older.

> They push your sandwich into your mouth.

> In the lunch queue I just stood by my cousin who's Year 9 and these two girls were mouthing off at me.

> When you're in the dinner line they push you out of the way.

> It's like we're ghosts. They ignore us and act as if we're not there.

> There's a little kid who's chubby. People go up and ask him for a pencil and if he says no, they just take it.

The majority of the comments concern dinner periods. Partly because of this many schools have tried to cut down on dinner times recognizing the period as a potential source of trouble. But there is another point of view in that Year 7 pupils also speak positively about school dinners at secondary level because, with its self-service cafeteria style arrangements it is perceived as something adult. Rushing pupils through lunch time in order to avoid bullying can therefore be counter-productive. What is needed is ways of dealing with the bullying problem directly.

Teachers are also perceived to be a problem. Many teachers are viewed as 'stressy'. Among the comments were the following:

> They get mad when someone speaks when they are speaking then take it out on the rest of the class.

> Good teachers explain things and don't accuse you of not listening. You can have a laugh.

> They listen to your reasons when you're late and don't pick on the whole class when just one or two are fooling about.

> Some teachers are nice to you and when you get stuck take time to help you. Basically you can be a friend with that kind of teacher and at the same time do the work.

> It's weird sometimes because if another teacher comes into the class they act a lot different to when the other teacher isn't there. They're really jolly and nice. When the other teacher goes out they're back to shut up and shouting like normal.

Here again, the two issues which most concern pupils are what they perceive to be the unfairness of being made to suffer because of one or two individuals and the positive things which come from these interviews are that the teachers who explain and listen to explanations are the ones who earn the pupils' respect. Perhaps the last comment here is of a pupil who said, 'I think teachers need a set of rules as well as kids'.

A constant complaint concerns supply cover. Although many secondary schools, as a result of the National Workforce Agreement (DfES, 2003) have now introduced cover teachers as full members of staff there are still problems in that teachers are not always able to carry on with the work that the pupils have been doing with their normal teacher (Galton and MacBeath, 2008). These comments collected during recent interviews make the point fairly forcibly:

> Supply teachers have to cover for all sorts of lessons so if you're stuck they maybe can't help because they don't know about that particular subject.

> Sometimes they can't control the class so they get another teacher. I think they kind of exaggerate the story so the teacher thinks we're worse than we have been. That way they don't look so hopeless but we get told off more for it.

> Basically the substitute doesn't teach. Most of the work set is written out of books. Like they tell us to do a page and write out the questions and answer them. Then people start misbehaving because they're bored and that leads to further trouble.

Despite these above concerns most students remain optimistic that things will get better once they leave Year 7:

> In Year 8 the teachers will trust you more.

> We hopefully get fewer supply teachers.

> We'll get to use computers more.

> We'll not be the youngest and I can look forward to seeing how some of my friends in Year 5 have changed.

> We will mix up classes so I can make a fresh start with new teachers.

> I will avoid some of the teachers I didn't get on with this year.

> I'm going to be nice to the new Year 7 because we've gone through it already.

While for the future cohort of Year 7 pupils the current ones have some valuable advice to offer:

> Don't cry in front of people or they'll take the mick.
>
> Don't worry all the big people won't bully you. Come here and settle in. It's just like your old school but bigger so don't be scared.
>
> Keep yourself to yourself and don't go round telling kids you don't like that, you don't like, just shut up.
>
> Don't say personal stuff out in class, you'll get laughed at.
>
> Don't get cheeky to older pupils or they'll have a go at you.

One pupil ended the interview on this positive note: 'Respect the teachers, respect your friends and be proud of yourself. Respect, like react to people how you'd want them to react to you'. The last point seems to demonstrate that pupils remain optimistic, despite the difficulties associated with the move from primary school and the disappointments over some aspects of their classroom experience, particularly in the core subjects. There is a sense that that things will get better, that, over time, they can forge decent relationships with teachers and with other pupils (provided one takes certain precautions and doesn't seek the limelight). This is a matter which we will return to in Chapter 5. It would seem important, therefore, to build on this optimism. One of the regular complaints pupils make with regard to pedagogy is that there is too much whole-class instruction and insufficient opportunities to take an active part in lessons. Even in science where there are often experiments to be undertaken, these usually occupy only a relatively short amount of lesson time, after which it is back to drawing the diagram in the books and writing out the experiment as it is set out on the board. Thus in the next and following chapter we examine the evidence that working in groups has both academic as well as social benefits. There, evidence will be presented which shows that with careful preparation working in groups not only appeals to pupils but helps foster better attitudes towards both school, in general, and learning, in particular. In later chapters we will then look at what is required to change this current teaching culture in order to promote more cooperative ways of working.

 ## Questions for discussion

1. Which of the two theories; 'transfer as person–environment fit' or 'transfer as a status passage' best explains the current attitudes and motivation of pupils entering Year 7?
2. What might you say to the argument that since results at GCSE are improving a slight hiatus in progress at transfer is of little consequence?
3. If you were in charge of transfer, what changes might you consider making to your current arrangements? Use the Five Transfer Bridges model presented in Box 2.1 to review the situation.

Box 2.1 The Five Transfer Bridges model

What some schools are doing	What *we* do now	What *we* may need to change or add
1. Administrative (designed to smooth the process of transfer): *Meetings of senior staff, Heads of Year, Subject coordinators, SENCOs etc.* *Transfer of attainment data and pupil records* *Communication with parents*		
2. Social (measures to ease pupils' anxieties): *Induction days and open evenings* *Use of secondary ICT, drama and sports facilities by primary schools* *Support for pupils 'at risk'* *Buddy schemes (Y7 with Y6)*		
3. Curriculum (maintaining continuity and progression): *Secondary staff observing and teaching lessons in primary schools* *Video conferencing lessons* *Bridging Units* *Summer schools*		
4. Pedagogy (helping Y7 teachers build on previous effective practice): *Joint programmes of teacher exchanges* *Joint training days* *Structured peer observation*		
5. Managing Learning (Helping pupils become 'professional learners'): *Extended induction programmes involving study skills, identifying preferred learning styles, thinking strategies etc.*		

3

Working Together – Learning Together: Cooperative Working in the Classroom

Maurice Galton

In this chapter we review the evidence concerning the use of cooperative learning as a way of improving pupil motivation and attainment. We then go on to describe the first major empirical study of group work which has been undertaken in English secondary schools. While the results were positive when the English, mathematics and science attainment scores of pupils who worked in groups were compared with others who worked as a class, we argue that further improvements could be achieved if teachers were prepared to give additional time to train pupils to work more effectively in group situations.

We ended the first chapter on a note of optimism. While in terms of attitudes to school and to key subjects such as mathematics, English and science there has been a regular decline over the past decade since these measurements begun, there was one area where scores were high. This concerned the pupils' attitudes towards working together cooperatively. Here pupils' liking for group work scores were uniformly positive (the average was around 80 per cent of the possible maximum score) and this high level has been maintained year on year. Other studies, notably that by Stoll et al. (2003), during the evaluation of the pilot stage of the Key Stage 3 strategy have also produced similar findings. Thus it is possible to argue that if group work could become a more central part of the pedagogy used with pupils in the lower secondary school then it might go some way towards helping to stem the decline in general attitudes to school and to key subjects.

There are numerous studies which attest to the value of group working as an effective pedagogy, both in terms of improving pupil attainment and also attitudes. A number of reviews testify to the value of this approach (Slavin, 1983, 1987; Kulik and Kulik, 1992; Lou et al., 1996). Group work generally results in academic gains as well as social and attitudinal improvements with moderate effect sizes in favour of groups. While the academic gains may be limited (although they can be higher if the task demand is cognitively challenging) they are usually accompanied by much greater positive changes in attitude. Most of the studies reviewed are, however, American based and have been carried out under fairly strict experimental conditions for relatively short periods. When attempts are made to undertake studies in more naturalistic settings where the students study the standard curriculum, where numbers in the class may be around 30, where the situation is liable to interruption from visitors bringing messages and when no allowance is made for the myriad of small interfering happenings that take place during a typical lesson, then the effects are less pronounced.

There are several possible reasons for this partly to do with the manner in which the experimental studies were conducted. Broadly speaking, two distinct theoretical positions influence the approach that researchers take when seeking to evaluate the effectiveness of collaborative groups. Kutnik et al. (2005a) for example, argue that the relevant psychological and sociological theories have been developed with different purposes in mind. Some researchers wish to emphasize improvements in school achievement while others tend to emphasize the development of pro-school attitudes. For example, the work of Robert Slavin in the United States has laid great stress on the processes of reinforcement in raising achievement and this approach can be said to have its origins in the psychology of behaviourism. In Slavin's (1995) earlier work great emphasis was placed on the idea of teams working together in order to secure rewards. In one particular form of what is known as 'teams-games-tournament' the goal is to achieve the highest group score on a mathematics test. The groups are of mixed ability so that to secure a competitive score it is necessary for those with knowledge and ability to work with slower pupils in order to improve the latter's performance. When the test is administered each pupil has to work through the questions on their own after which a joint group score is calculated. To have any chance of achieving the top score it is necessary for the slower pupils to improve their performance as a result of the teaching they have received from their more able peers.

Along with this approach is the belief that the children in the group need to acquire certain social skills through training so that they can support each other. According to Kutnik et al. (2005a) this is a key weakness of the approach because the behaviours to be taught are selected on the assumption that the social settings in which pupils are required to cooperate are non-problematic. These 'normal' group behaviours are broken down into component skills so that each skill can then be taught or reinforced for any pupil whose behaviour is deemed to lie outside these norms. Kutnik and Mason (1998) have criticized such programmes because they argue that to rely on a 'functional view of norms' which can be taught to pupils individually is to miss the point of working together in the classrooms. This is because it decontextualizes these acquired learned behaviours from the various kinds of natural interactions which, typically, take place within the classroom setting. Others (Damon and Phelps, 1989) also argue that the effectiveness of the groups will be limited if the sole focus remains on external rewards for success. Slavin's ideas have a strong following in the United States but do not seem to have taken root here in the UK.

In contrast to this behaviourist approach, Cohen (1994) has used a sociological perspective which argues that in order to work together effectively groups must first overcome certain problems. Among matters subject to negotiation are the individual's status and the power relationships which exist among pupils. Cohen identifies the high-status pupils as ones defined by their attainment or their social class, their race and their gender, and argues that if groups are to work effectively ways must be found for members of each group to learn to value the contributions of all participants. Thus in this approach, typified by the work of Johnson and Johnson (2000) the emphasis is not, as in Slavin's case, to have different members of the group take individual responsibility for different aspects of the task in order to add these contributions to a joint outcome. Rather it is to have all members contribute to a joint outcome from the start, although at some point the group might decide to delegate certain tasks to certain members in the interests of greater efficiency. Gillies and Ashman (2003) offer one possible explanation why the various reviews of American research do not always agree as to the outcomes which arise when working in groups. They argue that where the emphasis tends to be on promoting equality of status then it is frequently the attitudes which improve most, whereas when the emphasis is on peer tutoring of the weaker students it tends to be attainment where improvement is greatest.

This would suggest that a more effective approach is to draw on the different elements of both psychological and social developmental approaches. It is argued, for example, by Kutnik and Mason (1998) that since one of the main reasons for using groups is to maximize pupil–pupil talk, it is highly likely that such communication will only be effective if supportive relationships exist among the group members. This so called 'social-relational' approach emphasizes the need for participants to gain interpersonal sensitivity concerning their peers. Hence an important part of the training process is that pupils should learn to trust one another so that, for example, group members know that their contributions to the group, however trivial, will be taken seriously by others and that an individual will not be the subject of ridicule or scorn if he or she makes a mistake.

An interesting example of this kind of sensitivity occurred during the SPRinG Project into the study of grouping (which was mentioned at the beginning of the book and of which more will be said in a later section of this chapter). In the final part of Chapter 1 different types of students were identified. Type 3 pupils were described as *struggling loners*, who rarely became involved in group activity. They tended to be among the less able, had anti-learning attitudes and were poorly motivated. Typical of this type of pupil was Matthew as the following extract from an interview with him demonstrates:

Interviewer: When the teacher says, 'Right I want you to get into groups,' what do you think?

Matthew: Boring lesson. Supposed to have to think.

Interviewer: Would it be more boring if you did it as a class?

Matthew: Yeah but it wouldn't matter because I'd just sit there and do nothing still.

Interviewer: So you can't opt out in groups?

Matthew: I don't get myself involved. I never do.

Other members of the group, however, seem to have developed the kinds of inter-personal sensitivity that Kutnik and Mason (1998) suggest is a crucial part of effective group working. The following exchange subsequently took place with two members of Matthew's group, Michael and Gareth:

Michael: If we're in a group and had somebody who didn't think they were as clever and had an idea and the person who they thought was cleverest also had an idea they'd immediately go with the person who had the cleverest idea.

Gareth: That's what Matthew's like.

Michael: Because Matthew thinks he isn't any good at English but he is quite good.

Interviewer: Do you tell him that?

Michael: Yeah, we do tell him and he comes up with some good ideas sometimes. But if I say something that's different to him he'll immediately just go all wobbly.

Gareth: He just doesn't believe it.

Michael and Gareth, both Year 9 pupils, display remarkable sensitivity about Matthew and with further training might learn how to encourage him to get over this reluctance to participate.

The importance of adopting the social-relational approach can also be illustrated in another interview, this time with Zoë and Emily, both *group shirkers*. Although opting out for most of the time, they both agree that they will sometimes be prepared to participate on condition that their peers show a degree of sensitivity:

Emily: Yeah. I reckon we have [got better at working in groups] cos us two used to be really naughty and used to get put on report sometimes.

Zoë: I still do.

Emily: Yeah. But not in a group really. When we work on our own we do but when we're in a group we think that, well, we're allowed to be together.

Zoë: So we just try to work well.

Zoë: If we done it as a class then we all wouldn't be doing much. Like there might be certain people with their hands up like the boffs or something. And if we done it by ourselves then half of us wouldn't do it would we? The only bad thing about working in a group I reckon is if someone's doing the work and you're just sitting there.

Interviewer: So if you don't share the work out and they take over?

Zoë: Sometimes I don't mind. But sometimes I do and I just get in a stress. A couple of times I was with Hannah and Katie and they're, like, boffs so they were doing all the work and they were like 'Oh! I'm doing this' and 'I'm doing that' so I just got in a mood.

Table 3.1   The relationship between seating and working arrangements in the classroom (pre-National Curriculum)

Organization	Seating arrangement	Working arrangement
Small groups	56.0%	5.0%
Pairs	16.0%	4.0%
Individual	7.5%	81.0%
Whole class	20.5%	10.0%

Grouping and group work

Before proceeding further we need to establish an important distinction between working together and learning together. In primary schools, as was mentioned in Chapter 2, it is customary for pupils to sit together but rarely to work together. Indeed, around three decades ago it was established that the primary classroom displays an asymmetric relationship between the way the pupils sit and the way that they work as Table 3.1, taken from Galton and Patrick (1990) demonstrates.

It will be seen that there is an inverse relationship between the way that pupils sit and the way that they work so that, for example, although for 56 per cent of the time the class sat in small groups they only worked as a group for 5 per cent of that time. A further 16 per cent of classroom arrangements consisted of pairs but only 4 per cent of time was spent working in pairs. Whereas although children rarely sat alone (7.5 per cent) nearly 81 per cent of the work took place with children working at their own separate task. Finally when the pupils were grouped in a whole-class seating arrangement (sitting together at the front of the room hearing a story etc.) they only worked in this manner for about 10 per cent of the time. Since these figures were produced there has of course been a drastic change because of the emphasis in the Literacy and Numeracy strategies on whole-class teaching. More recent reviews of the situation (Galton, 2007) show that the use of whole-class teaching now occupies around a third of the lesson but much of this whole-class teaching is not a cooperative class activity but still involves each individual pupil listening to the teacher and absorbing as much of what is said as he or she can. This contrasts with the situation where working as a class involves extended interaction between the teacher and the pupils so that, for example, when a pupil replies to a question they answer not only for themselves but for their peers. Interestingly when pupils are asked how they learn most in classrooms they often reply that they do so by listening to the exchanges between the teacher and other pupils.

Use of groups in the secondary classroom

For various reasons there are few similar studies in secondary schools concerning the different modes of working but there is no reason to believe that whole-class teaching is any different from that taking place in primary schools as indeed, the data on transfer produced in the previous chapter confirms. In developing the Key Stage 3 National Strategy the then DfES produced training and guidance materials concerning the use of group work in the teaching of numeracy and literacy (DfES, 2004c). However, in the pilot evaluation study of the Key Stage 3 Strategy, Stoll et al. (2003) found that whole-class teaching continued to dominate the pedagogy of the core subjects, although when pupils were asked about their preferred way of learning 90 per cent of the sample of Year 8 pupils expressed a preference for working in groups rather than for whole-class teaching. This finding was supported in a study by Kutnick et al. (2005b) who surveyed a mix of 250 Year 7 and Year 10 classes from 47 secondary schools. The result of this 'mapping' survey showed that the pupil groupings in these classrooms were rarely determined by the nature of the task demand. When pupils worked in groups they were often allowed to choose their composition which, because they were based on friendship, tended to be strongly associated with the attainment level, gender and ethnicity of the pupils, although the latter variable was not included in Kutnick et al.'s (2005b) analysis. In science, the determining factor which decided whether group work would be carried out was the availability of equipment. In other cases the decision to move to group work was often arbitrary. For example, in one instance reported in Kutnick et al. (2007) the rationale for changing from 'class' to 'groups' was 'because children were becoming bored with the class work and I thought they needed a change'.

Possible impediments to the use of group work

The seeming reluctance on the part of secondary teachers in England to use groups specifically to facilitate desired academic outcomes rather than merely for social, practical, or convenience motives, may be thought surprising, given the evidence referred to earlier in the chapter that there have been a host of comparative studies, particularly in the United States and Israel, comparing the use of cooperative and collaborative groupings against more traditional classroom structures. Given the expressed concerns of teachers about the decline in the conduct of pupils, it might be thought that the use of groups to encourage more cooperative behaviour might have become more frequent since the introduction of the Key Stage 3 Strategy.

There may be a number of reasons why this transformation in teaching methodology has not occurred in addition to the one cited earlier that the comparative studies of group work and class teaching have often been carried out under circumstances that do not reflect conditions in a typical classroom. Teachers claim that they are under too much pressure, because of the demands of the curriculum, to find the necessary time for setting up and carrying out group tasks (Kutnick et al., 2007). Other practitioners may have concerns about loss of control over the learning environment since it is often difficult to be certain that the talk among pupils is productive, or even on-task. This contrasts sharply with the situation during whole-class discussion where pupils generally only speak when requested to do so by the teacher. Teachers may also see the need for mixed-ability groups as an additional source of difficulty, since it often means placing a disruptive pupil among others who work well together with possible problematic consequences. However, Putnam et al. (1996) found that when such children are placed with others there are positive socializing effects. By way of contrast, however, Brinton et al. (1998) suggest that aggression or withdrawal is a more typical response. There is also some evidence that suggests that different personality types react differently to the groups. Webb (1989) for example found that introverts were more likely to withdraw from groups and in Kutnick et al.'s (2007) case studies many teachers said that they did not know what to do with the 'loners' who withdrew from group activity completely. Entwistle (1977) also suggests that anxious pupils learn best when materials are highly structured as in whole-class direct instruction so that the more open-ended problem-solving approach which researchers such as Sharan and Sharan (1992) claim facilitates cooperation within groups may not be so appropriate for such pupils.

Another key reason for teachers' reluctance to use grouping to enhance academic performance may be the requirement that to work effectively pupils need to be trained in communication skills (Mercer, 2000). In the United States, Webb and colleagues (Webb and Farivar, 1994; Webb et al., 1997; Webb and Mastergeorge, 2003) have studied the communication processes that are required to ensure effective group work. They emphasize the necessity of having pupils in the groups who can undertake focused questioning, explore alternative answers and provide explanations for these answers if groups are to be proficient in their problem solving. To be able to operate at this cognitive level requires appropriate training, not only to enhance this exploratory talk, but as Kutnik and Mason (1998) suggest to provide the necessary levels of trust among group members so that in subjects such as Humanities and English they can handle issues which are likely to be controversial such as those that concern issues of race, gender or politics. Kutnick's et al. (2005a) review of secondary school teachers' approach to group work, found that teachers were provided with little advice about training pupils to participate effectively in either social or communicative interactions.

Social pedagogic research into group work

The SPRinG (Social Pedagogic Research into Group work) Project was part of a wider initiative, The Teaching and Learning Research Programme (TLRP). The main impetus for SPRinG was to build on earlier studies and address the gap between what research findings recommend and what classroom practitioners in schools typically do. We sought, with the help of teachers, to develop a programme of group work that could be successfully integrated into school life and to subsequently evaluate this programme by examining pupil progress in comparison to a control group in terms of (a) attainment, (b) motivation for group working, and (c) within-group interactions. The project took place on three sites (School of Education, University of Brighton; Institute of Education, University of London; and Faculty of Education, University of Cambridge) with each site taking responsibility for a Key Stage. Our concern here is with the research in Cambridge which was responsible for the study at Key Stage 3. Given the relative dearth of UK studies at secondary level, a notable exception being that of Cowie et al. (1994), Cowie and Rudduck (1988) and Mercer and Littleton (2007) the inclusion of Key Stage 3 classrooms was particularly important.

The study had five phases, the first three of which concern us here. Following an introductory Phase (Phase 1), there was a developmental Phase (Phase 2), which involved working closely with teachers in seeking to develop the most effective methods of implementing group work and included development of the programme and research tools for evaluation. The main evaluation Phase (Phase 3) was designed to test the effectiveness of the group-work initiative by means of experimental comparisons. The project ran for four years.

During Phase 1 (the introductory stage) 30 Key Stage 3 teachers (14 English and 16 science) were recruited to the project. Subsequently 12 mathematics teachers were invited to join the study. Teachers were recruited either as a result of a recommendation by colleagues in the Faculty or by local advisors. The period was also used to develop the various attitude, attainment and observation measuring instruments to be used in the experimental comparisons. Phase 2 consisted of a year-long collaboration between the research team and teachers to develop a set of usable practices, based on existing research evidence but which at the same time promoted effective group work in everyday classroom settings. There were regular meetings with teachers to discuss emerging ideas concerning effective group work, to test the various measuring instruments and to observe and give feedback on initial attempts at group work. Valuable lessons were learned about, for example, group size, group composition, what activities worked well and what strategies needed to be adopted to encourage good working habits in the groups. These ideas were incorporated into a number of training activities (described in the following chapter) which were guided by three key principles:

1. *The use of a relational approach throughout the study.* Behind this statement was the belief that group work skills had to be developed; that teachers cannot just place pupils into groups and expect them to work well together. Group work therefore requires an extended period of preparation. As well as improving pupils' skills to communicate effectively through listening, explaining and sharing ideas it is also important that pupils should learn to trust and respect one another. They also need to acquire various planning, organizing and evaluation skills in order to maintain group work activity.
2. *Involvement of teachers in the design of the project and in group work.* Programmes developed in one context or one country may not readily transfer to others. Only teachers have the necessary experience to be able to judge the *fitness for purpose* of a particular course of action within their own classroom context. As

Anderson and Burns (1989) argue,' Contrary to some people's opinions, evidence does not speak for itself. The translation of evidence into thought and action requires people who understand both the research and the classroom'.

3. *The need to situate group activity within a particular classroom context.* Our approach required that any proposal for working in groups should take into consideration the main dimensions governing all classroom activity. This includes 'fixed factors' such as classroom layout, class size, normal seating arrangements and so on. It also includes pupil characteristics and the class composition (mixed ability, broad bands, sets etc.) the curriculum content and the manner in which such content is organised.

Having thus set out the background to this research, the remaining sections of the chapter will describe the methodology employed, then present the main results and finally discuss the implication of these findings for both future research and current practice.

Design of the Key Stage 3 study

As explained previously, only English and science teachers were initially recruited but in the second year of the study a further cohort of mathematics specialists were added. Originally it was hoped to conduct a 'true' experiment with teachers randomly assigned to two conditions (use of group work versus a combination of whole-class and individual work) but this proved not to be feasible for a number of reasons. First, and most importantly, few teachers were willing to be part of the whole-class and individual seat work treatment group. All said that they had joined the project in order to discover how to use group work more effectively and that they therefore did not wish to be excluded from participating in the various training programmes. Second, teachers argued that in some cases, particularly in science, where for some experiments there was limited amounts of equipment, bringing pupils together in groups was the only feasible strategy.

After some discussion with the participating teachers it was agreed that the key difference between the use of groups for, say, practical tasks and for promoting cognitive development was in the use of groups for developing new concepts or for problem solving. Typically, the former was usually done through class discussion involving what Edwards and Mercer (1987) have described as 'cued elicitations'. It was agreed, therefore, that the essential comparison would be that in all cases where it was intended to introduce new concepts, develop ideas and find solutions to problems, then this would be done either by means of whole-class activity or through the use of small groups. At other points in time where the tasks involved were practical or relatively low level, as in mathematics, where pupils might be comparing answers or solving different aspects of a problem individually and then bringing the final result together, then groups could be used. The essential distinction here was between different types of grouping as defined by Galton and Williamson (1992). In their study group activity was defined in three different ways. The first kind of grouping was designated *collaborative*. In this situation there was complete social inter-dependence so that pupils worked cooperatively to complete a common task. For example in English, pupils might have to make predictions about what certain characters in a story might do next while in science, faced with certain results, they might be asked to come up with an acceptable hypothesis and way of testing it.

The second kind of grouping was termed *cooperative*. Here pupils work independently on their own tasks as a contribution to a common goal. In mathematics, for example, each pupil, having worked out a number of examples, might then come together to share these results, while in science pupils might take measurements of a chemical process at different temperatures and then come together to produce the overall graph showing the rate of reaction.

Finally, pupils could be placed in '*seated*' groups where individuals worked on their own but helped each other by checking and comparing answers. In English this might involve pupils reading each other's stories while in mathematics it would involve group members checking their respective calculations. Essentially in this study, therefore, comparison was between collaborative forms of group work and whole-class discussion.

In accordance with the principles of social pedagogy the situation was designed to follow the normal pattern of events as closely as possible. In mathematics and science, for example, units of work usually lasted for around six to eight weeks. In each subject teachers were randomly assigned to one of two groups. The first group then chose from four units, two which were part of the school's scheme of work for the participating class. This group then taught one unit using collaborative group work and the other unit using a combination of whole-class teaching and individual work. The situation was then automatically reversed for the second group so that whenever the first group taught a unit using collaborative group work the second would use the combination of a whole-class and individualized teaching approach.

The assessed tasks

Table 3.2 shows the topics chosen for each subject. In mathematics the topics consisted of number patterns (from the Algebra strand) interpreting data (Data Handling strand), ratio (from the Number strand) and areas and volumes (measurement of Space and Shape strand), thus covering the four curriculum Attainment Target areas. In science the topics involved the study of particles, electric circuits, forces and living cells, and were chosen to cover both physical and biological aspects. English presented more difficulties in that often the goal of the teaching is for pupils to gain an understanding of certain general processes and to acquire certain skills rather than as in mathematics and science where the understanding usually relates to specific content knowledge. It was decided therefore to focus on four forms of writing genre (narrative, response to text, persuasive and descriptive). Teachers of English were free to choose their own content but the end product would be a piece of work which could be assessed using appropriate National Curriculum levelling criteria.

Table 3.2   Measures used to assess pupils' performance

English	Science	Mathematics
1. Narrative writing	1. Particles	1. Number patterns
2. Response to text	2. Electronic circuits	2. Interpreting data
3. Persuasive writing	3. Forces	3. Ratio
4. Descriptive writing	4. Living cells	4. Areas & volumes

In each case pupils were given a test prior to beginning a unit and the same test was administered once the unit had been completed. This typically took six weeks. The Science Attainment Measures were mainly taken from a series of diagnostic tests (Millar et al., 2003) constructed as part of another TLRP Project (Towards Evidence-based Practice in Science Education). Where items covering the particular topic were not available others were selected from the Key Stage 3 statutory tests and from the optional tests created by the Qualifications and Curriculum Authority (QCA). In mathematics the number patterns for algebra were largely taken from the *Dime* (Diversity in Mathematic Education) set of mathematics enrichment resources published by Tarquin Press. Items were generally investigative in style testing higher-order thinking. Questions about interpreting data from the Data Handling strand were taken mainly from the Secondary Mathematics Independent Learning Experience (SMILE) pack. Again, there was a mix of items, mainly testing higher-order thinking. Ratio from the Number strand was again constructed from the SMILE pack and from other QCA test examples. These items mainly demanded knowledge application rather than problem solving. Areas and volume from the measurement for space and shape strand were also constructed from the SMILE pack and like the ratio material the items mainly demanded knowledge application rather than problem-solving skills. In the case of both mathematics and science all the items chosen were assigned a level by two expert judges and a mix of items selected which covered Years 7, 8 and 9. The pupils' overall levels score was then converted into a number using the NFER numeric conversion scale. This is shown in Appendix B.

In English the procedure was somewhat different in that pupils were given an assignment initially involving various kinds of writing. This was marked by a small group of SPRinG project teachers, all of whom had had experience of public examining at GCSE and were therefore familiar with the process of levelling work. At the end of the six weeks pupils again were asked to complete a similar piece of writing and this was again marked by these experts. In each case the marking was 'blind' so that teachers were unaware of the school where the scripts originated and did not mark work from their own school. Levels were again converted to numeric scores using the NFER scale.

Prior to carrying out the evaluations all teachers had taken part in a programme designed to help them hone their pupils' group-working skills. It has been shown by Kagan (1988) that with training the pupils can improve both the quality and the effectiveness of their work in groups. The SPRinG training programme was an amalgam of various approaches including the development of group dynamics (Kingsley-Mills et al., 1992) the development of suitable attitudes (Farivar and Webb, 1991) and the improvement of various communication skills (Wilkinson and Canter, 1982; Mercer, 2000). In the event, unlike their colleagues in the primary sector, the secondary teachers found it difficult to give the time to the full training programme. In particular, some of the participating science teachers questioned the necessity of pupils needing to spend time on trust exercise designed to improve the dynamics of groups. As a compromise, it was agreed that training should concentrate on a few selected areas. These included setting and improving rules governing both the behaviour and the conversation in groups, exercises designed to improve group maintenance skills (summarizing, time-keeping etc.), exercises designed to improve decision making by consensus rather than voting and, at a later stage, exercises designed to support better reasoning and explanation within the groups. Most of these training exercises were taken either from Kingsley-Mills et al. (1992) or from Cowie and Rudduck (1988). More details of these training procedures will be provided in the next chapter.

Key Stage 3 comparisons

It proved difficult for teachers to carry out all four tasks during the course of the year. This emerged during the first year of the fieldwork when a trial of the design was carried out among some members of the English teaching cohort. During the construction of the training programme it was found that many of the activities designed to promote better group cohesion were a natural part of pupils' developing response to English text. In many English lessons there was an emphasis on sharing feelings as well as ideas and this required the development of empathetic relationships between pupils during both class and group discussion. English teachers therefore felt ready to undertake the comparative study before either their science or mathematics colleagues. Having found that four writing tasks were too many, the English teachers agreed to collapse the categories into two, that of imaginative and discursive writing for the second year of fieldwork. Data collected in the first year on all four forms of writing was then collapsed with response to text and persuasive writing being combined into the imaginative mode and descriptive and narrative writing into the discursive category. Data for both years was then aggregated to give the results shown in Table 3.3 where the means, standard deviations (in brackets) and effect sizes are presented. It can readily be seen that in the case of imaginative writing the classes taught through the use of collaborative grouping outperformed those in which whole-class teaching was the dominant methodology. The pupils taught mainly through the use of groups raised their performance by nearly a whole level (from level 5– to 5+) whereas the scores of those taught as a class barely changed. The result produces a small to medium effect size using Cohen's (1988) criterion which according to Hattie (2005) represents upwards of one-third of a year's progress. For discursive writing those taught in groups again do better than those

Table 3.3   Progress in English by topic and by gender (*SDs* in brackets)

Topic/gender	Mode	Pre-test	Post-test	N	Effect size
Imaginative	Group	31.17 (5.27)	32.57** (5.30)	200	0.43
	Class	29.73 (7.90)	30.31 (6.50)	137	
Discursive	Group	29.32 (6.06)	31.19** (5.34)	185	0.37
	Class	31.12 (5.61)	31.80* (5.28)	178	0.18
Boys	Group	29.29 (5.35)	30.66** (4.93)	211	0.38
	Class	28.37 (6.19)	29.13* (5.62)	186	0.18
Girls	Group	30.87 (5.60)	32.79** (5.38)	223	0.42
	Class	32.31 (7.17)	32.84 (6.08)	211	

* = $p < 0.05$; ** = $p < 0.01$.

taught mostly through whole-class teaching. In both cases the gains are significant (at the 1% level for groups and at the 5% level for class). The effect size for groups is nearly twice that for students taught by the whole-class method. Overall therefore the findings are very positive in terms of using an approach based on collaborative group work.

Support for these findings comes from Mercer and Littleton (2007). In their study Year 8 pupils in two schools were put through a special training programme, *Thinking Together*, which was designed to improve the quality of reasoning for joint problem solving. Prior to training pupils completed a written task which required them to 'assess the persuasive quality of non fiction text', in this case a selection of public service advertisements. At the end of the school year the pupils were retested using a similar exercise and the results compared with those from another Year 8 cohort in a control school that had not been trained to work together in groups. Whereas the pupils in the control school made no improvement over the period, those in the two schools who underwent training did much better such that the difference between their mean scores and that of their peers in the control school was significant at the 5 per cent level.

In the second half of Table 3.3 a similar analysis is presented, this time by gender. In the case of boys the gains between pre-test and post-test are significant for both groups and class, but the effect sizes in the case of groups is again almost twice that of that for pupils taught mainly by a whole-class approach. In the case of girls, however, it is only the approach based on the use of groups that alone achieves significance level, giving a small to medium effect size equivalent to one third of a year's progress compared to the results for whole-class teaching. On this evidence therefore working in groups to develop pupils' ideas in English has much to recommend it, certainly for girls but also for boys.

At the end of the first chapter four different pupil types were identified. For each form of writing (*discursive* and *imaginative*) a regression analysis was performed to examine the effects of type, gender and year group on post-test scores. For discursive writing being in groups, particularly in either Year 7 or Year 9, had a positive effect but having a positive disposition towards group

Table 3.4 Progress in mathematics by task demand and by gender (*SD*s in brackets)

Task demand and gender	Mode	Pre-test	Post-test	N	Effect size
Low-level demand	Group	30.35 (4.14)	30.53 (4.62)	133	
(ratio and area/volume)	Class	34.64 (4.37)	35.08 (5.64)	167	
High-level demand	Group	33.54 (4.56)	34.98* (5.22)	185	0.70
(number pattern and	Class	29.78 (3.78)	30.45* (4.26)	178	0.48
data handling)					
Boys	Group	31.16 (4.26)	32.00* (4.90)	124	0.56
	Class	32.67 (4.88)	32.96 (6.15)	134	
Girls	Group	32.33 (4.91)	32.90 (5.82)	108	
	Class	33.08 (4.69)	33.87* (5.04)	127	0.54

* = $p < 0.01$.

work made little difference irrespective of the type to which the pupil belonged. With imaginative writing, however, the *active collaborator* pupils of both gender (type 2) were the only ones to produce a highly significant gain in scores (large effect size > 1.0). It is largely the superior performance of these pupils that compensates for the remaining types and gives rise to the positive result for group teaching in Table 3.3.

In dealing with the maths attainment scores a similar procedure was adopted to that used for English, in that the scores on different topics were combined according to the perceived task demand. Scores, based on low-level cognitive demand, mainly consisted of items from the ratio and areas and volumes tests while high-level scores were mainly taken from the number pattern and data-handling items. Here the results, shown in Table 3.4 are not as clear-cut as were those for English. When the cognitive demand was low level neither pupils taught in groups or mainly through whole-class teaching made significant progress. There is clearly an ability teaching mode interaction in that on the tasks of lower cognitive level the pre-test score indicates that the pupils who worked in groups appear to be of lower ability than those taught by whole-class methods. The situation is reversed when the higher-level scores are considered. It is unclear how this inbalance arose since with four curriculum Attainment Targets available there are six possible combinations of two units that an individual teacher could select. One possibility is that most teachers tended to use group methods with pupils of lower ability when the task was of a lower level. Another possibility is that there were more Year 9 classes in the whole-class teaching cohort and they naturally had higher pre-test scores. This situation then reverses when the higher-level cognitive scores are considered. Table 3.4 shows that when mathematics tasks are concerned with investigations involving higher-level thinking both results are significant (at the 1% level) but the effect size achieved in the groups is higher than that achieved through whole-class teaching, although in both cases the gains are sizeable and represent considerable progress. When the scores are looked at in terms of gender there is a surprising interaction effect in that boys did better when taught in groups (effect size 0.56) while the reverse was true for the girl pupils (effect size 0.79). There is a some support for the view that this is a genuine effect, in the case of boys since those taught in groups have the lowest pre-test mean, and previously, Pell et al. (2007) have detected a slight tendency for less able boys to have more positive attitudes to group work although the correlation of −0.06 was very modest. These positive attitudes to group work were also positively correlated with pupils' anti-learning and anti-school dispositions. These boy pupils are precisely the kind whose achievement has been the source of so much national concern (Warrington and Younger, 2006).

The result for girls runs counter to other recent research. Boaler (1997a, 1997b, 1997c) for example, has carried out a number of studies on the effectiveness of ability grouping in mathematics. More able girls disliked the rapid-paced whole-class interactive teaching which was the norm in the higher sets because it provided too little thinking time. It could be that the result in Table 3.4 is simply due to the pre-test differences, where the more able girls do better than slower-learning ones irrespective of teaching mode. Certainly, a regression analysis on the two areas testing lower cognitive demand (area/volume and ratio) shows that pre-test scores predicts around 90 per cent of the variation in post-test scores with no significant group versus class effect. Since in the second half of Table 3.4 there are more able girls in the 'whole-class' category this results in a superior post-test score overall. However, when the cognitive demand is high, as in *interpreting data*, then being a type 2 pupil (the *active collaborators*) and being a girl working in groups elevates the post-test scores above all other types, irrespective of gender, by one-fifth of a National Curriculum level. This is in accord with Boaler's (1997c) conclusion that able girls with positive group-work dispositions will do better when allowed to work together collaboratively rather than taught by means of interactive whole-class teaching. With *Number Patterns* there is a similar positive effect for type 2 pupils, this time for both genders. There is also evidence that older pupils in Year 9 cope better with these higher-level tasks. Being in Year 9 improves the post-test score by over one National Curriculum level.

With science, the results are again more difficult to interpret, partly because the decision over which topics to attempt was largely governed by the way the syllabus was constructed and in particular, the year in which a topic was dealt with. This tended to vary from school to school. In the event the decision to offer only two out of the four topics resulted in certain anomalies in that no teacher undertook the Living Cells module. Because of the different points in time when topics were taught in various schools, most teachers eventually undertook the Electricity topic as a whole-class activity but had more flexibility in their choice of either particles or forces for the group activity. As a result, there was considerable difference between numbers in the group and class cohorts in each of the three topics. A second problem occurred because in the case of science, the teachers were concerned that the

Table 3.5 Progress in science by topic and by gender (*SDs* in brackets)

Topic/gender	Mode	Pre-test	Post-test	N	Effect size
Electricty	Group	26.85 (4.19)	30.62** (5.25)	26	0.71
	Class	29.25 (5.15)	33.58** (5.49)	106	0.73
Forces	Group	26.21 (7.57)	29.79** (8.06)	28	0.98
	Class	31.76 (8.51)	33.35* (9.74)	66	0.27
Particles	Group	29.32 (5.27)	31.93** (6.27)	94	0.48
	Class	31.21 (4.81)	31.92 (5.15)	39	
Boys	Group	28.56 (5.46)	31.30** (6.09)	54	0.53
	Class	29.87 (7.87)	33.64** (9.23)	53	0.69
Girls	Group	26.81 (5.86)	29.89** (5.86)	53	0.58
	Class	30.00 (7.86)	33.70** (8.23)	54	0.49

* = $p < 0.05$; ** = $p < 0.01$.

test items, particularly the diagnostic type, covered too large an ability range. It was therefore agreed that each teacher should recommend the items for their class test which they believed matched the average ability level of the pupils that they taught. Initial analysis of the results showed that some teachers had tended to underestimate the ability of their pupils and as a result 'ceiling' effects occurred at the post-test and some pupils achieved the maximum possible score on the particular test used.

The results are shown in Table 3.5. In all three tests the pupils taught using collaborative groups made significant gains with the same magnitude of effect size in the case of electricity (both group and class cohorts achieving effect sizes approaching 0.8, the 'large' Cohen (1988) criterion. However, in the case of both Forces and Particles it is the pupils working in groups that do better (in terms of effect size) compared to those receiving whole-class instruction. Thus, overall, in science, the trend was only marginally in favour of group work. When gender comparisons are examined there were significant gains for both boys and girls when thaught by either group or whole-class methods. In terms of the effect sizes boys and girls do equally well when taught by either method.

Looking once more on the influence of the different pupil types only the *struggling loners* (type 3) failed to make significant progress on the Electricity test and this is also true for Forces where the *anti-boff shirkers* (type 1) and *quiet collaborators* (type 4) do particularly well, although the former type still display negative attitudes to science. For Particles it is the type 2 pupils (*active collaborators*) who do best followed by the *quiet collaborators* with the other two types showing no significant changes between pre- and post-test scores. Overall, therefore, in relation to these different types of pupil, no clear conclusions emerge apart from the interesting result that pupils of anti-learning disposition, such as Matthew in the earlier episode, made significant positive progress in two out of the three tests.

What can one make of these findings?

These findings in themselves do not therefore constitute an overwhelming case for the use of group work rather than whole-class teaching. As Alexander (2006) observes, part of the weakness of the Government's initiative to encourage the effective use of what was initially termed whole-class interactive teaching has lain in the failure to define the terms precisely so that in much of the Government literature, the advocacy of this approach was often accompanied by an injunction that lessons should maintain a rapid pace. Recommendations of this kind represents a confusion between the use of questioning as in *direct instruction* (Gage, 1978; Rosenshine, 1979) and its use to enable pupils to engage in *'thoughtful discourse'* as a means of teaching for understanding rather than transmission (Good and Brophy, 2002). In direct instruction rapid question and answers are used by the teacher to find out what pupils remember from previous lessons in order to decide whether previous material needs to be retaught or new material introduced. This is very different from interactive whole-class teaching which is designed, as with group work, to promote thinking and problem solving and which therefore requires pupils to have extended *wait times* or as Alexander prefers, *'thinking times'*, in order to process and organize information before providing an answer. Alexander (2006) has developed these ideas into a programme which he describes as *Dialogic Teaching* which in its principles mirrors many of the purposes of group work, although with greater teacher participation. According to Alexander's initial results reading and writing has benefited from the increased emphasis on dialogic talk during classroom discourse particularly for the less able pupils but not all teachers are able to change easily from the dominant process of cued elicitations. Nevertheless, a truer comparison between whole-class and group instruction should perhaps seek to make comparisons between two treatment groups, one trained in group-working skills and one trained in the use of dialogic talk during whole-class teaching sessions. Even so, there are grounds for suggesting that if in this study the structure of the group activities had been better organized then the differences in terms of pupil progress between whole-class discussion and talk in groups would have been even larger.

There are a number of reasons for making this claim to do mainly with the context in which teachers had to operate when taking part in this study. First, as part of training pupils to work effectively in groups it is vital that teachers brief and debrief the class so that they can begin to gain meta-cognitive awareness of what it means to be part of a group. Debriefing sessions therefore are particularly important because they not only evaluate how individuals responded in the groups but they also call for participants to make suggestions about suitable strategies for improving the situation on future occasions. It was noticeable however, particularly in science (which had the least positive results in favour of group work) that teachers rarely found time for these debriefing sessions. It was comparatively rare, for example, to see a science lesson where the teacher with, say, five minutes of the period left preferred to keep discussion of the results over until the next lesson and instead engaged in a debriefing exercise. More often teachers preferred to use an evaluation sheet which they handed to pupils as they left the class. Thus the exercise then tended to take the form of an additional homework task rather than generate a debate on the consequences of the previous classroom activity. Some teachers also skipped parts of the training, again on the grounds of time, and justified this action by arguing that similar training procedures were also part of the school's PHSE programme. This raises questions concerning transfer of training where there is strong evidence that if transfer is to be effective it has to be contextualized (Good and Brophy, 2002) so that developing the rules for working in groups in PHSE may not the same as developing rules for working in groups in science. Indeed, there was evidence for this within the study in that in some schools the same pupils were observed participating in groups in both science and English where their levels of cooperation were noticeably different.

The second factor which tended to diminish the effectiveness of the groups involved the quality of feedback which often emerged during the 'reporting back' session. Built into most teachers' antennae is the notion of equity, particularly with respect to the opportunity to learn. Thus in the earlier Oracle Study of primary children and their transfer to the first year of secondary school, when at that time the most common form of teacher–pupil interaction was through individual attention, it was noticeable that the quantity of teacher–pupil interaction received by each pupil was very similar (Galton et al., 1980). This came about because even when teachers devoted an extra amount of time to a particular pupil on any one day they tended to compensate by giving more attention to other pupils subsequently. In the same way teachers in the present study appeared to feel that if children had produced work in groups then all groups should be given the same opportunity to tell the rest of the class what they had accomplished. Given the limited available time these reporting-back sessions by the various groups tended to be short and to consist mainly of reporting what had been done and the results of this activity, rather than giving explanations for the group's chosen approach since this would have taken considerably longer. Yet the key purpose of using group work to develop the quality of pupils' thinking rests in the increased use of explanations as part of the reasoning process (Webb, 1985). Part of the value of group work is therefore lost if this kind of reasoning is not present and not shared by all the pupils during the reporting-back and debriefing stages.

Only in a few cases did teachers attempt to solve the shortage of time problem. In one particular case in a school well endowed with IT equipment, laptops were brought into the classroom and each group presented their experimental results and their reasoning in the form of a small Power Point presentation which was then emailed through a wireless connection to other groups. These presentations were then the object of the class discussion, with the result that a degree of repetition which often occurs when groups present their experimental findings was eliminated.

The third factor which inhibited greater progress within the groups concerned the manner of scaffolding the various activities. There is good evidence to suggest that in teaching for understanding and for problem solving requiring meta-cognitive reasoning, the scaffold should be built into the task itself rather than teacher directed (Rosenshine et al., 1996; Brown, 1997; Palincsar and Herrenkohl, 1999). Within the present teaching culture, however, teacher-directed scaffolds such as demonstration and guided discovery are promoted as the most effective means of support rather than building supporting cues within the task, an approach often advocated in the cognitive developmental literature. Guided discovery, in particular, has come to be associated with pupil dependency (Doyle, 1983; Galton, 1989) in that pupils become adept at pushing teachers to give more and more guidance until they provide the required answers. Thus in terms of Doyle's analysis, the guided discovery approach reduces the risk of pupils failing by lowering the ambiguity of the task. When cues are incorporated into the task instructions, on the other hand, it becomes possible to maintain the task's ambiguity but reduce risk of failure by framing the task in such a way that pupils feel that their initial efforts have some relationship to what is ultimately required. During observation of the group lessons it was noticeable that teachers gave pupils very little thinking time before they intervened within the groups, and during subsequent interviews pupils often complained about this saying that they wanted to be left 'to work things out for themselves' until they had arrived as a group at some initial consensus. Then, when the teacher came to the group, they felt collectively strong enough to argue for their view. On the other hand, when teachers intervened too early to give some guidance, pupils tended to see this as a sign of 'teacher take-over' in which s/he was seeking to impose certain of their own ideas. Pupils strongly resented this perceived loss of ownership (Galton and Williamson, 1992).

As a response to this problem some teachers in the study in a particular school created the idea of responding to pupils in what was termed 'neutral space'. As Neil (1991) has demonstrated both space and posture have major implications for the way that pupils interpret the teacher's actions within the classroom. While textbooks often show teachers operating at the same level as the pupils within the group (by kneeling at a table or sitting down on a chair) this, if done too early, may reinforce the notion of take-over because the adult is seen to be imposing himself within the group's space. On the other hand, the area near the teacher's desk or at the front of the class is one where it is customary for teachers to offer direct instruction and this space is therefore clearly seen by pupils as belonging to the teacher. Neutral space on the other hand (near the door, by the window, at the back of the class) can be conceived as belonging to neither teacher nor pupil and therefore does not carry the same overtones of ownership and direction. In the present study some English teachers devised a strategy where, when joining a group to listen to the discussion, they would often sit at an angle to the table so that they were not directly in eye contact with the group members. In this situation one teacher sometimes sat with her hand over her mouth, as if indicating that she was intending to listen but not speak. At some point when these teachers had visited most of the groups they would then go to a position of 'neutral' space, tell the class that that they had been listening to various ideas, that some of these were very excellent and that they would like to share them with all groups and also include one or two comments of their own. Subsequently when visiting the groups it was then possible to ask whether any of those ideas had been useful to the group and in this way it appeared that pupils were more ready to accept outside advice when attempting to reach a conclusion.

Finally, as discussed earlier in the chapter Kutnick et al. (2005a) have commented that theories of group work tend to divide into those which emphasize the social applications of collaborative working as opposed to those that emphasize academic outcomes. Because social relational elements tend to dominate, teachers are often not precise enough in defining their learning goals and in deciding whether these goals are worth the time and effort involved in setting up and managing group work effectively. All too often in this study, because the purposes of working in groups were not clearly delineated, teachers failed to carry out the necessary activities such as briefing and debriefing to ensure the effectiveness of the procedures adopted. Thus if group work is to play a greater part in the pedagogic repertoire of teachers there is need to put more emphasis on training classroom practitioners in how to train pupils to work collaboratively, perhaps not so much at the initial training level, where students have enough to contend with, but rather during later professional development. Nevertheless, despite the limitations in current classroom practice described in the previous paragraphs, and the attitudinal and motivational consequences outlined in the first chapter, the findings presented earlier are sufficiently encouraging to suggest that greater efforts with respect to professional training would pay rich dividends.

There is also a further dimension which needs to be taken into consideration when evaluating the consequences of using group work. This involves the promotion of 'thoughtful discourse' designed to develop pupils' conceptual understanding and the capacity for productive reasoning when engaged in problem solving. We turn to this issue in the next chapter.

 Questions for discussion

1. What do you consider to be the main problems in implementing group work?
2. In your opinion, in which of the three subjects discussed (English, mathematics and science) does the use of group work present the greatest challenge?
3. Which do you think should be the primary aim of group work, to promote better attitudes or to improve attainment?

4

'It's Good to Talk!': Improving Communication between Pupils and Teachers and Why It's Worth the Effort

Linda Hargreaves

The chapter will show you how working in collaborative and cooperative groups can improve students' engagement with their work, allow them time to discuss their tasks, raise the quality of their discussion and, critically, even out some of the interactive imbalances that characterize more traditional organizational settings – provided that teacher and pupils give some thought to the process of working in groups, and the kinds of tasks that are appropriate for group discussion and collaboration. Some examples of research and schemes on group work at secondary level will be presented. Finally, you will see the key points and three basic tasks used by the SPRinG teachers to prepare themselves and their pupils for effective group work.

Communication between pupils and teachers has a notorious tendency to be one-sided. Teachers, complying with national curricular objectives, decide the subject, format, medium and content of the communication. The medium is very likely to be speech, dominated by the teacher, complemented by graphics and 'powerpoint' text. Often, after a brief question and answer session intended to provoke recall of the previous lesson, to stimulate pupils' curiosity or awaken their prior knowledge of a new topic, teachers set about transmitting information to a more-or-less receptive crowd of youngsters. Many teachers would probably argue that lively and effective communication in the classroom is not difficult to achieve, as shown by their pupils' successes in tests and exams. Yet, despite these successes, pupils' attitudes to school subjects appear to decline as they move into Key Stage 3 (see Chapter 1). Their motivation, paradoxically, seems to remain fairly stable in spite of the declining attitudes, but closer inspection shows that it is driven by extrinsic rewards and instrumental goals, such as the need to pass examinations rather than by intrinsic factors such as curiosity, challenge or fascination with a subject. Indeed, their intrinsically motivated pursuit of new learning and/or effort to establish their personal identities would seem more often to reside in out of school activities. This is no more evident than in their rapid assimilation of digital technology, or dedication to sport whether as fans or players (see Mayall, 2007). Of course, pretty well all of us prefer leisure to work but, in the face of increasingly attractive and interactive distractions from school learning, how might teachers engender more positive attitudes to school learning, and perhaps even foster their own love of their subjects, in today's youngsters?

One approach, as this chapter title suggests, would be to improve communication in classrooms between pupils, and between pupils and teachers. But this is an old story. Educationists have been saying this since the 1960s and 70s (e.g. Barnes and Todd, 1977). Researchers have shown repeatedly, in a variety of ways, that what passes for 'communication' involves a great deal more 'transmission' than 'reception' by teachers (Flanders, 1970; Galton et al., 1980; Edwards and Mercer, 1987; Mercer, 2000; Hargreaves and Galton, 2002). Even when teachers are trying hard to achieve a more interactive style, the imbalance persists (English et al., 2002; Mroz et al., 2000). Not only is the talk one-sided, but as Alexander (2008) suggests, it resides predominantly in the rote and recitation domains of his five categories of teacher–pupil discourse. Alexander's five types of teaching talk and the organizational settings in which they are likely to be found are as follows:

- *Rote* (teacher–class) the drilling of facts, ideas and routines through constant repetition;
- *Recitation* (teacher–class or teacher–group): the accumulation of knowledge and understanding through questions designed to test or stimulate recall of what has been previously encountered, or to cue pupils to work out the answer from clues provided;
- *Instruction/exposition* (teacher–class, teacher–group or teachers–individual): telling the pupils what to do, and/or imparting information, and/or explaining facts, principles or procedures;
- *Discussion* (teacher–class, teacher–groups or pupil–pupil): the exchange of ideas with a view to sharing information and solving problems;
- *Dialogue* (teacher–class, teacher–group, teacher–individual or pupil–pupil); achieving common understanding through a structured, cumulative questioning and discussion which guide and prompt, reduce choices, minimize risk and error, expedite 'handover' of concepts and principles (Alexander, 2008).

As we shall see later, Alexander's method does not involve training per se, but even with video-stimulated reflection, understanding of purpose, motivation, and practice, classroom talk at the levels of discussion and dialogue, of two-way mutually respectful communication, can be elusive. Why is it so difficult?

So far, among many things, the preceding chapters have shown that

- pupils' attitudes to school and school subjects tend to decline from year to year;
- collaborative group work helps to maintain more positive attitudes;
- collaborative group work is associated with positive performance outcomes;
- group work is particularly beneficial for certain types of task, especially when these are cognitively challenging; and, as if to complicate things even further, that
- when the attitudes, motivation, personality and teacher-rated performance of around 800 pupils were combined in a cluster analysis, four types of response to school were picked out, while a few pupils (35 in this case) had such unique combinations of characteristics that they did not fit any type;
- these types subordinate gender as a way of analysing pupil responses to school;
- ideally teachers need to take account of these pupil response types in their planning and the way they teach.

As noted in Chapter 3 successful group work depended on teachers' skills and procedures in implementing group-work strategies, on their appreciation of pupil characteristics, idiosyncracies and work styles, and on pupils' levels of training and familiarity with working in groups, among other things. In this chapter we shall look more closely at why the use of collaborative group work may be a particularly important pedagogical strategy, and at what kinds of interaction and conversation take place when pupils work in groups and whole-class sessions. In trying to improve communication in classrooms we shall look at how pupils can be trained to interact more effectively in groups, and with their teachers, and try to see what it might be that sustains attitudes and facilitates achievement when pupils work and learn in groups.

All of this presupposes that teachers themselves are willing to let go of their 'transmitter' roles and adopt a more co-constructive, 'learning together' stance. Many researchers and writers have commented on the powerful role of the teacher, and the way that teachers control the flow of communication not only explicitly, but also implicitly. For example, when a pupil tries to ask or answer a question, Edwards (1980) suggested that the process is akin to people bidding at an auction: pupils compete for the chance to speak, often merely to reflect back the message they have just received. The other increasingly recognized but curiously irresistible constraint on effective classroom communication is the 'IRF' (Initiation-Response-Feedback) pattern of exchanges (Sinclair and Coulthard, 1975). We shall consider these twin barriers to productive talk later, as recent years have seen a strong resurgence of research interest in classroom interaction, in the analysis of teacher–pupil discourse, and the development of strategies to improve its quality.

In this chapter, we shall consider recent attempts to achieve two-way communication, and in particular how collaborative group work might be developed, and how it can support improved pupil teacher communication and contribute to more positive attitudes to school work. First let us see to what extent group work is already used in secondary schools, and then revisit the theoretical foundations of the quest for more two-way communication, both between teacher and pupils, and among pupils.

How much is group work used in secondary classrooms?

Baines et al. (2003) carried out a survey of classroom organization using a novel technique which they called 'grouping mapping'. They asked teachers of Years 2, 5, 7 and 10 to record the location, curriculum area, interaction type and task of the boys and girls in their classes, at pre-determined times (from a range of times so that breaks, assemblies and so on could be avoided) on a pre-drawn plan of their classrooms. Analysis of the 16,000-plus mappings showed that the primary children were located in groups of 4 to 6, in about 50 per cent of the mappings, and 7 to 10 in about 20 per cent, and so were located in groups for 70 per cent of these mappings. The interaction types recorded, however, revealed that the children were involved in 'individuated' interaction types in 66 per cent of the mappings, in whole-class interaction with the teachers in 22 per cent and in peer interaction in a mere 12 per cent. In other words, the children were subject to the same organizational asymmetry identified by Galton and the ORACLE teams in the 1970s and 1990s between seating and working teams (see Chapter 3). In secondary schools, around 6,000 mappings were returned. The spread of grouping locations was more evenly distributed between pairs (28%), trios (12%) and small groups of 4 to 6 (25%), with 30 per cent of the mappings showing groups of over 10. Furthermore, the interaction types also showed a better balance between individuated inter-action (39%), peer interaction (33%) and class interaction (29%). Even so, although the secondary pupils were organized or seated in groups for 65 per cent for the time, they were involved in peer interaction for only 33 per cent of the records.

Baines et al. (2003) showed also that about a third of the mappings included an adult in both the primary and secondary classes. Three types of grouping defined by Galton and Williamson (1992) were listed in Chapter 3. These were labelled cooperative (children work on independent tasks towards a shared common goal), collaborative (children work together on the same task towards a shared common goal) and seated (children sit together but work individually towards individual goals). Alexander (2001) identified an addi-tional grouping, which he labelled 'collective', to refer to the situation when a teacher or adult is seated with a group, either to teach them directly or to lead a discussion, thus rendering this type of grouping a 'mini class'. This collective grouping will have become more common in primary schools since the introduction of the National Literacy Strategy and use of 'guided reading' (DfEE, 1998). We shall consider later what happens to talk between pupils in cooperative and collaborative groupings, and in whole-class and collective groupings, but now let us revisit the theoretical foundations supporting the case for more two-way dialogue between pupils and between teacher and pupils.

Why try to improve communication in classrooms?

Few would argue with idea that cognitive challenge leads to new learning. Here we shall argue that this has particular importance for 11 to 14 year olds in Key Stage 3, as peer relationships take on increasing importance for them, and as they begin to demand greater independence and to challenge authorities that have (more or less) satisfied them during childhood.

As we have seen, Vygotsky's theory is generally invoked to support the use of group work as he argues that children learn by solving problems with people more capable than themselves, who take them through their zone of proximal (or potential) development (Vygotsky, 1936; Cole et al., 1990). While this explanation provides roles for teachers and more capable children, as Mercer (1995) points out, it does not provide support for how children of similar cognitive levels might advance each other's learning. We can see this, however, in a less often cited area of Vygotsky's (1935/1986) writing that concerns his work on the development of concepts and complex thought. Like Piaget, he proposed a series of phases of cognitive development. After criticizing the work of his contemporaries including Piaget, Vygotsky went on to say,

> What we are interested in is the general conclusion, that real concept formation and its abstract reasoning do not appear before children reach adolescence. These findings challenge the position of some psychologists who claimed that no radical changes in the intellectual function occur in adolescence and that all basic intellectual operations, which will be active later, are already formed by the age of three. (pp. 98–9)

Vygotsky (1934/1986: 110) saw the 'ascent to concept formation [as] made in three basic phases, each divided in turn into several stages'. Vygotsky labelled the first phase, 'syncretic', because the child's understanding of a word's meaning is '*a vague syncretic conglomeration of individual objects* that have somehow coalesced into an image in his mind' (p. 110, emphasis in original). The second phase is when a child thinks in 'complexes … [when] … individual objects are united in the child's mind, not only by his subjective impressions but also by *bonds actually existing between these objects*' (p. 112, emphasis in original). He described five types of 'complex' which lead eventually to the third phase in which true 'advanced concepts' appear when the child reaches adolescence, and can *abstract* or *single out* elements of a complex and

> view the abstracted elements apart from the totality of the concrete experience in which they are embedded. In genuine concept formation, it is equally important to unite and to separate: Synthesis and analysis presuppose each other as inhalation presupposes exhalation *(Goethe).* (pp. 135–6)

Parallels might be drawn between these phases, and Piaget's pre-operational, concrete operational and formal operational stages, but while both psychologists saw social interaction as an essential factor in progress towards advanced thought, Vygotsky saw it as *the* essential factor (see Smith, 1996). Further, unlike Piaget, Vygotsky did not postulate accompanying neuro-physiological changes, a view subsequently refuted by neuro-scientific studies (see Goswami and Bryant, 2007–9; Alexander et al; 2009). The crucial link and justification for the use of group work in Vygotsky's developmental process is language – hence the importance of social interaction with peers as well as more advanced thinkers. Vygotsky (1934/1986: 107) argues that all forms of learning are relevant to this process, but that 'real concepts are impossible without words and thinking in concepts does not exist beyond verbal thinking. That is why the central moment in concept formation, and its generate cause, is a specific use of words as functional "tools"'. He goes on to say that

> The investigator must aim to understand the intrinsic bonds between the external tasks and the developmental dynamics, and view concept formation as a function of the adolescent's total social and cultural growth, which affects not only the content but also the method of his thinking. (Vygotsky, 1935/1978: 108)

Of course, words and interaction are just as important in the earlier phases. While Vygotsky emphasizes peer interaction as a cooperative process in the co-construction of knowledge, Piaget draws attention to the power of the cognitive conflict created when same-aged children disagree about a problem, in improving the less advanced child's level of thinking (Wood, 1998). Empirical studies of children in groups by Christine Howe, Neil Mercer and their respective colleagues, (e.g. Light et al., 1979; Howe and Mercer, 2007) illustrate this process as regards conceptual development. Our principal concern, however, is with improving the process and quality of classroom interaction, and so we turn now to the evidence gathered by the SPRinG project at Key Stage 3 about classroom talk in whole-class and group-work settings.

How were the classroom observations made?

Our observations were based on two kinds of record: a detailed time-based schedule for records of the organization, behaviour and interaction of six pupils per lesson, and a set of three-point ratings of various features of the lesson such as task demands, task suitability for group, individual or whole-class organization, teachers' introduction and debriefing, and classroom climate. These relatively crude ratings provided a rough and ready overview of the main features of the lesson and were completed at the end of the lesson.

We are concerned here with the organization, behaviour and interaction observations. These recorded:

1. how the *target* pupils (i.e. those pre-selected for observation) were organized into seating and working groups;
2. for each 30 second period, whether they were:
   a) mostly on task, off task, or partly-on, partly-off task and so on;
   b) working quietly or interacting with the teacher or with other pupils, and if so how many boys or girls were involved;

Table 4.1 Main categories used to observe pupils' classroom behaviour

Target's behaviour	Target interaction/dialogue	Target–adult
On task	Listening/watching	Group
Routine-wait	Nonverbal	Class
Distracted	Question	Individual
CODS/RIS (Partial on-task)	Suggests	Content
Intermittent	Explain/reason	Task
Sustained	Agree	Routine
Other	Argue/disagree	Monitor
	Seek help	Other
	Maintain	
	Block	
	Social/off task	
	Other	

3. their verbal and non-verbal interactions such as whether they asked questions, made suggestions, explained things to others, argued or disagreed, facilitated or obstructed group activity. These behaviours were recorded once if they occurred during a 30-second interval;
4. whether an adult was interacting with the target pupil, individually, or as a group or class member, and what the interaction was about;
5. after each 30 seconds, ratings of the target's group as a whole, being on or off task, working collectively or individually, and whether the task was more abstract or more practical in nature.

A list of the behaviours coded is shown in Table 4.1. After observing one 'target' pupil for four consecutive 30-second periods, the observer then observed the pupil sitting beside the target. The observer then observed two more pairs of pupils, before returning to observe the first two pupils in the same way in the second half of the lesson. Observations of group-work sessions were made over the course of two school years, or six terms in all, and resulted in a total of 1,204 two-minute observations of pupils in groups, but comparisons between group work and non-group work lessons were conducted only in the second year. Twenty-one teachers worked with us for two or three years, but ten more joined the project in its final year. Over the two observation years, we collected 1,515 complete two minute observation sets.

What do we know about pupils' interactions as they work in different organizational settings?

If, as theory suggests, children's thinking, or ability to analyze, synthesize or criticize concepts, improves through their conversations with peers and adults, then we need to look for evidence about how much opportunity children are given in school to hold such conversations. This can be assessed by considering the mean length of their utterances (MLU), a measure that is used by psychologists as a measure of young children's spoken language development. Unfortunately, observations of lessons at Key Stage 2 in several research studies have shown that pupils rarely have the opportunity to make extended utterances in class. Alexander's (2001) detailed study of lessons in five countries, revealed that pupils' MLU in England was two words, with a range of one to nine words, whereas the teachers' MLU was 4.6 words, and their range was one to 40 words. Russia, Vygotsky's native land, was the only country in which the pupils' range and mean were greater than their teachers' (pupils' mean 5 words, range 1–40; teachers' mean 4 words, range 1–30). English et al. (2002) similarly, found that 95 per cent of children's utterances were of one to three words. If group work is to contribute to an improvement in classroom communication, and ultimately to help children develop their conceptual understanding, then we need to demonstrate that it allows for extended interactions. We need to find out, also, whether such interactions are associated with relatively high or low levels of cognitive challenge – thus reciting a poem, repeating a list, or recalling simple facts would be regarded as having low cognitive complexity, whereas formulating an explanation, challenging a point of view, or making a suggestion represent a higher level of cognitive engagement.

Do pupils work harder in groups than in whole-class settings?

Our observations showed that by the summer term when teachers and pupils had become used to working in groups, pupils at Key Stage 3 were more likely to be wholly on task across all three subjects when involved in group work than when in whole-class or individual working sessions (Figure 4.1). In the spring term, however, they were more likely to be on task in non-group work settings, especially in mathematics lessons. The switch to being on-task more often in groups in the summer term in all three subjects may be explained by various factors, including teacher and pupil greater familiarity with working in groups, through teachers' better matching of topics and/or tasks to group work, pupils improved skills of cooperation with or tolerance of others, or possibly less pressure of impending tests or examinations, for example. Whatever the reason, Figure 4.1 illustrates clearly the benefits of group work.

Gender made no difference to levels of engagement whether in groups or not, but working in groups showed marginally higher time on task for all four of the pupil types introduced in Chapter 1 (Table 4.2)[1].

Table 4.2 Time on task and pupil types

Pupil type	Not in groups (M ± SD)	In groups (M ± SD)
Group shirkers	3.00 ± 1.38	3.19 ± 1.67
Active collaborators	3.26 ± 1.00	3.29 ± 1.08
Struggling loners	2.65 ± 1.27	3.45 ± 1.10
Quiet collaborators	3.23 ± 1.20	3.62 ± 0.87
M	3.13 ± 1.20	3.34 ± 1.07

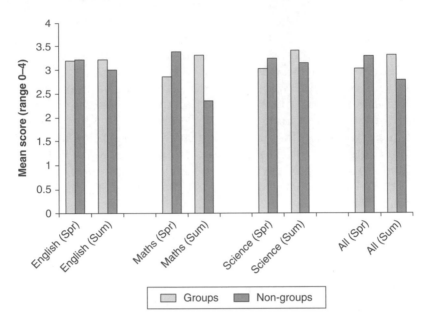

Figure 4.1 Time on task in groups and not in groups

As we all know, everyone spends some time when we are supposed to be concentrating, either trying to concentrate, perhaps looking as though we are concentrating, but actually thinking about something else, fiddling, doodling or day-dreaming. The more passive our role, the more this is likely to happen. When observing we refer to this part-on-, part-off-task behaviour as '*cods*' (partly concentration/partly distracted), or to day-dreaming as '*ris*' (responding to *i*nternal *s*timuli). These two categories of behaviour typically took up less than a quarter of each two-minute observation 'set'. Nevertheless, the difference between the group- and non-group-working conditions is dramatic, as shown in Figure 4.2.

Sometimes inevitably, there will have been mis-classifications of 'cods', when the pupil was actually thinking deeply about the task, or attempting to solve a problem but, by the same token there will have been mis-classifications of pupils giving the impression that they were wholly absorbed in their tasks, especially when they were in passive modes, such as listening and/or watching. In other words, the more active roles that pupils must adopt in a group setting would appear to reduce partial distraction, and so contribute to on-task behaviour. This is further borne out by the positive correlation between 'cods' and team size, where team refers to the number of pupils assigned to work together on the task: the bigger the team the more often the observers recorded 'cods', or, conversely, the smaller the team, and hence the bigger part played by each pupil, the less daydreaming or doodling we saw.

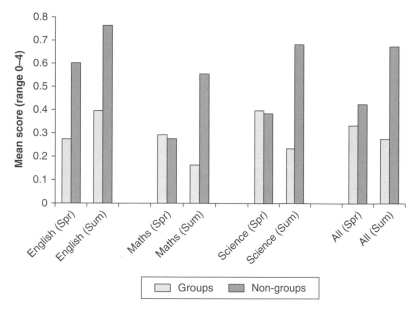

Figure 4.2 Incidence of partial distraction or 'cods' in group-working and non-group-working organizations

What kinds of interaction take place in group and non-group-work settings?

While there were general quantitative benefits in terms of time on task, especially in mathematics, during group work in Key Stage 3, there were also qualitative benefits in terms of how the pupils interacted with each other. For example, when involved in group work, the pupils were more likely to engage in extended, or 'sustained' interactions and were more likely to engage in higher-quality dialogue as we show later. Sustained interactions were those that involved the target pupil in an interaction that lasted beyond 30 seconds. Not surprisingly these occur relatively infrequently but, importantly, they were much more likely to occur in group-work settings, as Figure 4.3 shows. Sustained interactions were not only significantly more common in group as opposed to non-group sessions, and in all three subjects, but they also increased between spring and summer terms. Furthermore they were more common among older pupils, whose tasks may have demanded longer interactions.

'Open dialogue' refers to the kinds of things pupils were saying to each other, such as raising questions, imagining or explaining things as well as when they were agreeing or disagreeing with each other's ideas. Open dialogue was recorded when pupils during science lessons said things like, 'I think the chocolate under the black paper will melt more quickly because it absorbs more light', or in English, 'Maybe we should make this bit more scary'.

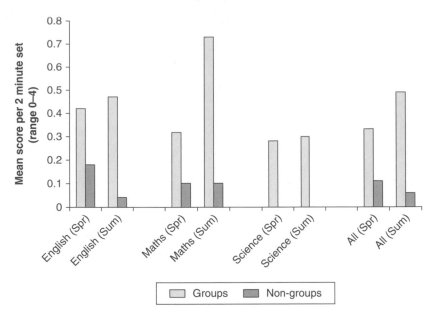

Figure 4.3   Observations of sustained interactions in group and non-group settings

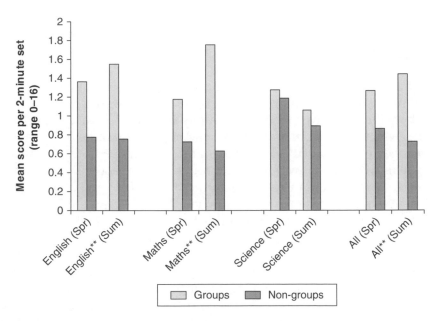

Figure 4.4   Open dialogue in groups and not in groups

We found that this kind of higher-quality dialogue was observed more often during group-work settings, significantly so in the summer term, in mathematics and English, though not in science, as shown in Figure 4.4.

Taken together, the findings in relation to sustained interactions and open dialogue, which are of course quite likely to coincide, reveal that group work was clearly working as expected, particularly by the summer term. It gave pupils more opportunity to make longer utterances, and participate in more extended discussion with their peers. In other words, group working allowed them to articulate their ideas and develop their concepts, as Vygotsky suggested that pupils of this age need to do. In mathematics, for example, we found that cognitive gains were more likely to occur when there were sustained interactions, and when there was more open dialogue, in both group- and non-group-work settings, but the higher prevalence of these kinds of interaction in groups suggests that group work may be particularly beneficial in bringing them about.

Does sustained interaction in groups really mean higher cognitive dialogue?

Sceptics might suggest that the sustained interactions in groups happen simply because the pupils have the opportunity to speak at greater length than in whole-class settings, or because they have more opportunity for social chat. The social chat theory was disproved when we checked for the coincidence of sustained interactions and higher-order on-task talk in the separate 30-second observation intervals as well as the aggregated two-minute intervals. When we looked at the quality of on-task pupil dialogue during sustained interactions during whole-class, individual work and group work, only the group work organizations achieved consistently high correlations, as shown in Figure 4.5. There are no correlations for individual and class working in 2002–3 because at that stage we were focusing only on group work.

We found that sustained interactions coincided with pupils raising questions, making suggestions, giving explanations, more frequently during group work than individual or class work in every term. Open dialogue, which includes higher-order dialogue, showed similar relationships. These findings in particular support the value of developing group work strategies in the classroom.

When is disagreement a good thing?

The inclusion of instances of pupils' disagreeing with each other in the open dialogue category might raise eyebrows. This was recorded when pupils said things like, 'No I don't think we should do that', or even 'I don't want to do it that way', as part of a constructive discussion or debate. They might or might not go on to give a reason, but the critical aspect was that the pupil felt free to disagree without disrupting the flow of activity or conversation. If the target pupil refused to participate, or prevented others from doing so, and was being generally obstinate and uncooperative then the observer recorded the behaviour as blocking the group. In the event we found that group-blocking behaviour occurred very, very rarely. Constructive argument or disagreements were significantly less likely to occur in non-group-working situations, and

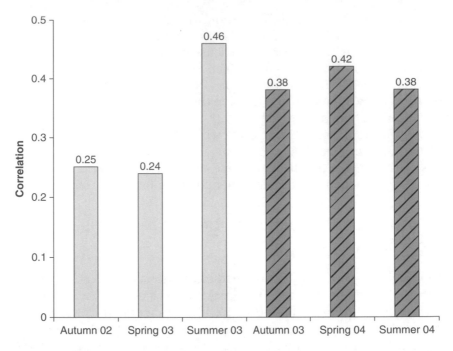

Figure 4.5 Relationships between sustained interactions and high cognitive dialogue during group work
(Bars in different patterns indicate the first and second years of the project)

were more common in English than in science or mathematics group working. When they did occur in mathematics group work, however, they were associated positively with residual learning gains. 'Blocking behaviour' in mathematics, on the other hand, was negatively correlated with learning gains in class/individual work sessions. Disagreements were also significantly more common in English than in maths or science. It seems that having the freedom, and confidence to argue or disagree in this way could be regarded as a crucial aspect of a 'learning conversation'. It signifies a relationship which is *not* dominated by the more typical power imbalance between teachers and pupils.

Group working would appear to permit better balanced power relationships although gender and achievement levels seemed to make a difference as regards agreement and disagreement dialogue. Lower-achieving girls were more likely to utter disagreements of this kind while higher-achieving pupils were less likely to agree openly by saying things like 'Yes, I'm happy with that', or 'OK let's try that'. The point is that in group-work situations, these girls perhaps had the confidence to contribute something to the conversations, rather than remaining silent, or blocking the group. This speculation is supported, arguably, by the findings that lower-achieving girls were also more likely to make suggestions when in groups, than in non-group situations. High-achieving boys, on the other hand, were significantly more likely to make suggestions in non-group, whole-class settings.

Our observations of *agreement* and *disagreement* would be classified as aspects of *exploratory talk*, in Mercer's three types of talk between children in groups (as described in Chapter 2). In Mercer's (1995: 104) words, these are

1. *disputational talk* ... characterised by disagreement and individualised decision making
2. *cumulative talk* which build positively but uncritically on what the others have said
3. *exploratory talk* in which partners engage critically but constructively with each others ideas.

Our observations of *group blocking* would fit into the *disputational* category. Mercer's research shows learning gains associated with exploratory talk, but, as he and his colleagues point out, children rarely get any guidance on how to communicate effectively with each other (Mercer et al., 2004).

Mercer (1995) reviews previous research which argues for, and demonstrates, the benefits of socio-cognitive conflict for learning. He and his colleagues (Dawes et al., 2000) have carried out extensive work on getting children to develop the quality of their discussions in groups, and explicitly encourage children to air their points of disagreement as they seek to agree on a solution (to a moral dilemma, for example) by the end of their discussions. Their 'Thinking Together' scheme offers procedures and problems designed to encourage productive discussion, argument and 'exploratory talk' in groups and rejects an outcome of agreeing to disagree, because

> the imperative to reach consensus ... is designed to motivate the children to engage, and keep engaging, with each other's ideas and suggestions in a considered and critical way ... whereas the option of not reaching agreement can offer and easy way out of continued debate. (Mercer and Littleton, 2007: 72)

Disagreements aside, the finding that group work seems to encourage longer interactions, and pupils giving explanations and making suggestions when in groups, has the potential to improve whole-class teacher–pupil dialogue as well, by giving pupils the confidence to offer extended answers to teachers' questions. In this way it can challenge the 'recitation script' (the Initiation–Response–Feedback (IRF) mentioned at the beginning of the chapter).

But not all pupils are alike: pupil types and group work

Apart from reference to some gender differences we have presented the characteristics of group work as if all pupils behaved in the same way in class, yet we know that pupils differ in personality, achievement, motivation and attitudes to school and to group work. Chapter 1 introduced four pupil types whose characteristics are just noted here:

1. Type 1 (*shirkers*) low-attaining passive extroverts with increasing anti-school attitudes: 32.2 per cent (264 pupils);
2. Type 2 (*active collaborators*) high-achieving, stable extroverts, who are positive about school learning and very positive about group work: 41.3 per cent (338 pupils);
3. Type 3 (*struggling loners*) low-attaining, anxious introverts with below-average motivation and a dislike of group work: 6.5 per cent (53 pupils);
4. Type 4 (*quiet collaborators*) average-attaining, stable introverts, well motivated especially in English and science, neutral towards group work but like cooperating: 19.9 per cent (163 pupils).

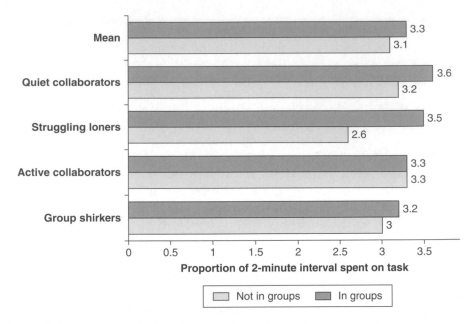

Figure 4.6   Time on task of pupil types when working in groups and not in groups.

Figure 4.6 shows how the different pupil types responded in group-work and non-group-work organizations in terms of their time on task, or task engagement. It is based on the proportion of each two-minute observation interval the observer judged that the target pupils had spent on task. (The two-minute observation period was divided into four 30-second intervals. The observer awarded one point if the child was on task for the majority of each 30-second interval. A pupil who was fully engaged for most of each 30 seconds would therefore score 4.) Working in groups resulted in increased time on task for three of the four types, and made no difference for the active collaborators. The small but significant group of *struggling loners* appeared to gain most from working in a group, with time on task up from 2.6 to 3.5 points, while the quiet collaborators also increased their concentration levels from 3.2 to 3.6 points. The active collaborators meanwhile maintained the same, high, level of time of task whatever the setting, while the other pupil types achieved higher, equivalent or close levels in group work.

Group work smoothes out the differences between pupils

There are other indications too that group work affords greater learning opportunities for some less dominant pupils. When the observations are broken down into the separate categories concerning time on task, distraction, sustained interaction and so on, by pupil type, the overall effect is that the large and often statistically significant inter-type differences observed during non-group settings are evened out during group work. As Figure 4.6 shows for time on task, a very uneven profile across the types when not in groups

Table 4.3 Group-work and non-group-work interactions by pupil type: how groups smooth out imbalances in participation

Observation category	Notes
Waiting/routine task	Significant difference between types when not in groups disappears in groups. Struggling loners spend less time 'waiting' and in routine activities when in groups.
Distracted	Significant differences between types when not in groups disappear in groups. Shirkers are the most distracted type in a non-group setting but group work reduces this difference and evens out levels of distraction across types.
Sustained	Sustained interactions increase for all types during group work, and significant differences emerge between types, with active collaborators showing the lowest level, high levels for group shirkers and loners, and highest for quiet collaborators. Despite the differences, all types are more involved when in groups.
Questions	Group work increases the questions pupils ask, and results in a more even distribution of question asking.
Suggests	More suggestions made in groups; boys dominate in all types in non-group settings; group work removes the gender imbalance except among the active collaborators.
Giving and seeking info	No significant differences when in, or not in, group work. Working in groups raises giving/seeking information overall and irons out the gender imbalance that active collaborator boys dominate when not in groups.
High cognitive dialogue	No significant differences between types in or not in groups. Group work removes gender imbalances that boy shirkers and quiet collaborators dominate, and girl active collaborators when not in groups.
All dialogue	Groups remove considerable gender imbalances in which boy shirkers, loners and quiet collaborators, and active collaborator girls dominate interaction when not in groups.

Note: all significant results here have small effect sizes.

becomes smoother in groups. Furthermore gender imbalances which typically involve boys taking a more active part in interaction when not in groups, are removed in groups. Thus, group work appears to reduce differences between pupil types. The figures are too detailed to include here but the following list of selected observation categories should reveal the general pattern (Table 4.3). Time spent 'waiting' or doing routine things (such as sharpening pencils) is reduced for the 'struggling loners' when in groups.

Attempts to improve communication in secondary classrooms

Recent attempts to improve the quality of classroom interaction in secondary schools in England include our own SPRinG research, some of Neil Mercer's work, and the Cognitive Acceleration in Mathematics Education (CAME) and Science Education (CASE) devised by Michael Shayer and colleagues. Several studies which focus on particular aspects of group working have been conducted abroad, however, in Australia, and the USA, as we shall see now.

Terwel (2003) and Gillies (2003, 2004) have studied group work in secondary settings in Australia. Gillies argues strongly for the importance of 'structured' group work to achieve benefits to children's social learning. By 'structured' however, she is referring to school-level commitment to group work rather than to the specific nature of the group-work activity. Thus her three 'structured' schools in Brisbane had a strong active commitment to group work: pupils had received social skills training for work in groups, and used group work at least once a week in maths, science and English. The three schools designated 'unstructured' were schools where group work was used on an 'ad hoc' basis in which pupils were instructed to work together but had no particular group work skills training. Gillies found several social benefits in the structured groups including students being more willing to work on the task, more 'elaborately' helpful towards others, by giving more unsolicited explanations in mathematics, for example, and ultimately having a stronger perception of group cohesion and social responsibility than their 'unstructured groups' counterparts. In an earlier comparison of the effects of group work on learning Gillies (2003) had compared five studies (four primary, one secondary) which demonstrated also that structured group work led to better learning outcomes for children. In her words,

> when children work cooperatively together, they learn to give and receive help, share their ideas and listen to other students' perspectives, seek new ways of clarifying differences, resolving problems, and constructing new understandings and knowledge. (p. 35)

Webb et al. (2008) and Boaler (2008) offer examples of group-work projects from the USA. Webb and colleagues focused on the teachers' role when the class is involved in group work. In particular they found that teachers varied considerably in the degree to which they supported pupils' explanations of their thinking even after training, and further that the nature of the teachers' explanations was reflected in the pupils' collaborative conversations, and in their achievement levels. Boaler also in the USA and also in mathematics lessons, describes a four-year longitudinal study of group work in three high schools. She describes in detail not only the students' huge gains in mathematics achievement, but also their remarkable social learning gains, achieving 'relational equity' between different ethnic and social class groups for example. The teachers gave the pupils, working in groups, 'fairly open problems that they could solve in different ways' (p. 18). They encouraged a range of solutions to the problems, and made clear to pupils that listening to, and helping others, were also valued activities. One critical aspect, of several, was getting pupils to reflect on the teaching methods used and on finding strategies for communication and mutual support. The pupils here were unique in their concern for other pupils' learning.

Finally, we move away from mathematics to English, and to a recent example from the USA, which encourages children to plunge straight into the use of 'argument schema theory' (AST) when discussing the dilemmas faced by story characters. Reznitskaya et al. (2009) are developing and testing a strategy in what the researchers call a 'collaborative reasoning' (CR) session. The children are trained to use a variety of argumentation devices to justify their views.

The evidence presented which compares a typical class discussion of a fictional passage, with a CR discussion of the passage suggests that this technique very successfully shifts the 'centre of gravity' away from the teacher to the children themselves, creating a much more balanced discussion in which the teacher plays a much less central role. This method could contribute to the achievement of the elusive 'discussion' and 'dialogue' levels of classroom discourse in Alexander's work on dialogic teaching, which we revisit later.

Improving classroom communication in the UK

Finally in this section we shall consider some examples of group work with 11 to 14 year olds in the UK. We begin with a look at Shayer and colleagues' widely used Cognitive Acceleration Schemes in science and, more recently, mathematics known as the CASE (Cognitive Acceleration in Science Education) and CAME (Cognitive Acceleration in Mathematics Education). Adhami et al.'s (1998) CAME programme, for example, aims to fill the 'window of opportunity for rapid intellectual development' that exists in the lower secondary school (p. vii). The programme combines Piagetian and Vygotskian theory in its conceptual base. It offers an integrated package advising on the teachers' role and teaching style, the class management and layout required using pedagogical principles derived from established psychological research, such as metacognition and transfer across knowledge domains, and the task itself. It emphasizes the role of the teacher in finding the critical moments to enter the pupils' discussions to raise the level of discussion but not inhibit it. As we found in the SPRinG classrooms, many pupils resented teachers who intervened too early in their discussion rather than letting them work things out. At the same time, by avoiding intervention, opportunities to promote cognitive development and understanding may be missed.

What is the role for the teacher in improving classroom communication?

There is now a variety of strategies that secondary teachers might use to improve classroom communication. We considered earlier the work of Mercer and his colleagues in which children are trained in how to work in groups in order to ensure more productive and exploratory talk. Another approach is to develop Robin Alexander's (2008) work with teachers, which aims to raise the levels of discourse, when appropriate, from 'recitation' and 'instruction' to 'discussion' and dialogue'. Having studied teachers working with classes and groups in five very different cultures across the world, Alexander (2001) has worked with primary teachers in northern and southern England using 'intensive video-based intervention' to encourage the development of 'dialogic teaching', which 'harnesses the power of talk to engage children, stimulate and extend their thinking, and advance their learning and understanding' (Alexander, 2008: 37) in their interaction with individuals, classes and groups of children. He goes on to define five essential conditions for teaching to be considered dialogic. In brief, they are: *collective* (teachers and children address learning together); *reciprocal* (teachers and children listen to each other); *supportive* (children articulate their ideas freely and help each other to reach common understandings); *cumulative* (teachers and children chain their own and other's ideas into coherent lines of thinking and enquiry); and *purposeful* (teachers plan and steer classroom talk with specific education goals in mind (Alexander, 2008). His 'Talk for Learning' Materials (two DVDs) provide numerous video extracts of teachers and children in class and group settings throughout the primary age range, while the little book that describes and justifies the work provides a persuasive background for the development of dialogic teaching, and an extensive list of accessible principles, repertoires and indicators of dialogic teaching. Using these, the teachers can analyse the talk recorded in videos that they make of their teaching at regular intervals throughout the year. They then 'set and review goals relating to the conduct of classroom talk on the basis of their analysis of what they see and what they hear' (Alexander, 2004: 3).

A critical feature for successful dialogic teaching, however, is the teachers' willingness and ability to set aside their 'power' for a time in order to engage in a more genuine discussion with children, in which, from a long list of indicators of dialogic teaching,

- questions provoke thoughtful answers and further questions;
- answers provoke further questions and are seen as the building blocks of dialogue rather than its terminal point;
- individual teacher–pupil and pupil–pupil exchanges are chained into coherent lines of communication rather than left stranded and disconnected;
- turns are managed by shared routines rather than through high-stakes competitive (or reluctant) bidding;
- pupils – not just teachers – ask questions and provide explanations, and they are encouraged to do so; and among other indicators,
- children have the confidence to make mistakes, and understand that mistakes are something to learn from rather than be ashamed of (Alexander, 2008).

The last indicator in this list is perhaps more critical than ever when working with young adolescents in Key Stage 3, who might be particularly sensitive and self-conscious about speaking up in a class setting. Our observation, that high-achieving boys were more likely to make suggestions in class settings, whereas low-achieving girls did so in groups, underlines the importance of establishing a classroom ethos that will encourage all pupils to speak. Some of Alexander's teachers have found it difficult to achieve the higher levels of discourse, possibly because of the children's lack of confidence in participating at length, not least after years of being denied long utterances in class.

Although Alexander has worked with primary teachers, his principles apply equally to secondary-school classrooms. To this end, a mixed group of primary and secondary teacher-researchers in Stoke-on-Trent have been working to improve communication levels among pupils. These teachers were concerned about the poor level of classroom discourse as many of their pupils, especially in Key Stages 3 and 4, rarely uttered more than monosyllables even when encouraged. They decided that the teacher–class focus was too daunting and began their action research studies using the SPRinG group-work training to foster the pupils' group-work skills, increase their confidence to speak in groups, and ultimately to improve teacher–class discussion. Their result included significant gains in the end of year SATs at Year 6 in one class and compliments from an OfSTED inspector on how well some Year 10 girls spoke about their work. The oracy skills of these girls had previously been a major cause for concern.

Preparing pupils for group work: the SPRinG approach

So now let us look at how the SPRinG teachers prepared their pupils for productive group work. First, group work requires some planning. Second, a few group-work training exercises are needed. Team work is a common requirement in most occupations and areas of professional life (consider team work's importance in TV's popular 'Apprentice' series, for example – failure to work with the team tends to result in hearing, 'You're Fired' at an early stage!). Developing team work skills in school is therefore a preparation for the world of work, as well as a means to improve pupils' understanding of complex concepts and ideas. Working with teachers at Key Stage 3 on this generic aspect of pedagogy soon presented a problem, however, because the teachers hailed from three different, tightly timetabled disciplines: English, mathematics and science. Whereas our Key Stage 1 and 2 co-researchers were able to provide an extensive handbook of group-work exercises and activities which their teachers could use with their classes over a period of time, our Key Stage 3 teachers rejected this as impractical given their curricular constraints and as too time consuming. In response we worked with them to produce a form of 'training' and a short handbook that was easily adaptable for each different curriculum area and which was not too demanding in terms of time. Together with our first cohort of teachers, we identified some initial key points for those starting to use cooperative and collaborative group work and added to them as the research progressed (Box 4.1).

Box 4.1   Key points in planning group work (from the SPRinG Key Stage 3 handbook)

- **Timing:** It is important in the early stages not to under-estimate the time needed to carry out the task as a group. This will be recouped later, when groups are more established and cohesive. Some activities need to be developed over a number of lessons rather than crammed into a single one. And set target times and give warnings of time remaining. Pupils feel frustrated if they are rushed but will go off task if there is time left to waste.
- **Lesson length, the tyranny of the bell:** Some activities will fit into 50 minutes or even 1 hour but this period is not usually long enough for extended group-work. Try to do group-work activities in double lessons if you have them or break

(Continued)

(Continued)

activities down so they fit into a number of consecutive lessons. It can be difficult to pick up an animated discussion after a day or two but curtailing it is worse.

- **Open vs closed tasks:** Once pupils are comfortable with working in groups they need contexts to explore, discuss, and debate. At the beginning, pupils may find very open tasks too challenging and threatening whereas in very closed tasks they will reach conclusions too quickly and these may as well be done individually. Tasks need to be structured so that pupils can work through them systematically but not so structured that there is no room for creativity and independence.
- **Challenge:** This is related to the nature of the task. If the task is too complex initially and lacks a clear structure pupils will not know where to start and the less confident ones will avoid participating whereas if it is too easy other pupils may become bored and demotivated.
- **Task outcome – individual or group?** In general, once pupils have to produce their own individual work in a lesson the group work breaks down. Similarly, if pupils have to share materials/worksheets they are forced to collaborate whereas if they have their own worksheet, etc they may opt to work individually, thus compromising the benefits of group work.
- **Tensions between competition and collaboration – assessment:** Individual assessment is likely to be competitive – there may be an unintended tension between asking pupils to collaborate to help each other and then giving them individual scores. One possibility in this situation is to give individual scores but add them to produce an overall group score – in this way it is in everyone's own interest to work together.
- **Other adults in the classroom – support teachers, teaching assistants:** Other teachers or helpers have not necessarily thought about group work (or, if they have, do not necessarily endorse it). Therefore, if the same adult comes into all lessons with your class you may want to talk to them about working in groups. Learning Support staff, who often have a special responsibility for a statemented pupil may naturally want to step in to help the pupil and the pupil's group. This can hinder the development of the pupil's group work skills. It is crucial therefore, that other adults coming into the classroom are clear about the role you would like them to adopt. Encourage the 'guide on the side' role.

The handbook then included some of the different activity paradigms used by the SPRinG teachers that could be adapted to work in any curriculum area. These are shown in Box 4.2.

Box 4.2   Examples of generic group work tasks and formats

Here are different forms of Group work that can be considered:

DISCUSSION – groups of pupils work to share understandings and ideas. The focus may be an interpretation of something ambiguous (e.g. poem, picture, set of data), an exploration of different responses to the same event or the pooling of ideas. Discussions may lead to individual understandings or may require negotiation to arrive at a consensus.

PROBLEM-SOLVING ACTIVITIES – usually these depend on discussing alternative strategies to solve a problem. Groups may be asked to compare and criticize each other's solutions at the end. Alternatively each member of the group may work on a different aspect of the task and combine contributions at the end.

PRODUCTION ACTIVITIES – these result in a concrete outcome such as a magazine, film, construction, or building. Often each member of the group will have a different role and these will be brought together at the end.

SIMULATIONS – pupils take on the situation of a supposed real-life group. They have the opportunities to contribute from their own strengths and perspectives rather than being assigned more specific roles.

ROLE PLAY – pupils are assigned a character from drama or a perspective over a contentious issue. The characters interact depending on their interpretation of the role.

Together with the teachers we identified three basic tasks that would help to introduce group work to the pupils and help both pupils and teachers to get started. Again, these tasks can be incorporated into any curriculum area. Our teachers implemented these three tasks during the Autumn term, hence, we would hope, the improvements in group interaction in the Spring and Summer terms. The three tasks introduce rules, argumentation skills and roles for group work. They are presented here as they appeared in the handbook.

Task 1: Pupils work in groups to devise their own rules for group work

Box 4.3   Making rules for group work

Pupils work together to devise

'Rules for Group Work'

They may like to present these as posters that can be displayed in the room and referred to during the year.

It may be worth doing an initial activity first to see what sort of skills your pupils have in your subject area and/or having a class discussion of what they understand of group work and their experiences of it.

Some examples of the rules pupils set for themselves appear in Box 4.4. An anecdotal but fundamental observation that emerged was that the children in secondary classes may not know each other's names. This became obvious when observing and asking children to tell us others' names for a seating plan. It is sometimes assumed that it is just the teacher who needs to get to know the pupils' names. Setting arrangements can throw pupils together in unexpected ways and even within settled tutor groups there can be new admissions and changes. Pupils can reach the end of an academic year either not knowing, or never having had to use and pronounce other names. It can be useful to have a 'getting to know you' game at the beginning of the year (even in Year 9) and to make sure that pupils work with others outside their tutor groups or friendship groups.

Box 4.4   A selection of the pupils' rules for group work

Ground rules for group work

- Don't leave anyone out
- Listen to each other's ideas
- Agree on what you would like to do
- Leave friendship problems behind
- Don't laugh at others
- Deal the work out evenly
- Be considerate
- Work as a team
- For the group to work together properly they have to compromise and be able to work with other people.

Task 2: Argumentation – encouraging debate and the skill to conduct an argument

Osborne et al. (2001), among others, have pointed out that science education lacks the debate and discussion that is more characteristic of, say, English or history lessons. Science, which by its very nature should continually contest its findings, is often presented as a series of facts. Osborne suggests that teachers might put competing scenarios to pupils and encourage them to discuss and debate the evidence before them, basing their arguments on the data themselves. Osborne's curricular focus was science but the same 'argument' can be applied in other curriculum areas as well. With our teachers we devised several topics in English, maths and science which could be used to develop pupils' debating, argumentation and negotiation skills. Box 4.5 shows the basic task.

Box 4.5   Task 2 – argumentation

We ask you to set a task that develops pupils' debating (argumentation/negotiation) skills within your own subject area. You can proceed in one of two ways:

> EITHER
>
> Carry out a brainstorming exercise as to the best way to conduct debates within the group, including how to establish consensus or agreement and what to do if it is not possible to agree. Then proceed with the task.
>
> OR
>
> Begin with the task and then attempt to establish the best ways to conduct such debates as part of a debriefing exercise with the class.

Within each curriculum area several topics were suggested to get things started – and a few more appear in the Appendix.

English

- Puzzle solving: pupils are presented with a picture or a description of a scene and have to decide what has happened by using the evidence available to reconstruct events and arrive at a solution;
- Provide paragraphs or section from a story, newspaper or magazine article. Pupils have to place them in a sequence in order to construct a narrative or define a genre (e.g. thriller, romance).

Science

- Construction of a typology or classification system (e.g. is the whale best described as a fish or a mammal?);
- Using ideas about the nature of matter (atoms, molecules) to explain or predict various phenomena such as conduction, melting or evaporation.

Maths

- Justification of solutions in investigative work;
- Statistical representation of data within newspapers, outside world. How should it be reported?

Task 3: Group roles

After some initial experience of working in groups, it is useful for the pupils to consider how a group works and how to make it more effective. In discussing an issue and reaching a conclusion the group will go through a process that will be enhanced if the pupils are able to take on different roles. First, as we have seen, Vygotsky's theory suggests that discussion with peers (as well as adults) is important for young teenagers as they develop the ability to process and understand advanced and complex concepts. Good communication, involving both speaking and, critically, *active listening* is an essential element in the initiation of group discussion as the group begins its task. As discussion, and/or practical activities proceed, a key aspect of the intervening process (middle) is the pupils' ability to engage in various maintenance functions which help sustain group activity. Then, attempting to reach a consensus and bring the work to a successful conclusion (ending) is a third part of the process. In the SPRinG group work project, pupils were encouraged to seek consensus but this was not a condition, whereas in Mercer's 'Thinking Together' scheme, final consensus is a requirement. It helps the group if members can adopt appropriate roles to initiate, sustain and conclude the process. Some writers divide roles into two kinds:

- *Active or Doing roles.* This involves initiating or 'starting things off' (often by the person seen as leader), giving information, clarifying other peoples' ideas (mostly by asking clarifying questions), summarizing and prioritizing and in so doing pulling together people's contributions, facilitating by getting on with the team's task and ensuring the task is completed and providing the creative input as the *'ideas person'*.
- *Supporting roles.* This involves encouraging others to participate, using humour to diffuse tense situations, gate keeping (making sure everyone, including quiet or shy participants, is involved in some way), sharing personal experience relevant to the task in order to reduce emotional tension and by suggesting ways in which the group can set about the task in hand.

Pupils need to be made aware that they can adopt different roles depending on the task. One SPRinG teacher made her pupils aware of the roles they had adopted spontaneously, and the class then used these to construct new groups which included one pupil from each 'type'. Box 4.6 includes the roles task. Box 4.7 includes a list of statements that might help pupils recognize and reflect on these roles in relation to their spontaneous statements. Box 4.8 provides a sample role-evaluation sheet used in the project but, as our teachers pointed out, it is important not to try to evaluate every group-work session – evaluation then becomes a bore and is not taken seriously.

Box 4.6   Discussion of roles in group work

Taking different roles

We would like to work on helping pupils to become more aware of these different roles and to develop these maintenance functions. Pupils need to realize the importance of the various roles needed for successful group work. We have added an evaluation sheet for the idea of 'roles' to be explored. There is also a 'Statement Bank' which may be better discussed as a whole class.

Box 4.7   Statements made by pupils in groups

Statement Bank

Did anyone say any of these things?

                    'that's a good idea'

'we need to get on'

'what do you think?'

'we haven't done this bit yet'

'let's see how far we've got'

'who's going to record?'

'what do we need to do first'

'she said that'

'let him say something'

When people make these kinds of statements how do they help the group?

Box 4.8   Evaluating group roles

PUPIL EVALUATION SHEET – ROLES

Who in the group (could be more than one person)	How did they do this?
Got the group organised?	
Acted as an 'ideas' person?	
Pulled together ideas?	
Kept us on task?	
Asked key questions?	
Made sure everyone had a chance to say or do something?	

Did the group work well? Why/Why not?

....

....

What would you do differently next time?

....

....

Briefing and debriefing

We finish the chapter with a final extract from the handbook on the teacher's role before, during and after a group-work session. Pupils told us that teachers often get involved in too soon rather than leaving the group to sort out its disagreements – in other words, they tend to intervene at the very points where, according to Piaget, learning could be at its height. The teacher's role plays an important part in the effectiveness of group work. In particular it proved to be important for the teachers to 'brief' and 'debrief' pupils before and after a group-work lesson, to explain

- The Group Task – what the group has to do, how members will co-operate
- The Learning Task – the content or context to be learnt, discovered, investigated (Box 4.9).

Box 4.9   Briefing and debriefing

BRIEFING

Both the Group Task and the Learning Task have to be made explicit for any group work.

Everyone needs to know:

- What the task is – what has to be done, how it has to be done;
- The aim of the task – what will be learnt, discovered, etc; how the group will work;
- The expected outcome at the end of the task;
- The time in which they have to do the task;
- What the group has to do to get the task done;
- What each individual has to do to get the task done.

And above all

- Why the task is being done in groups rather than individually or as a class.

DURING THE TASK

- The teacher's role needs to be more of 'the Guide on the Side' rather than 'the Sage on the Stage'; at the beginning of the task encourage group work by observing and monitoring rather than intervening and directing. Groups may need to come back together as a class before being able to move on again.
- Activities need to be carefully structured and broken down into manageable parts – timing is crucial. Allow enough time for real group work to take place but not too much that pupils lose focus.

DEBRIEFING

At the end, the work and the process need to be reviewed:

- Was the task done – both at the group level and at the learning level?
- Does everyone feel they have gained something from the task – both in terms of content and of working as a group?
- Is everyone happy about the outcome?
- Was the time managed well?
- How did the group work together?
- How do individuals feel the group worked?
- How could our group do better next time?

Conclusion

This chapter has argued that collaborative and cooperative group work organized to encourage discussion and debate is of particular value for 11 to 14 year olds, and yet is relatively rarely used. Vygotsky's less often quoted writing on this subject supports the idea that in this age range peer-group discussion makes a vital contribution to the ability to deal in advanced and abstract concepts, while Piaget's work emphasizes the importance of cognitive conflict for intellectual development. Cooperative and collaborative group work provides opportunities for both of these processes. Our observations in science, English and mathematics show that group work increases time on task and decreases distraction and routine waiting time. It increases sustained and higher-order interaction and smooths out differences between pupils of different types. The achievement of these effects depends on both teachers and pupils having attended to: some minimal rules concern ground rules, argumentation and group roles; planning tasks so as to optimize scope for debate; and the various roles that it is possible to take. The chapter ends with extracts from the SPRinG handbook intended to provide (almost) at a glance training in the development of group work. The next chapter looks more closely at the pupils' and teachers' experience of working in groups.

 Questions for discussion

1. Why is it so difficult for teachers to make the move from 'centre stage' and the IRF script, and hand over discussion to pupils? What practical or organizational changes need to be made to facilitate the achievement of 'the discussion' or dialogic levels of teacher–pupil discourse described by Alexander?

(Continued)

(Continued)

2. What do you see as the risks (if any) associated with introducing more collaborative group work into secondary classroom practice? What strategies would you introduce to minimize or accommodate such risks?
3. Suppose that you had introduced more group work, and/or were working on the improvement of cognitive challenge and quality of pupil contributions to class or group discussions, and yet test results did not reflect these pedagogical developments. How would you explain this? What would you do to find out whether your strategies were working in practice – whether pupil contributions were perhaps longer, better articulated, more analytical, giving reasons, and so on?

Note

1   A child scored one point if they were on task for the clear majority of a 30-second time interval. The percentages therefore are slight over-estimates of the actual amount of time spent on task in every two-minute set of observations.

5

Teacher and Pupil Development in Different School and Classroom Contexts

Susan Steward and Charlotte Page

In this chapter we explore the potential for group work in different school contexts and across different subject areas. We consider the school structures that either help or hinder effective practice and the strong 'subject cultures' that exist in secondary education which make sharing teaching experiences and expertise difficult. We argue that while differences between subjects do exist – particularly between the core ones of English, mathematics and science – there is also potential for teachers learning from each other as well as a need for a more common approach towards teaching and learning that embraces issues of citizenship and pupil equity within all subject areas. We conclude by considering the positive outcomes of effective group work, both for pupils and for teachers.

In previous chapters we have discussed the declining attitudes of Key Stage 3 pupils towards the core curriculum subjects of English, mathematics and science. Clearly if these negative attitudes are to be changed we need to radically change pupils' learning experiences within them. Our observation results from the SPRinG project also indicate that, through training, teachers' questions and interactions can also develop from the merely procedural to the conceptual level and while we do not argue that group work provides 'the answer', nor that it is appropriate to use in every context and in every lesson, nevertheless we want to explore commonalities across subject areas and different school contexts.

Unlike the data presented in previous chapters much data in this chapter is qualitative in nature. To support and attempt to understand the survey and observation results we carried out interviews with groups of pupils and a number of teachers in the SPRinG project. In total we interviewed 36 groups of pupils and 12 teachers with the interviews taking place on the same day as the classes were observed. In all cases the interviewer had observed the class on three previous occasions so could refer to previous lessons, incidents that took place in them and other pupils in the class. We have supplemented these interview data with issues and experiences discussed at the teacher development sessions and from a 'final evaluation' open-ended questionnaire. Subsequent to the SPRinG project the team also carried out a project into grouping and group work (Kutnick et al., 2006) and for this used not only different schools in one of the areas of the SPRinG project but also other departments in a SPRinG school that had not been involved with the initial project. Thus we can compare teachers experiences in using group work within the SPRinG project with those who were not.

Different schools, different teachers, different timetables, different classrooms ...

The SPRinG project recruited English, mathematics and science teachers at Key Stage 3 from schools that were not only geographically and socially diverse but also in Local Authorities with different approaches to school organization. Thus we had teachers from middle schools (for pupils aged 9–13 years: Years 5–8), high schools (for pupils aged 13–18 years: Years 9–13) and secondary schools (pupils in Years 7–11 as well as pupils in Years 7–13 and Years 8–13). Also within the four LAs used we had a range of academically high- and low-performing schools. All these factors brought a range of different perspectives and experiences to the project.

Schools are organized very differently, even for schools in the same area, and a crucial consideration for lesson planning and organization is lesson length. We did not set out to prescribe lesson plans or schemes of work – we could not have done so even if we had wanted to. However, the difference in planning a 40-minute lesson compared to one that goes on for 95 minutes is enormous, and teachers have to develop their own strategies for dealing with the timetable in their own schools. To some extent this made the comparison of observation data difficult because shorter lessons necessarily had a very different structure and 'feel' to longer ones. Teachers in schools with shorter lesson lengths therefore often needed to 'carry over' activities and discussion so that activities could be done in enough depth as well as the 'group-work training' that was needed.

The focus on 'the lesson' in the English education system is perhaps particularly relevant here. From the beginning of their initial training teachers are required to produce 'lesson plans' and although there is a requirement to place these lessons into a larger unit of work both Ofsted and formal observations by assessors focus on the 'lesson' and the performance of the teacher within it. Now that the three- (or even four-) part lesson is standard and recommended this emphasis on 'the lesson' is even more pronounced. In contrast, other countries' (e.g. Australia, Hong Kong) Initial Teacher Education programmes emphasize the planning of the 'unit' of work that will stretch over a number of lessons and encourage students to see a single lesson as only a part of a whole. Therefore there is a corresponding shift of focus from the individual lesson to the unit when teachers consider learning outcomes – we tried to encourage our own teachers who worked in schools with shorter lessons to adopt this perspective.

While the challenge for many teachers is having too many pupils (and therefore furniture for them to sit on and around) in too small a space, science labs often present the opposite problem. Teachers in the SPRinG project were often adept in changing the classroom layout very quickly and would choose to organize desks and seating to suit tasks – often it was found that discussion was most effective around a smaller table rather than pushing tables together (i.e. a group of four pupils around a table for two). However, moving the furniture for group work was not usually possible in science labs where benches are fixed. Observations in other classrooms often shows desks (or tables) put together, and suggests that pupils are expected to work in groups, although this does not usually follow; studies in group work in primary classrooms often show the same disparity between seating and working arrangements (Galton and Williamson, 1992). Discussion of arranging the furniture may seem trivial but it is an essential component for successful group work, that is, allowing pupils to form distinct groups, to develop a group identity, to hear each other without shouting and sometimes to share written work.

The question 'What's the best number of pupils to have in a group?' is often asked. We did not prescribe group size, as teachers can best judge their own classes and how each task requires pupils to work. We observed some groups comprised of eight down to groups of just pairs our definition of group work was 'any activity that allows collaboration and discussion'. We also made the distinction between a 'collaborative' activity (one where pupils worked on the same task) and a 'cooperative' one (where pupils worked on different aspects of a task). Teachers found that collaborative activities were more effective in promoting interaction and discussion whereas cooperative ones could be done almost independently.

We were keen that teachers in the study were encouraged to use their professional judgement as to what worked best in their own schools and the activities that would best fit their schemes of work. At Key Stage 3, unlike primary level, teachers do not have the same class for extended periods of time therefore many developed their own approaches and pace within the project; any prescription by us would not have worked.

School ethos and management expectations

Not all schools were supportive of the group-work project and some of our teachers felt isolated in their departments or by their school's expectations as to what constituted a 'good lesson'. In particular, in the more 'traditional' schools the senior management was sometimes unsupportive of teachers who chose to arrange their classrooms so that pupils sat in groups and where extended discussion took place – the view of some school managers still being that the only effective classroom is a silent one. Another view was that the only effective way to learn is for pupils to write individually in their own books. A mathematics teacher commented on a lesson where he had been observed by the Deputy Head using computers in a group work context:

> ... [the class] were doing the stuff on spreadsheets and he seemed quite ... perplexed and concerned that there wasn't any evidence actually going into their books 'cos it was all going on the spreadsheet.

In other cases, teachers who adopted an alternative teaching approach to other subject areas felt isolated, in that they seemed to feel they could not change pupils' attitudes to learning when they had only three hours of teaching a week compared to 22 other hours of a less challenging approach. An English teacher summed up her frustration that other teachers did not even attempt group work:

> I often feel that I'm in there battling on my own as the only member of staff trying to do group work with that particular band [of pupils]. The other members of staff think I am completely and totally mad. They don't even attempt to do group work with these children. The only place where it is done is in science where they work in pairs. But it's not a language communication thing. They are given something practical to do and I've seen them work in silence just literally pouring things in. So although they are together in pairs they're not doing what I'm asking them to do. So I feel very on my own in the school trying to do it.

The teachers who were able to work together in a department felt that continual dialogue with colleagues around them really helped move their practice on and supported them when lessons might not have worked as effectively as they had wanted (e.g. we recruited all of the science department in one school and most of the English department in another). Where a momentum for change was generated, teachers in other departments became interested in the approach and these Heads of Department were asked to lead whole-school INSET sessions.

Experience and evidence from another study (Schools Facing Exceptionally Challenging Circumstances – SFECC; MacBeath et al., 2007) indicates that a cross-sectional group of teachers can instigate and manage change to whole-school approaches to teaching and learning. This model of school improvement can be described as: '"middle out" since its influence is designed to flow "upwards" to senior leadership as well as "down" to individual classroom level'. (MacBeath et al., 2007: 91).

In many of the schools in this study the members of such 'school-improvement groups' gained the support of other staff members because they were highly regarded and seen as particularly effective teachers, that is they were succeeding at the 'chalk-face level' and so had credibility. By contrast, in schools where approaches are initiated at senior-management level but not understood or endorsed by classroom teachers the opposite results often occur (e.g. other, less successful initiatives in the SFECC project). This highlights the need not only for teachers to feel supported (the ones in the SPRinG project got support from each other and from the Cambridge Team) but also not to expect real change to happen overnight – our teachers often benefited from an unsuccessful lesson because they could discuss what happened with a non-judgemental observer and therefore could move themselves and their practice on.

In some schools, particularly in those with low performance data, teachers often feel under more pressure to 'just survive' and innovation does not seem possible. While the research into group work did take place in a few schools that were classed as being in 'challenging circumstances' (i.e. high FSM, high SEN, low academic outcomes) we only worked in one that had recently come out of 'special measures'. The science teacher from that school who joined the project in its final year was observed to have particularly positive relationships with pupils in her classes and was acknowledged by her peers as an exceptional teacher. We do acknowledge other research that indicates that it is often difficult for teachers in very challenging schools or those under Ofsted scrutiny to innovate as they are constantly being inspected and monitored:

> Staff felt that the improvement process imposed rigidity on their teaching practice. This was felt by teachers to undermine their confidence. However, the new systems seemed to work in helping the schools get out of Special Measures, even if the process risked disrupting the flair of individual teachers. (Hargreaves et al., 2007: 253)

In the next chapter a teacher, who recently moved from an 'academically successful' school to a more 'challenging' one, discusses how she had to adapt her practice to suit the new classroom circumstances that she encountered. While she argues that group work is possible and does lead to improved teaching and learning (even if more slowly) she found discussion with colleagues from her own subject area in other local schools invaluable in sustaining her commitment to implementing this innovation within her own more challenging school environment.

Is group work possible in all subjects?

The view is often expressed that group work is 'usual' and 'easy' in subjects like English and the humanities but very difficult in other subjects such as mathematics where the individual needs time for private reflection while all of our teachers recognized that there was a place both for class and individual work, the above stereotypes do prevail and need unpicking. Indeed the front covers of the KS3 National Strategies (DFEE, 2001a, b, c) tend to reinforce these underlying assumptions associated with mathematics, science and English in pictures portraying either pupils engaging in a typical lesson (e.g. sitting in rows facing the front and putting up hands to answer teacher questions or working individually from mathematics; sitting on desks having an informal discussion from English) or portraying typical lesson content (no pupils shown but rather aspects from the science content such as a plant and a cell). For each of these subjects therefore, we want to focus on a teacher and his/her class that was particularly successful in promoting more positive attitudes to that subject and 'better learning' within it. We want to explore from the pupil interviews how group learning and working was understood differently in these three core subjects.

Mathematics

Interestingly, a number of pupils from English and science classes mentioned mathematics as the one subject where they just could not imagine working in a collaborative way (because they never had experienced a different approach). Another recent study looking at the reasons for widespread 'quiet disaffection' with Key Stage 3 mathematics lessons also highlighted 'isolation', that is, limited opportunities for working collaboratively, as a feature of mathematics learning and therefore a cause (Nardi and Steward, 2003). These attitudes towards and experiences of mathematics lessons were echoed by a mathematics teacher who had not been part of the SPRinG project – he questioned whether the nature of the subject itself works against collaboration or whether he, and many other mathematics teachers like him, had no previous experience as a learner himself in this subject to draw upon:

> Maths tends to be much more didactic, well especially me. It tends to be more individual work ... I struggle to find ways to get them working successfully in groups that will help each other develop their learning. I'm slightly envious of what the other [subjects] do. Now whether that's because, as a teacher, I'm unable to come up with a solution or whether it's because it is a more individualized way of learning ...

This quote points to the need for training and for same-subject teachers to be brought together so that they can talk about the perceived constraints of their subject and strategies that work. A mathematics teacher, having been in the SPRinG project for some time, put forward the opposite viewpoint about the nature of mathematics teaching and learning:

Teacher: I think in many ways there are actually more advantages with doing group work in maths than probably any other subject because there is so much that can be learned through peer teaching ... I'm not sure that that is the case in English and science ... Maths is that sort of subject where you have to understand the concepts – like Pythagoras's theorem, you either understand Pythagoras' theorem or you don't. If you understand it you can teach it to someone else. And isn't it better that a pupil can do that for another pupil rather than me standing at the board ...

Interviwer: Sometimes people say this about maths and science because of the view that there's an answer, there's one answer. In English everybody can have opinions.

Teacher: But as I show with the question today, it's not actually about the answer, it's just about the method and it's about saying, well ... and I think that sometimes maths teachers, and certainly non-maths teachers, get hooked up with the fact that there is only one correct answer and therefore there's only one method, which isn't the case. And I think, you know, if you look for diversity that's why I got Luke to come up and talk through his method 'cos his was completely and utterly unique. ... And I think that's what this brings out. And it also means then that if a pupil doesn't see something in the same way as everyone else and they see it in a different way they actually feel quite positive about themselves and about the fact that they can get the right answer in an alternative way. And they'll still feel confident, whereas often in the past people have been, well, I haven't done it that way therefore it's wrong.

Jo Boaler, who recently conducted a comparison of the mathematics departments in three Californian high schools, focused on one of these departments which, atypically for mathematics, used group work as its predominant teaching method in heterogeneous (i.e. mixed-ability) classes. She comments:

In previous research ... I have interviewed many hundreds of students who have worked in groups ... but the students in all the other schools in which I have researched have listed benefits that were exclusively about their own learning. At [the group work school] students also talked about the value group work added to their learning, but students' descriptions were distinctly reciprocal and they voiced a clear concern for the learning of their classmates. (Boaler, 2008: 179)

From the pupil interviews we too have evidence of this 'reciprocity' in mathematics learning through group work. In particular 'helping others', peer tutoring and 'learning through interaction' feature much more strongly in mathematics classrooms (and in particular the ones we want to focus on).

The other feature of learning in mathematics is that of 'more ideas' – this implies a different approach to teaching mathematics where traditionally only one method and approach have been encouraged. The fact that these pupils were exchanging ideas implies that they too (like their teacher) had learnt that while there might be one 'numerical answer' to a problem there were many ways of getting there. The excerpt in Box 5.1 illustrates how pupils have learnt to support each other in mathematics and how group work has moved their learning on.

Box 5.1 Girls discussing working in a group of six in mathematics

G1: I like it when we work in groups.

G2: Well, what we do is we normally work in a group but then kind of do the main work in pairs.

G3: Yeah and then we discuss it

G2: And if we don't get it we'll ask.

G1: Yeah, we help each other and like sort things out and ...

G2: Yeah. But today's lesson ... normally we're working on exactly the same thing, but today we had different questions so then ... we all did different ways to do that ...

G5: Well, what we do is sometimes Mr V doesn't like us working in groups and he'll often say it's just, you know, pair work or individual work but, erm, we often just discuss it anyway because we like it.

G4:   Yeah, it helps us to work really better.

G1:   'Cos then you can ask other people.

G3:   And then if you are stuck …

G4:   Putting your hand up and asking.

G2:   And also then you can see different points of view and you get different answers. So say I rushed ahead and then I would say, 'Oh Harriet, hold on, this calculation is wrong' or I would ask somebody else and they would say, 'Oh look this is what we've done wrong as well'. It helps.

G5:   Because we've been following … what we've each been doing, but if we get Mr V in or someone he … we might have to start again from the beginning and read through it 'til he knows what we're doing.

When asked about working individually on computers:

G3:   But yeah, if Olivia hadn't been there then I would have been completely stuck and then I would have asked another pair to help.

G4:   And also it's far more creative 'cos you have different ideas and then you can get them together and it's like a large scale idea.

G5:   I would have found it much harder because there's a lot of stuff that Amy remembered that I completely forgot about.

Int: With the laptops?

G5:   Yeah.

G4:   But then when she remembered it – that meant I remembered it as well so it was much better.

Int: What about the understanding of areas of different shapes?

G4:   I know more about it now.

G2:   I think it was easier in groups 'cos we each had our own idea.

Science

When group work is mentioned in the context of a science lesson it often centres around 'the practical' and indeed there is a persistent perception (from both pupils and teachers) that the science practical is group work. Practical group work however, does not necessarily raise the levels of scientific dialogue between pupils. The science teachers involved in the SPRinG Project were particularly interested in exploring how best to encourage discussion in their classes and a learning together culture – that is, where pupils support each other and build on each other's knowledge to develop scientific understanding. The science teachers involved in the project were keen therefore to provide more opportunities for pupils to talk about science and to explore science concepts together.

Over the course of the project, teachers noted that developing group-work skills over a prolonged period allowed many more pupils to become actively engaged learners in the classroom and also changed pupils' understanding of what science is about. Rather than concentrating on the correct answer or the result, pupils started to ask many more questions and to interrogate the science concepts as can be seen in the following quotes from their teachers:

The questions they ask have improved in quality. Rather than asking for an answer they make an observation and ask, 'Why?' this has happened.

Sometimes I have given pupils only a brief outline of how to set up and carry out a practical. Initially they just wanted to get everything finished as soon as possible,

> but increasingly they are looking back over how they have carried out the task and making improvements themselves.
>
> Confidence among the lower-ability groups has definitely increased. They are more willing to share their ideas, and in practical tasks are more self-assured when setting up and carrying out investigations.

There are, of course, very real challenges for science teachers wanting to bring a more collaborative way of learning into their classes but these challenges are not necessarily particular to science. However, more than their colleagues from other subject areas, science teachers spoke about the constraints of time and a packed curriculum, especially during the initial training stages of group work; like colleagues in other subjects they too also found it difficult working within a department or alongside colleagues who were not interested in group work and how best to engage disruptive or disengaged pupils. Despite all these challenges, SPRinG science teachers were positive about the benefits group work brought to science enquiry in their classes both raising the levels of scientific discourse (questioning, justifying, analysing, clarifying) and raising pupil confidence and motivation for science.

Three main types of science lesson were highlighted by SPRinG teachers and researchers as being particularly successful for group work and particularly raising the level of discussion between pupils. Teachers stressed that in all group-work tasks adequate time needs to be set aside to discuss *how* the group work went – and not only the science. The three main types were:

- building discussion time into and around the science practical – working to plan an investigation, to test, to record, analyse and evaluate;
- debates/discussions around ethical and controversial issues – opinions, justifications, implications;
- peer tutoring – questioning, analysing, explaining and clarifying scientific concepts and theories.

By way of illustration we will focus on one Year 7 science class that showed particular success in developing positive attitudes to learning and science. Attitudes in this class towards group work improved significantly more than other classes taking part in the project. Not only this but the quality of group work also improved significantly. From tests carried out before and after group-work input, these pupils were also among the few classes to show the highest achievement gains. So what exactly happened in this science class to bring out such positive attitude and attainment results?

From lesson observations and pupil interviews a very clear pattern emerged indicating that pupils liked being in this science class. In our lesson observations, this class consistently scored the maximum for quality of lesson environment and atmosphere – meaning that the pupils were happily engaged in their work, understood what the task required and the need for collaboration and relations between pupils and also between pupil and teacher were respectful and calm. The pupils felt good about themselves regardless of ability and this positive class feeling spilled out into how pupils treated each other. There was a genuine desire to help each other and a sense of pride and responsibility to act in this way. Group work was not just about sharing out the task and learning in a social way, it was also about giving something to the group. Here too was a very real sense of 'relational equity' (Boaler, 2008) between pupils and between teacher and pupils in the class, that is, there was a respect for others' ideas, a commitment to the learning of others and a shared sense of how to support and communicate with each other (Boaler, 2008):

Int: What makes a group work?

M: I think if you've got a variety of people …'cos if you've got like all people who like get stuck a lot then you're not going to get very far, but if you've like got people who like know the answers, you've got people who don't and then you've got people who struggle a little bit but they think they know the answers who are a bit like shy …

Int: Mm.

M: Then you have people who don't really want to take part, but you try and get them to anyway.

As the quote suggests pupils took responsibility for their own and others' learning, even when some pupils did not want to participate. This sense of responsibility and care for each other was something the teacher modelled with the class and something that was spoken about and valued in all lessons. Pupils' ideas were encouraged and respected and the teacher guarded against telling information but rather encouraged pupils to find answers. Coupled with this type of communication was a careful planning of science tasks appropriate to the level of group work competence and science knowledge. Time for discussion was built into lessons – not only discussion about the science concepts but also discussion about the group-work processes. There were also options, other than the teacher, for groups to turn to when they got into difficulties that is, prompt sheets helping pupils through a task and modelling asking others in the group. In this way pupil resilience was built up as well as confidence in their own abilities to overcome social and learning problems. The excerpt in Box 5.2 illustrates this resilience and confidence in their own abilities.

Box 5.2   Pupils talking about group work in science

Int: Have your views on group work changed over this year? Did you like group work as much as you do now?

L: I didn't like it when we first came in because I thought it was going to be boring, but now …

K: Yeah, 'cos we didn't know anything.

L: We do practical stuff, it's better.

K: And I think … I weren't too sure at the start of the year, but now we do … We sort of do more fun stuff and now we know like what to do and how to put out the equipment and everything and everything that we need. I think Miss trusts us.

Int: Yeah. I think she does as well. ... you don't need her as much do you?

L: No.

Int: When do you need her to come in?

L: Like when we're stuck on a word or something and if we don't get the question don't we? But most of the time we just figure out ourselves.

Int: You do, that's good. And has that changed do you think?

L: Yeah. We used to always put our hands up didn't we and say, Miss I want some help and really you know ... deep inside you can do it ... but you just want Miss to do it for you.

K: I think we'll be even better in Year 8 as well.

M: Yeah.

K: We're just getting better and better ...

And talking about their attitudes to science at the end of the year compared to the beginning:

L: I thought it was boring and like ...

M: I like Miss much better now.

L: I didn't think that Miss would trust us to do practical work.

Int: Why do you like it now?

M: 'Cos we like working in groups to do all practicals.

L: Yeah. It makes the lessons more interesting.

K: I thought it would be really, really boring, but Miss makes it fun as well as what we do in the lesson. So that's really good.

L: I think it's well better working in practical stuff.

The success this science teacher had was not a fluke. The teacher worked very hard to model with pupils how to respect everyone's contribution and also how to encourage those who opted out or disrupt a group. The difficulties of group work were talked about openly. Pupils therefore learnt to become more articulate at thinking and talking about others' needs as well as their own. Pupils in this class gradually became more emotionally literate which raised the levels of effective group-work learning (high levels of on-task dialogue and support for each other) and raised attitudes towards science itself. The response of the pupils in this science class closely reflects the research by Matthews (2004) and Morrison and Matthews (2006) who looked at the effects of integrating emotional learning alongside science learning. Year 7 pupils involved in these studies worked in mixed-gendered groups within science classes where social and emotional discussion was encouraged as well as cognitive discussion (Matthews, 2004). The research showed that working in this way improved pupil attitudes towards science and increased their tolerance and understanding towards each other.

English

There is an assumption that English as a subject lends itself to group work as discussion is a key feature of this subject; indeed there is still an oral component of the GCSE at Key Stage 4. However, as one English teacher reflected in an article for the SPRinG newsletter on 'the hidden benefits' of taking part in the project, group work in English was not as 'natural' or as easy as many think (or as he himself had initially thought):

> When we were nominated to be part of the SPRinG project, we were a little surprised to say the least. Over the years, the English Department at [our school] had relegated group work to a minimum. On the whole we tended to use it for oral work at GCSE. For us this was where it seemed to sit best. The move by the government to a whole-class approach had also had an effect on the way we planned our curriculum. That and being a 13–18 High, with examinations in every year bar Year 10, meant that we were very much in production-line mode.
> [...]
> To begin with, during the first year when researchers visited school, I became aware that group work was not the picnic I had thought it would be. Wanting desperately to provide showcase lessons with my lively new Year 9 group for my researcher was turning out to be a bind and success across the board was proving to be more than elusive. It was clear that I had to go back to the drawing board and rethink a whole series of issues before planning group work.

The nature of English, as one teacher described, is 'explorative' – 'we're not always looking for right answers'. Another remarked that '[group work lessons] don't work if they're too structured and they don't work if they're not structured enough. If you have a definite outcome you can often be disappointed'.

Pupils too talked about group work in English in qualitatively different ways to mathematics and science. In particular they talked about 'opinions' and 'generating different ideas' and 'points of view' that they would not have thought of individually. The importance of someone's opinion is that 'it can't be wrong' and so the pupil giving that opinion in the closeness of the group can gain confidence that they are also able to contribute and that their views are valuable too. Other pupils in the group not only learnt to listen but also learnt to respect views different to their own and to develop skills of argument when they did not agree.

Many English teachers talked about poetry in particular as a rich source for group work – the ambiguity and different interpretations that arose out of discussions were a surprise to some teachers who had used class-centred discussions in the past; in particular they realized that they had taught one interpretation whereas their pupils, if allowed, understood the poems differently (see excerpt in box 5.3). Where group work is more difficult (and perhaps not recommended) is for imaginative/creative writing – 'you can't do that in a group as much because you have different ideas', although as the results in Chapter 3 showed, putting pupils into groups to discuss ideas and to plan prior to the actual writing worked well. It was rare to find a situation where pupils were asked to write collaboratively (script writing is cited as one example where professional writers work collaboratively but there are few others). Nevertheless many pupils felt that the quality of their written work did improve over the year and were surprised by their own progress – 'sometimes you do long pieces of writing without any help'. This exchange between four girls illustrates how group working supports individual writing:

Girl 1:   I think if you're, like, sitting like how this is like sitting next to one person and if you're writing a story or something and you don't know what to put next so you can like ask a friend what you could put next.

Girl 3:   Yeah. What I think is quite good is when we write stories we just …

Girl 2:   Yeah we write a little bit. Or plan it out. And if you are, like, stuck, you see what everybody else is doing.

Girl 3:   We read each others don't we?

Girl 4:   Yeah get, like, ideas but don't copy just, like, get ideas. That sort of helps you.

The English teachers recruited onto the project were often ones recommended to us by their Local Authority advisers or through the training link with the university and so were known for their distinctive approaches and expertise. However, despite this, all English teachers in the project had to develop their approaches to and thinking around group work as well as re-evaluating their classroom roles – regular meetings with others in the project gave vital time for this reflection and learning:

Int: And has your attitude to group work changed over the years. Like, are their aspects of being in the project that have surprised you?

T: I think it's just more consciously thinking about the impact and the effect and the usefulness of it. I mean I've always done [group work] but I actually now think it's more valuable than I thought it was before. Simply because I have thought about it more and I've observed it more closely and observed the impact of it more closely.

Int: So in some ways you've developed as a teacher? It's made you think about teaching and learning much more than you wouldn't necessarily have anticipated?

T: I think part of it might have happened anyway as I say in a very different environment [a change of school] I've had to think about things in a different way in any case. And part of it has come from that and part of it has come from being on the project. And also you know going to Cambridge and hearing other people talking is very useful. I mean that's one of the most useful things for us as teachers that we get out of that day listening to what other people do.

Int: And also time to reflect?

T: If you don't get it, you do something. You're too busy and you've moved on. You've gotta do something else. Yeah. You don't get that time.

Another English teacher who had used group work more recently and was very positive towards it remarked, 'I could see the benefits of doing group work [before] but now I can see the benefits of doing group work well'.

The excerpt in Box 5.3 illustrates how group discussion can engage pupils with a text and develop their understanding of it. The poem by Grace Nichols, is about a black slave giving birth in a field: the ending is particularly ambiguous.

Box 5.3   A teacher and a group of boys talking about a poetry lesson in English

T: And it was a hard poem, and I was absolutely amazed at what they came up with [in their groups]. And then when we got to the class where they had to make their notes on the poem, the input was much richer. Not just the one-word sort of short answers. What were your thoughts on this line or this the ending? What did you think she was talking about? Much more sophisticated answers and developed answers. And original. They weren't all mine. You know and I thought, 'Oh I hadn't really thought of that'. Poetry is wonderful cos it's not definite is it? You can interpret it how you like …

Some weeks after the lesson the researcher asked a group of boys who had worked together about the poem:

Boy 1:   We looked at several lines that could have double meanings so if one person has a view and another person follows it on with their view then that fits them together.

Int: So you didn't have a big argument about it?

Boy 3:   No I can't remember any arguments.

Int: Because at the end it's not clear what happens to the baby is it? So what did you all think?

Boy 1:   She's young and she hadn't given birth yet had she? She was in labour wasn't she?

Boy 2:   She was free.

Int: Sorry. Richard, what did you say?

Boy 2:   It was something to do with freedom so … so I thought that I wanted her to let it swim away and not be asleep like her.

Boy 1:   I had a feeling she wanted to kill the baby or something.

Boy 2:   Yeah that's it at the end, people weren't sure whether she wanted to kill it to save it from slavery and whether she did or not in the end.

Boy 3:   I'm not sure about the end of that.

Int: So you don't come to a decision about that? In your group you just said it could have been this or that?

Boy 1:   Yeah.

Boy 3:   Yeah.

Other school subjects

Observations in the Grouping and Group Work Project raise issues around some other non-core subjects. For example, many design and technology lessons are very individual, with pupils carrying out their own project over many lessons (with interesting repercussions for the notions of 'pace' and 'challenge'). An observer noted the relaxed atmosphere in the room (with the radio on) and how pupils appeared focused and engaged over a task whose finished outcome came about after a number of weeks. This might lead us to question prevailing orthodoxies for a 'good' lesson in the core subjects, that is how there often appears to be little continuity from lesson to lesson and the lack of pupil ownership of the finished 'product'. By contrast other subjects such as drama often expect pupils to work in groups throughout and the outcome is often a group 'production'. One of the SPRinG English teachers said that he had learnt many techniques from working with a colleague in drama (also raising interesting questions around whether English teachers are natural drama teachers).

We did not set out to promote citizenship values such as greater respect and equity among pupils but as in other studies (e.g. Boaler, 2008 – mathematics, Matthews, 2003, 2004 – science) we also found these unexpected outcomes. It is often assumed that young people learn respect and tolerance as well as group working skills in PSE (Personal and Social Education) but our study showed that even if these issues were covered they were not necessarily transferred to other subject areas. We would argue that citizenship and its implied values of collaboration, respect, tolerance and so on cannot be 'bolt on'; dealt with only in the one hour a week given over to PSE or seen merely in terms of student representation on a School Council. Education for citizenship and democracy, whether in school or society, needs to be based on core shared values and on interaction between different social groups. John Dewey (1916: 97–8), who applied many of his ideas around democracy to education, argued that:

> in order to have a large number of values in common, all the members of the group must have an equable opportunity to receive and to take from others. There must be a large variety of shared undertakings and experiences.

Therefore, among other principles, democratic education allows opportunities for students to actively collaborate and learn from a range of other students different from themselves (Osler and Starkey, 2005). Others have argued (e.g. Noddings, 2005) that this implies the need for a more 'holistic' educational approach where each subject or discipline in a school not only teaches its own skills, competencies and knowledge but also takes responsibility for teaching students to be 'active citizens' in the broadest sense. All school subjects can aim to promote equity between students and can offer opportunities for discussion around 'moral, social, emotional and aesthetic questions', that is, this has to be a whole-school approach centred around the needs of the 'wholechild'. An important component of this is a different learning environment where active collaboration and valuing others' views are an integral part.

Why do group work? Views of pupils

Despite these strong arguments for a greater use of collaborative learning that promotes 'relational equity' between students and more 'active citizenship' the norm in most schools is either a whole-class teaching approach or individual working (even if pupils are seated around the same table). The pupil interviews indicated, in many cases, a quiet antipathy towards these approaches and, among a few individuals, overt disengagement and alienation from school and learning. Here we outline some of the reasons why these normal approaches are not really working to the advantage of most pupils.

The negatives of whole-class teaching tended to focus around the issue of 'exposure': some pupils did not want to look too 'smart' and 'keen' in front of their classmates:

Boy 1:   Yeah, and you get called boff, when someone calls you a boff then you don't answer as many questions because you think that people don't like you because you're ...
Boy 2:   Too clever.
Girl: Yeah, you get bullied.

or they did not want to appear 'different':

> Girl: I don't think it's not wanting to be wrong. I think it's more, like, not wanting to be embarrassed if you're thinking the opposite to everyone else.

and the need for collaboration and sharing were sometimes perceived differently at class and group level:

> Girl 3:   [... If] you're having a class discussion about some work you've got to do later, and you've got to, like, write it down then if you keep the opinions to yourself then no one else in the class is gonna be able to write down your opinion ... I think if you say your opinion in the class and someone else thinks it's better than their opinion then they're gonna use it. Which isn't very fair on the person that thought of it and that means someone will be accused of copying. So it's not very fair.
> [...]
> Girl 3:   Sometimes it's better to work by yourself because sometimes when you work in a group and other people get your ideas so it's all, like, all the things I've sort of been saying.
> Girl 2:   Yeah, but if you work in a group then you're supposed to share your ideas. It doesn't matter if they nick your ideas because you're in a group.

Again, while many of the negative comments around individual working could be applied across subjects pupils did, however, recognize types of activity where this approach was useful in some subject-specific activities such as revision and practising calculations in mathematics, creative writing in English. The main reasons for not much liking individual working for other activities was because it was isolating and 'harder on your own'. It was also frustrating having to depend only on the teacher for explanations:

> Int: So what if you don't understand in [this subject]? What do you do?
> Boy 1:   We have to ask the teacher.
> Int: What happens if lots of people have got lots of different questions they need to ask?
> Boy 1:   They normally do! Then you're just waiting there for ages and then he tells you to sit down.
> Boy 2:   Yeah. If you get up and ask then he goes, go and sit down. And then say, 'if I see you up again you'll come to my room at break'.
> Int: So actually he can't manage?
> Boy 2:   No.

And sometimes it was easier to quietly subvert the rules to gain understanding:

> Boy 1:   In French you can't really talk as well – last year, we had to be silent and then if you're stuck there's nothing to do and ...
> Boy 2:   But in French I would ask my mate next to me ... like, quietly, so I didn't get into trouble.

The theoretical arguments given earlier around the need to embed citizenship values and particularly discussion and collaboration in all school subjects are also reinforced in a more 'grounded' way by pupils and teachers themselves. The attitude survey, discussed in the first chapter, showed that, in general, pupils were positive about group work. The pupil interviews tried to probe the reasons why. Within the pupil interviews the positive reasons for liking groups from pupils were put into four broad categories:

- **Learning**: 'sharing work', 'helping each other', 'more confident', more ideas/opinions', 'time to think', 'do better work', (223 statements);
- **Task**: 'more interesting', 'do more work', 'given better work', 'less pressure', 'greater participation', 'because of talk', 'more fun' (71 statements);
- **Social**: 'stability of group', 'being with friends', 'becoming friends', 'managing disruptives', 'better relationship with teacher' (55 statements);
- **Economy of effort**: 'sharing out work', 'less work to do' (54 statements).

Again, many of these 'positives' were independent of the subject being discussed. It is often assumed that pupils are positive to group work because of the opportunities to work 'socially' and to be with friends. However, our interview results show that pupils actually appreciate the different learning environment and tasks more than these more superficial reasons. Most importantly, a large number said that they 'learnt better' in groups compared to whole-class teaching or individual working. The nature of this 'better leaning' reflects some of the aspirations of active citizenship – in particular the right for all students to participate fully, to be included, to be free to express themselves and to be valued by their peers and the teacher (Osler and Starkey, 2005).

Teacher development: the changing role of teachers

Overall teachers in the project were extremely positive about using group work and the ways in which it had begun to transform their practice. Not all teachers were equally effective and nor did some find the approach easy. We have already discussed one teacher who thought he 'did group work' but then realized after being in the project that he did not and therefore had to reassess its rationale and planning. Another teacher responding to the question, 'Do pupils benefit from working in groups?' replied,

> What is one of the interesting things is that it forces you to remember that group working is often one of the most constructive things you can do in a classroom. Because the whole point about teaching is to create autonomous learners. And you are giving autonomy if you are working in groups.

Referring again to our observations we would argue (as would many teachers) that teachers need to spend less time planning activities and more time planning for group work. Teachers introduce tasks by saying *what* pupils should do and what the expected outcomes are rather than *how* pupils should work and *why*. Similarly at the end of the task the focus is on *what* was discovered/ produced/and so on rather than *how* pupils worked to produce that outcome or what went wrong when they didn't. Some teachers talked of the dangers of overplanning and being overstructured 'rather than allowing the group work to develop itself'.

The key for success for many teachers was when they began to re-evaluate their role in the classroom. Many recognized that they needed to move from the role of 'sage on the stage' to 'guide on the side':

> *Int*: You said when you were talking about Year 9 that you had to learn to stand back. Do you think that you did jump in much more at the beginning of the year? Is that to do with where they are and sort of assumptions about them not being able or old enough or mature enough all those sorts of things.
>
> *T*: Yeah. I kind of think that they just need me. You know and I think teachers are quite egotistical like that. I really do. And sometimes you like the sound of your own voice as well and you just ... Yeah I've got a really good idea and I want to enforce it on you. You know. I want to tell you. Now if I just shut up they might come up with that idea themselves. It's just waiting and that's been quite hard for me but if you're quite a gregarious person and you want to help them and you want to get them moving with it and sometimes if you just stand, maybe a prompt but not actually telling them ... I think that's my fault and I can't speak for everyone but I think a lot of the time we tell them too much.

Many teachers, like some of those mentioned earlier, started to realize that anticipating the outcome of pupils' responses to a poem, how a mathematical investigation would be carried out and so on did not allow for alternative interpretations, strategies or solutions. Being open to different approaches and giving that autonomy to pupils allowed them to achieve much more.

When teachers should step in and intervene in a group became an increasingly important question for project teachers as they developed their group-work practice. Teachers talked about 'getting a balance between intervening and leaving it' because if they intervened too much they 'run the risk of being too interventionist, too shaping and too controlling'. The English teacher quoted earlier highlighted a common problem, which is that many teachers expect pupils to need their help and that perhaps many pupils have learnt to rely on their teacher's input for the answer. Stepping into and directing pupil groups too quickly was something that most project teachers battled with partly because they found it hard to gauge the levels of learning and engagement actually taking place in those groups. The excerpt in Box 5.4 indicates that pupils often expect teachers to intuitively know when and how to intervene. However, this is not always the case. Many of the SPRinG teachers had to resist their own impulse to take over a group that appeared to be making less progress than other groups and to allow that group to learn at its own pace and to develop real autonomy over time.

Box 5.4   A group of pupils talking about when teachers should and should not come to the group:

Int: So going back to the poetry lesson that you did. What did the teacher do when you were working in the group?

Girl 1:   He'd come round and listen to us.

Girl 2:   Yes. He'd come round each group for about five minutes.

Girl 3:   And then if you were stuck he'd just sort of talk to you. And make sure you know what you are you doing.

Girl 2:   And like if you have any questions or you're stuck then he'd help.

Int: But he didn't butt ... Did he butt in?

Girl 2:   No he did listen ... Well to us anyway.

Int: And is that what you wanted him to do?

Girl 2:   Yeah. Because you get sometimes ... some teachers if they hear something that they don't agree with then they always butt in and don't let you finish. [...]

Girl 2:   But then Mr W he does listen and then he speaks afterwards ... so that's better.

Int: Does he give his point of view?

Girl 2:   Sometimes. Yeah.

Girl 1:   If that helps.

Int: Are there times when you want the teacher to come to your group?

Girl 1:   Sometimes ... if we're stuck.

Girl 4:   Some teachers let you be more independent and do it for yourself.

Girl 3:   Yeah but the trouble is if you know what you're doing and the teacher come along it just annoys yer. No, not annoy yer but like gets in your way.

Girl 1:   If you've got your own opinions and points, and you think they are right then tell him

Girl 4:   But like some people don't say like, you know they're wrong.

Girl 3:   Some teachers don't ask you how you're getting on they just kind of basically try and help you instead of asking.

Int: Even though you don't want any help?

Girl 3:   Yeah. Mr W. asks us 'are you all right?' sort of thing and 'do you know what you're doing?' and if you say 'no' then he'll help if you say 'yes' then he'll just move on to the next person.

Int: So do you think he sort of judges it right?

Girl 3:   Yeah.

The issue of student participation and engagement in a whole-class setting is also difficult for teachers to gauge, as a vocal group engaging in a whole-class discussion can be misleading. As one teacher reflected,

> If I think about, say some of the classes I have taught where, because of the nature of the group, they were good at listening and you didn't have to do a hands-up, they were actually, it could be over to them. Still 40 to 50 per cent of the people would not be involved in that. But because you'd have 12 to 13, 14 people in a group

discussion you'd let it go. But talking to some of the kids who never used to take part, they said they found that dreary and were just waiting actually to get on with the work. Whereas I was sitting there thinking, 'Oh this is good stuff. Look at the tangents we're exploring …'. So although half the class were having a good time and I was thinking it was pretty good, there were a whole of bunch of other clients who are not being catered for. Whereas at least in the group work, the bulk of the kids are engaged and on-board and discussing it.

Similarly, pupils engaged in individual work but sitting in pairs or in groups can be equally misleading as to the extent of their real engagement with learning (e.g. Nardi and Steward, 2003, considering quiet disaffection in mathematics).

Through the interviews with pupils involved in the SPRinG Project there is evidence of better pupil engagement and learning as a result of group work. As highlighted earlier, 223 statements from the pupil interview data indicated that group work was 'better for learning' implying that, after a year in the project, many pupils were more interested in these core subjects and were more actively involved in lessons than they had been before. As a boy in Year 8 remarked,

> I've always had Mr X as a teacher, but I think he's changed his methods or something because I enjoy it now and it's not because I enjoy [this subject], it's because he's done something to change it and I don't … I couldn't explain what but he has done something and it's now a better lesson.
>
> Before I would try not to take part. I would sit back and let other people do the work … But now I feel I should try and help out and I've found it easier now and I find I'm learning more.

At the End of Project Evaluation all teachers also referred to 'better learning' through group work and it was interesting for us to note that again most comments from teachers were *not* subject specific. The attainment tests that we developed were subject specific and took place very soon after the topic was taught, and while we have no quantitative measures of 'deeper' learning or understanding, (some test items were designed to assess higher cognitive thinking). Other studies have empirically looked at whether learning through group work is more embedded and is more likely to remain over time. However, our teacher and pupil interviews could only qualitatively indicate that better understanding had taken place. For example a mathematics teacher commented that when she revisited topics the recall from the class was quicker and one of her students said that if he had worked on the algebra in a group 'it would have been in my head more 'cos I can't remember it now'.

The attainment measures devised to test whether group work did result in higher cognitive scores when taught through group work (described in Chapter 3) were perhaps too blunt a method to measure the more subtle learning described above. Indeed when asked how individual pupils had benefited many teachers talked about 'increased confidence', 'raised levels of self-esteem', 'better social skills', and so on. While we were unable to look at group attainment outcomes that also have an impact on the individuals within them the following give some teacher responses to the question,

'When pupils work together on tasks to produce a group outcome what from their work has surprised you?':

English:	• 'A sense of pride lacking in individual work';
	• 'More original, more insightful than individual response';
	• 'Weaker students grew in confidence and then were able to express and explain their own ideas'.
Mathematics:	• 'Depth of understanding and ability to open up the task';
	• 'Generalizations in algebra';
	• 'Oral presentation and discussion of their work';
	• 'They have been able to attempt and complete tasks they would not normally do if working on their own'.
Science:	• 'Looking back over how they carried out the task and making improvements themselves';
	• 'The questions they ask have improved in quality';
	• 'Rather than asking for an answer they make an observation and ask 'why' this has happened'.

In the real world of the classroom, the SPRinG experimental design that asked teachers to teach a topic either using a group-work approach or with a whole-class/individual approach is artificial; in reality all methods are appropriate at different times during the teaching of any topic. As a long-term strategy to improve student learning in any subject we too would argue that a more holistic approach to developing whole units of work that integrates rather than 'adds in' group work is needed. From their involvement in the project, the Head and Deputy Head of one English Department decided to revise their schemes of work so that an element of group work was embedded alongside a variety of other strategies within each unit. This resulted in a more holistic series of lessons where collaborative working was seen as more natural and expected way of working and after which each student produced their own individual work. For these teachers, the result of this change in planning was certainly more effective and considered:

> T: [My colleague and I] have both said that we have benefited immensely from having to think about putting group work into our schemes of work. And we have found that the group work has actually given the students a better understanding of whatever we were doing. Now because they go through a journey to an assignment which they write individually, I would be very hard-pressed to say that because we did group work that it was better. What we would say is that the global approach to that assignment has been enhanced. You know, in other words our scheme of work has been enhanced by group work. And somewhere along the line, I don't know whether we could ever find that out, it will have made their understanding, when they come to write it, clearer ... but I think what we're doing, because you know it is a journey, I have to describe it as a journey, we will do several things and then eventually we'll bring them together, and that will bring about the assignment.

This approach, as discussed earlier, shifts the focus from the individual lesson to the series of lessons that make up a coherent whole. It can also be argued that the act of collaboration between these colleagues led to improved understanding of the learning process for them as teachers as well as better learning and written outcomes for their students. The following quotes also highlight how other teachers developed their own practice and confidence:

> I have become much more confident in trying new approaches to teaching particular topics and more skilled at self evaluation of those new approaches.

> I have approached teaching in a different way and thought a lot more about how pupils learn.

Conclusion

In this chapter we have argued that group work is possible in most school contexts and across all subjects. We also highlight that most pupils acknowledge the benefits of 'good' group work and enjoy learning in this way. However, we do recognize that group work is not easy, is not a 'quick fix' and, depending on various contexts (school ethos, department ethos, lesson length, colleague support), can present a real challenge for teachers. In the more successful schools in the project, the group-work innovation did develop a momentum of its own and was taken up by a number of teachers and sometimes by the management team as a vehicle for real cultural change across the school. We would argue that this change embraced many of the components of real citizenship education that schools have had a responsibility to deliver over recent years in that it supports many of the recommendations for success such as a greater emphasis on 'pupil voice', on democratic and participation with a clear appreciation and understanding of individual difference (Ajegbo, 2007). The cultural shift requires by more collaborative classroom learning also requires teachers to reflect not only on their own role in the classroom but also on their relationships with pupils. In the next chapter we explore the challenges that teachers and pupils encountered in introducing and using effective group work in their secondary classrooms.

 Questions

1. What conditions have to be in place in a school before teachers can attempt to organize student learning in small groups?
2. Are secondary school subjects as distinct as is often supposed? How can teachers be brought together more effectively to discuss common issues around teaching and learning?
3. What are the core values of citizenship education? Should 'citizenship' be taught as a stand-alone subject with its own slot in the school timetable or should it be integrated across a range of subject disciplines? Should citizenship education be primarily concerned with content or with pedagogy?

6

Why Were Some Classrooms More Successful?

Susan Steward

> In this chapter we not only explore why some classrooms were more effective (and enthusiastic!) through the qualitative insights that pupils and teachers gave us but also a number of particular issues that need further consideration and exploration. We explore some key challenges that face most teachers in most classes to a greater or lesser extent whether at the class, group or individual level. We argue that an effective classroom is one where there is a climate of 'co-learning' between teacher and pupils and where relationships, whether teacher–pupil or pupil–pupil, are key to real and transformative learning.

In the previous chapter we concluded with the positive outcomes for both pupils and teachers of using group work, in this chapter we look at more negative experiences for both, and explore how the challenges presented can be reduced, if not overcome. Again the data presented in this chapter is qualitative in nature either from SPRinG lesson observations, teachers feedback or pupil interviews. We were able to compare the schools and teachers in one of these areas with data collected from teacher interview data from the subsequent 'Grouping and Group Work' project (Kutnick et al., 2006). This second project also focused on school and classroom grouping practices at KS3 and compared three schools in one area that had very different approaches to school organization: a school committed to mixed-ability teaching, a school using more conventional organizational approaches to setting within the core subjects and a school providing alternative provision for a 'nurture' group outside of the main timetable for that Year group. The school committed to mixed-ability teaching was also a SPRinG school but this allowed data from other teachers not involved in that Project to be collected.

Previous work examining secondary teachers' working lives (MacBeath and Galton, 2004: 17) highlights challenging pupil behaviour as an overriding concern for teachers and the biggest obstacle to effective teaching. One of the reasons cited by teachers in this study for this increasing disaffection was 'inappropriate curriculum' and perhaps implicitly 'inappropriate pedagogy'. Therefore we were particularly interested in whether group work could change the behaviour and attitude of not only overtly disaffected pupils (i.e. that teachers would identify themselves) but also of a much larger group who appeared outwardly compliant but, as we would suggest from our attitude survey (and that other researchers would support), were inwardly disengaged (e.g. Rudduck et al., 1996). Therefore to gain insight into the range of pupil attitudes we used the results of the SPRinG attitude questionnaire to identify pupils who were either very positive or very negative to group work as well as those who were potentially disaffected from school and schoolwork in general. Having identified some of these extreme pupils we aimed to observe and interview them with their normal working group and so therefore the groups of pupils interviewed contained a range of classes, subjects and types of pupil. We also deliberately chose classes that appeared to have a number of extremes within them and where group work had been observed to be relatively effective.

Teachers, in their feedback on group work, indicated that there were particular types of pupils who had improved learning outcomes in their subjects, for example,

English T: … helps less able students to participate and access lessons thus improving their self-esteem.
Mathematics T: … less confident girls have really made progress both in terms of performance and confidence in giving answers.

However, despite particular advantages for some pupils and general advantages overall, some individual pupils clearly did not respond well and in many interviews teachers discussed in depth the behaviour of these individuals in their classes. We were aware from both the attitude survey and the qualitative interviews that not all pupils were positive to working in a more collaborative way. Teachers also recognized that changes to their practice brought other challenges in the classroom to the fore – specifically issues around particular types of pupils in that class. In the previous chapter we discussed subject-specific issues particularly around 'subject cultures' and expected forms of teaching and learning in those subjects not only from management and other teachers but also from pupils themselves. We have also discussed the difficulties of working in a school whose ethos does not lend itself to collaboration and discussion in classrooms. Therefore we will now look at particular issues and types of pupils who can be found in most classrooms whatever the subject being taught.

In the end of project review teachers identified particular pupils or groups of pupils who presented them with key challenges such as

- the disaffected, who are difficult to engage in any task;
- disruptive and 'naughty' students;
- including dysfunctional students in the groups;
- socially inadequate students who find group work difficult despite a year of trying;
- including some students with Special Educational Needs (SEN);
- students who choose not to interact;
- groups who are off task at least part of the time;
- some boys who see tasks that are of interest to girls as being pointless to themselves;
- very low-ability students and very high-ability students;

These different 'types' of pupils and the challenges they present will be discussed at individual pupil, group and class level.

Particular individuals

The disaffected and alienated
There is a minority of pupils, identified in the attitude questionnaires, who can be described as extremely 'disaffected and alienated' both from school and from learning in general. These pupils may be able to subvert what is going on in their group because of their strong personality or, in other cases where they are not so confident, they may disengage and absent themselves if not physically then mentally. An English teacher talked about the behaviour of the first group who, he recognized, may not immediately benefit from group-work approaches.

> There are individuals for whom education is a, not a competition, but an area of conflict. And that's the way they deal with it, then group work is threatening because it actually undermines their approach to the classroom. Because for them the classroom is conflict, teacher and peers. And if you put them in a situation where they have to work with their peers, and alter the dynamic of their relationship with their teacher, you are actually undermining the structure they like to work with.

Many teachers offer pupils the choice of working on their own if they cannot work productively with others – teachers reported that no pupil had taken up this offer. But this strategy is more of a containment; a better solution would be to try to use their influence positively. While these pupils are difficult to 'get on side' one teacher argued that, with time, the teacher–pupil relationship can be improved if such pupils are given a role:

Int: [in the classroom] he was slightly sending it up, you know, '*Oh right we've got to share ideas you know*' but in here [i.e. practising outside the class], given a different context, given space, given time, performing to me, performing to that he was different. Why?

T: Because … Because in there he's alpha male isn't he? He's the alpha male of the group. He is the one that … the boys look up to and the girls fancy, so in that space he's taking on a role isn't he?

Int: But how do you tackle that?

T: I think you can tackle it in lots of different ways … One is to do something like what happens to him in here, which is to give him a context to perform positively. And I think another thing that you do is that you try and channel that energy and that enthusiasm and that intelligence and that alpha desire for the good of the group … He's quite a maverick figure in some senses and I think you have to find ways of involving him in the process of what you're doing … because he will then lead for you if you get him on your side. He will then be involved and lead for you and be a useful spokesperson for the teacher. Often in the past the way I've approached people like that is to get them on your side. And they then disseminate it for you because if you get that kind of pupil who has that kind of influence on a class then you're 90 per cent home because they're going to be saying to the rest of the class, 'Well I'm up for it, why aren't you?'

The 'quietly disaffected'

The second group referred to earlier are the more 'quietly disaffected' – the less confident, who may try to undermine other pupils' work in groups but often defer to stronger personalities or opt out without trying. Matthew, from an English class (described in Chapter 3), talks about never being involved in group work. However, when the interviewer asks him why, he goes on to talk about his issues with school and English in particular:

Int: Why don't you get involved?

M: Because I never do.

Int: What in English or in anything?

M: In any group work. I just sit there.

Int: So you don't like English as much now as you did in Middle School?

M: I liked it in Middle School.

Int: You liked it more in Middle. Why is that?

M: Probably because I don't like this school. Everything was better in Middle. I didn't have teachers on my back all the time.

Having to manage disruptive, dysfunctional, lazy pupils causes other pupils the most problems and is the main reasons why they report that they do not like group work (poor group work skills and poor social skills are the main reasons for not liking group work for pupils). However, in some cases other pupils are happy to manage and support a peer who is having difficulties. In this case the other boys in Matthew's group did try to support him and, despite functioning less well than other groups, the teacher could see progress at these pupils' own pace. The teacher had actually thought very carefully about where best to place Matthew, showing that a knowledge of pupil relationships and personalities is key:

T: … but even that group you see, I think has come on. When you first saw them, you know, they were totally off task and talking about God knows what. They are far more on task. You know, I mean just, they just function in a, in a relatively positive way.

Int: Because you also said to me that you think that their level of writing …

T: Yeah, well they've improved. I mean they've all, come on, even Matthew. And Matthew reads. He reads because Luke gave him a book. Because Luke is a fanatical reader. And so he is now onto his third Terry Pratchett novel. So this is a guy who would normally say, 'I don't read, reading's rubbish'.

In a class with much low-level disruption a teacher stressed pupil responsibility towards the group as his lever to address behaviour. In effect he promoted pupil–pupil relationships over and above the teacher–pupil one and so a potential source of conflict was dissipated. The establishment of class and group rules by pupils themselves all help to promote what could be described as a 'democratic' classroom where pupils and teacher share responsibilities:

> *T*: I think again you are hoping that the group thing is actually going to give them some responsibility for their behaviour. And so therefore they will improve their level of behaviour because they will feel that it is not the teachers they are upsetting, it is actually their peers.
> *Int*: So you can actually go in there and intervene and talk about responsibility and say, 'Look what do you feel about this?'
> *T*: Particularly. Like in the project where people have set up rules, there are rules outside of the school that you can draw on. These are the rules we have agreed together as a group. You are breaking those rules. And those rules are not about me and you, they are about you and the group. So I think you can call on all of those things, and I think the difference is in a whole class situation, you know ... the conflict is a theatre. It is a smaller theatre if you are in a group situation. And I think the biggest punishment is removal from the group.

Pupils with Special Educational Needs (SEN)

Working with SEN pupils, especially around emotional and behavioural issues, can also present teachers with problems. In some cases other pupils do not want to include those with SEN, who are different from themselves, but in other cases they do recognize how to manage those who have emotional outbursts. In other cases teachers can help this process by recognizing when not to push students:

> *T*: I thought it was interesting that Steven and Sian decided that they wanted to work on their own. Steven has Asperger's and Sian is an emotionally deprived child. I asked her, 'What do you want to do?' and she said that she wants to work with Steven. And then when she got there, she wanted to work on her own. I said, 'Well what would make you happy?', 'Working on my own'. And she looked happy. So ...
> *Int*: And she succeeded really well, didn't she?
> *T*: She did. She did. Yes and that was because she couldn't, wouldn't have been able to cope with the other pupils distracting her.

It was important that this teacher recognized these children's needs in that lesson and that he considered the composition of groups carefully. He argues,

> You have to use your knowledge of the pupils' personalities, to see what will work. So for instance if I tried to enforce the group rationale on Sian or Steven, then I could have blown my lesson. Because that way there could have been tears, crying. Five or ten minutes could have gone.
> [...]
> I think it is crucial to be sensitive to the needs of the individuals within the group. Because you are dealing with the security that they have as individuals, so that you know they come into a room, the place they sit. Where they are is part of their individual and emotional security. And if you are going to play with that you have to realise that that has an impact for certain individuals, for whom that space is where they feel secure in that room. So that is important.

In another case a pupil with a disorder on the autistic spectrum wanted to work with his group but was prevented from interacting as an equal by his learning support assistant (LSA). The issue of the role of LSAs was brought to the fore in a number of classrooms – for while teachers were recruited to the Project these staff members were not and therefore could not be expected to understand the need for different adult roles in the classroom. They were often very protective of the individual in their care and either directed the whole group or isolated the pupil with special needs. In one instance the interviewer talked to the group including Tom, the boy with SEN, about the helper working with Tom all through the lesson:

Tom: I would have preferred to work with Callum.
Int: Why?
Tom: They're always … they're always following me. There's loads of people they always follow me.
Int: And because she was here working with you then Callum couldn't talk to you about what was going on either? Did she help you, Callum as well?
Callum: Not really.
Fred: It's kind of two separate work … Tom works with the helper …
Simon: 'Cos when Tom's helpers are around they, like, don't let him get his ideas across to us so, like, it's just like me, Fred and Callum just working and it's like as if Tom's not there 'cos he's just working with the helper and they don't let us give ideas to him or anything.
Fred: Normally the … the helpers, like, spend too long, like, explaining to him and he falls behind.

Another study looking at the inclusion of pupils with special educational needs also found that 'there can also be a tendency for TAs to isolate "their" child from group or whole class learning contexts' (MacBeath and Galton, 2006: 61).

It would not be fair to blame either teacher or LSA from the earlier excerpt – the problem is a lack of liaison time between the two so that they can agree roles in the lesson – the need for this is rarely recognized by the school management. Other teachers in the project also reported the difficulties of including support staff in their planning for group work as they saw a variety of staff (even different LSAs for the same pupil) who had different levels of expertise and subject interests. Unlike primary schools, where support staff work in the same classroom each day, in secondary support staff can be allocated work in different subject areas and responsibilities for different pupils each week (MacBeath and Galton, 2006) and therefore, in such cases, find it hard to build up any subject expertise or any relationship with the teacher. Some support staff take complete responsibility for the learning of the pupil or the group to which they have been assigned (and, in some cases that we observed, ended up taking over and doing most of the work themselves). We would strongly argue that teachers need development time and space to be able to plan for pedagogic and curriculum change and therefore time for collaboration with all colleagues must be included in this if any new initiative is to succeed.

The social loners

Social ability need not necessarily correlate with academic ability, and so socially inadequate pupils may be found among the most able or the least able classes in their year. These pupils may be those who do not want to mix and/or those pupils whom other pupils do not want to mix with. They may be either introspective and withdrawn or brusque and rude to their peers. Teachers tended to also refer to these pupils as 'dysfunctional', that is, not wilfully 'naughty' nor disaffected but somehow unable to function 'normally' within a group, which is to say that they were perceived as 'odd' in some way. At the extreme are those pupils who are on the autistic spectrum. From our interviews it was often mathematics classes that presented issues for teachers, and many of these loners were highly able mathematicians. A teacher admitted it was difficult teaching a class even if there was one such pupil of this type:

> And also if you get ... not so much disaffected, but a dysfunctional pupil, certain dysfunctional pupils within a group and if you've got more than one in the class I think it can be difficult. There are people in this class like X who would just say, 'Right well I'm going to do all the questions, I'm not going to be bothered with working with the rest of the group – I'm going to get on with it'. Yet when he was actually doing the [activity] he was quite happy to work with and learn from the others because they were teaching him something that he wanted to know. Yet he feels with the mathematics that he has the ability to do the things himself and so doesn't need the input from the others. So there's no one within that group that he values to give him a contribution. That may be putting words into his mind, but it's my perception that he feels that he is a good mathematician and I haven't given him anything suitably challenging yet that he has needed to use anyone else to learn from and he's not prepared to teach anyone else very often. He will do it very occasionally. Very rarely will he interact with the others in terms of helping them [either].

Yet in another class another good mathematician who usually works on his own did appreciate that he had benefited from working in a group and from explaining to others how to solve algebraic problems:

> Int: What about you John? What did you get out of today's lesson?
> J: Dunno. If I wasn't in the group I'm not sure that I would have spent so much time trying to find the best method of ... 'Cos she [didn't] set like a set amount of work which you can like go through quickly. So I could spend more time trying to find the best method as I've had time ...
> Int: So do you think that was of benefit?
> J: Er yeah. I haven't got quite as much work done as I would have if I was separate but I think I've found a better method.

However, John could not be described as 'enthusiastic' about this group work lesson and despite being a 'gifted' mathematician he also seemed quite unenthusiastic about mathematics too. It is difficult to see which other pupils to group individuals such as these with as their ability sets them apart and they rarely see the point of collaboration to extend their skills.

Mary Barnes (2000), exploring the issue of different masculinities in small group work, also identified a group of boys in a mathematics class that she described as 'the Technophiles' because of their interest in computers and science. She also noted that in group work these boys did not like working or discussing with others and seemed to be 'more interested in getting to an answer quickly than in exploring alternative approaches'; also when two such students were in the same group 'they communicated with one another in brief, rather cryptic remarks which others found difficult to follow' (p. 156). Yet their teacher reported that their written assignments were often 'inadequate and did not reflect their understanding'. She also argues that group composition needs careful consideration and that students like these

> need to be convinced of the importance of both written and oral communication skills and given assistance in improving them. The importance of listening to others also needs to be stressed to all students, but especially this group ... avoiding if possible placing two of these students in the same group. (p. 166)

The successful conformers

Much teaching and learning is either whole-class based or individually based, even though pupils might sit together rather than apart (the exception being low-ability sets where pupils are few in number so they are deliberately separated to allow greater teacher 'control' over behaviour issues (Kutnick et al., 2006)). Other studies have shown that higher-ability pupils can be more resistant to group-work approaches – perhaps because they have learnt how to be successful in conventional classrooms. We cannot blame pupils for not wanting to share their ideas as in most classroom contexts the emphasis is on competition rather than collaboration, on out performing your neighbour in a test rather than on helping them succeed along with you. A minority of pupils in the interviews did say that they preferred working on their own because they did not have to share, and resented having to work with those they considered 'less able' than themselves:

> Pupil 1:   Well, I've found being in sets much better 'cos I found in the higher set it
> really pushed me and I felt that I'd done my best.
> Pupil 2:   Same with me.
> Pupil 1:   And I feel that definitely in this class being in classes 'cos there's such a mixed
> ability there we're doing not as hard stuff and it doesn't really push me.

Teachers remarked that it was often the most able who were most resistant to new methods and could potentially undermine any innovation:

> I think there are pupils within the ability spectrum who have been encouraged to see themselves as high achieving individuals, who can be quite conceited about group work, and quite antagonistic towards it.

Teachers perhaps need to recognize that it may be those pupils who are usually the least 'trouble' and the more successful learners that may be most resistant. This change in the classroom dynamic and their relationships with such pupils can be a surprise. It may be worth considering whose voices are usually heard in classrooms and whether enabling the less vocal, the less confident and the more disengaged – perhaps the 'quiet' majority, makes up for the antagonism from the visible minority. Tasks that require sharing and collaboration, that is, where pupils cannot successfully complete them on their own need to be used so that such pupils do learn the value of learning in this way. However, such pupils may still resist these approaches.

Group issues

In the interviews, when asked, 'When is group work difficult?' pupils also focused on their relationships with other pupils or others' behaviour and/or their own or others' lack of skills. The reasons for negative experiences of group work were as follows (interestingly it is poor group-working skills and poor social skills that are cited as the main problems):

- Non-functioning group – poor group-work skills: 'arguing', 'one person doing it all', 'always given same job', 'having to share', 'others get credit', 'too many ideas', 'not taking it seriously' (80 statements);
- Non-functioning group – poor social skills: 'not liking others', 'odd one out', 'off task', 'opting out', 'outside factors e.g. friends, rows etc.', 'bossiness' (74 statements);
- Task: 'not enough to do', 'no teacher input', 'not enough views', 'same sort of work', 'work more/too demanding' (16 statements).

This would reinforce the views expressed in earlier chapters that classes do need to be trained for group work and do need to understand the dynamics of an effective group so that pupils come to understand themselves and others. One teacher, for example, expressed surprise at how much pupils could understand about the dynamics of the group process itself:

> T: I think because I made too many assumptions about people being able to work in groups it perhaps taught me, over the years, the ground work in terms of what a group was for. What we want to achieve. And the class having an understanding or discussing what the group work is all about and how people at different times play different roles. Which I'd never considered before or that it was possible to actually discuss with them. That you can do that.
>
> Int: So are there things that surprised you?
>
> T: Yes. Surprised at the level of response to kids recognizing what groups are about. When you start opening up that discussion about what groups are for I think I had a pattern I thought they might have an understanding about what they thought about groups. And I remember those early discussions about setting up ground rules but when you push the rules a little bit further you just push methods of working a little bit further I was very surprised at what the kids could identify.

The most effective teachers found that relationships and interactions between pupils was key and spent a great deal of time thinking about maximizing these:

> But I mean the whole thing has made me think far more about the dynamics. I'm far more aware of the dynamics. I'm looking for harmony, all the time looking to create harmony. And when I think about some of the classes I've had I know that I wouldn't

have been in some of the situations I found myself in if I'd thought better and harder about where they sat and who was sat behind them, and how we might get people to interact. Because I just hadn't thought about it, simply because I arrogantly sort of said, 'Well I'll do it'. But then you give yourself work. You know, you're creating a scenario that you've got to deal with. Whereas this actually was all about massaging.

Classroom issues

Setting and streaming

The ability of different pupils seemed to be an issue in most classrooms. One teacher noted problems working with low-ability sets:

> *Int*: When is group work hard?
> *T*:   ... something about the ability of kids I think ... I think the lower the ability, you have to work more to pitch it into a way that will get them into the problems that you want them to look at. And organizing your groups 'cos often with low-ability pupils there are often other problems ...
> *Int*: Like 'I'm not sitting next to 'im ...'
> *T*:   Precisely. And I think you know there are those issues and I think an easy option is to cop out and sort of do it in a much more structured and a much more individualized way.

Whereas another teacher highlighted higher-ability sets as a problem:

> The 'middle- ' and 'lower'-ability classes seem to enjoy working collaboratively more than higher-ability students. The reason for this seems to be the recognition of achievement: the more able enjoy the kudos of individual achievement (the Tim Henmans) while the middle- and lower-ability classes are quite secure in team achievement (the David Beckhams)!

In a mixed-ability class an English teacher remarked that it was the higher-ability groups and the low-ability groups that were least effective:

> *T*:   I have noticed that groups that I thought would work well together haven't, for one reason or another. And actually for me the mixed-ability groups tend to work better. The last activity that I noticed that the worst two groups was a group of boys, low-ability boys, and the highest-ability group.
> *Int*: Was that mixed gender group the highest?
> *T*:   Yes, it was. They seemed to be quite happy *not* to talk to each other and just do their own thing. Because they thought, 'I don't need anybody else's help I'll just do my own thing'. And they virtually ignored each other. And the low-ability boys just didn't do anything. They didn't have anybody to keep them on track and kind of promote ideas. Even though they probably have got plenty of ideas but it was not obviously the done thing to be seen to work. So I actually split the boys up and I split the bright ones up as well. Today.

These quotes illustrate that ability grouping, whether between or within classes, can be an issue in every subject area. Given that one of the big issues for teachers at present is pupil disaffection and poor behaviour where these pupils are found in substantial numbers in any one classroom the result is that this class is very difficult to teach. While many schools do group classes purely by attainment (i.e. the school or department claims that behaviour is not taken into account), in other schools either low attainment and poor behaviour go 'hand in hand' or poor behaviour ultimately results in low attainment so the result is the same. One teacher, when asked which pupils were advantaged (or disadvantaged) by ability grouping commented,

> There are some students who gain – some of the more competitive ones who're in a higher set they do achieve more. It's mostly a motivational thing. You also get people put into a lower set not necessarily because of ability but those who are switched off and don't want to do the work and so they drop down even further. Out of harm's way is one way of putting it cynically – it's not right but sometimes you've got to think of the others.

Some subjects such as mathematics and modern foreign languages are more likely to be ability grouped than, say, English and humanties (although there has been a trend towards more setting and streaming in recent years). For example:

- at Key Stage 3 the majority (83%) of mathematics lessons in England are grouped by ability compared to 48 per cent for English and 61 per cent for science;
- by Key Stage 4 100 per cent of schools sampled reported ability grouping for mathematics compared to 63 per cent for English and 83 per cent for science (Ofsted, 2004).

Some of the reasons for ability grouping in mathematics were given as follows by teachers in the project:

> I think mathematics is a particularly difficult subject when you've got the full range. I know some people can do it but I can't – I think you are confronting them much more with failure in mathematics and they can see what others are doing and they are nowhere near to what you're talking about.

and:

> Kids come here with a very clear label that they've given themselves of where they are in mathematics. It's hard to shake off that label.

We had a concern that a number of teachers in the project chose to work with higher-ability sets (in schools and subjects where setting took place). Certainly the challenges are greater when working with lower-ability pupils – especially where more difficult pupils are concentrated. However, we would strongly argue that the potential for change and positive outcomes is greater with the lower-ability range and the more disaffected (where other initiatives appear to be having little success!).

Results from the Grouping and Group Work Report (Kutnick et al., 2006) that observed pupils in different sets across a range of subjects indicate that lower-ability groups (sets/streams) have a more restricted curriculum and pedagogical approach:

> The learning and general classroom experiences of pupils categorised as low ability differed from all other types of categories [i.e. high and middle ability]; they had less opportunity to interact with peers, were least likely to be asked to undertake 'new knowledge' learning tasks and were most likely to work with an adult in the classroom and not with their peers. (Kutnick et al., 2006: 59)

Ironically, different issues and challenges emerged from the higher-ability sets that might not have been anticipated, particularly in English. An observer to an English top set, which the teacher herself described as 'quiet and passive', noted the social and cultural homogeneity of the pupils, which led to a tendency for these pupils to agree with and to not challenge each other. Constructing an argument is central to the process of thinking and developing understanding. Reasoned argument allows pupils to develop logical thinking and is best developed through discussion and debate with others but this is less likely to happen if there is already consensus and a lack of different perspectives around an issue.

In working with lower-ability groups teachers may need to be very careful over the choice of tasks and may need to extend the period of training in using group work and alternative approaches, as results from Grouping and Group Work show that these pupils have the least opportunities to work in a collaborative way and so will need most support. Some teachers in the SPRinG project did feel demoralized when they tried to apply the 'rules' for group work to low-ability classes and to use similar techniques to those used with higher-ability classes:

> I really thought that if I gave a lot of thought to group work and I did all the group rules and I constantly reinforced it and I gave them activities which I hoped they would enjoy, I really thought that by the end of the year I would be able to look at the group and say there are definite areas of progress. Whereas at the moment I feel I'm searching for areas of progress. They are there. But they're hard to find. And that's made me rethink about me. That I don't feel so confident that I can just go in and just do things. I plan meticulously and I think for ages over it and it's still sometimes failing. As it did the other day. And that's not doing my confidence a lot of good at all.

When the interviewer asked if the same strategies had worked with the top-ability half of the same year group that this teacher also taught, the following comment was made:

> That's all fine but then anyone can do the top groups. [The strategies have worked] Yes they have. And they've enjoyed it. And probably there's a much more relaxed atmosphere in there and it's been lovely and I've enjoyed doing it. I've enjoyed doing most things with them. I certainly don't worry about doing group work with other sets.

This experience had made this teacher reflect on ability setting/banding in English:

> And the other thing that's really made me think is that banding, and this is a band not a set, is a complete no no for group work and they won't be in a band next year. Huge mistake. Cos there's not enough children there to support the ones who need it – there's too many needing support and I can't do it.

Another teacher, however, recognized that she needed to be less ambitious in her expectations and work more slowly with her classes. She had moved schools the previous year and was finding her current school much more challenging. Here she talks about the strategies needed for classes to be 'ready' for group work – in particular taking things more slowly and sticking with it allows a more positive relationship to develop based on mutual trust. In the following year this teacher stayed in the project and chose to work with a low-ability set in Year 7:

> T: They like the security of boundaries and knowing where the boundaries are and now they're in that place and I'm in that place with them it would work … And it does take quite a long time. But also I think the issue with me that I've come to a school that's a very different environment so I had to establish myself, not just with the class but in the school and I think hopefully in September with a similar group the process would be quicker. You know, cos certainly at the start of the year my expectations of them were too high and getting the work at the right level took several weeks and things like I do much more kind of kinaesthetic learning. I do much more drawing and visual because a lot of weaker kids are those kind of learners. I've had to adopt my teaching, not just the activities, but also my style to adapt to the environment. So it's me and them in a way, do you see what I mean? It wasn't just a straight-forward you've got a new class in September. I was dealing with a whole new ball game as well.
>
> Int: So are you saying is that actually it's not just a question of like wanting to do group work. It's also being able to. Feeling that you've got a reasonable relationship with the class you are going to teach.
>
> T: Because ultimately you've got to be able to pull them back haven't you. And you've got to know that you can do that and they've got to know that you can do that as well. And with some classes that happens almost immediately, doesn't it and with other classes that are more challenging it takes much more time to establish that relationship and that dynamic. So they can have a certain amount of autonomy but you know and they know that when you say, OK stop, turn round and listen and its whole class again and you get them back whereas with that difficult class any change or shift in the lesson caused fairly major disruption at first. Because they can't cope with it. You know if I drew breath they'd start nattering and it takes quite a long time for them to realize that's not how it's gonna operate. But I hope for September I'm much more clued up than I was when I first came here. Cos obviously [my previous school] is such a totally different environment. So I've had to develop skills that perhaps I hadn't needed to have before in the environment that I was in. So I am hoping that September will be easier than last year.

A mathematics teacher in the project also chose to work with a low-ability set of pupils who were often together for a number of their lessons; they had developed a 'group culture' of their own that many other teachers found difficult to deal with (he joked that other members of staff had thought him mad to invite a university researcher into his lesson with this particular group!). He also described the need to choose activities carefully – in particular those that re-enforced listening to each other and therefore developed pupils' language skills. He too used sorting and visual activities rather than traditional writing tasks. From our observations we noted here too that this approach was under-pinned by the positive relationship that the teacher had with this class.

Gender: 'girls are angels, boys are devils'

All of our research took place in mixed-gender classrooms, no schools were single sex and none had adopted a policy of single-sex classes in any subject to address the under-achievement of either boys or girls in that subject. Policies for between class grouping in the core subjects were either social – around heterogeneous tutor sets or were determined by perceived ability in that subject (i.e. ability setting). Within-class groupings were decided upon by teachers themselves (the research team promoted teacher autonomy for this) – sometimes these were friendship based, sometimes random, sometimes around 'learning styles and sometimes based on gender considerations (either deliberately mixed or single sex).

We have already discussed some issues raised by ability setting and streaming – these also throw up gender issues. In particular many low-ability classes in mathematics and science are dominated by boys (e.g. as observed in our own studies) and high-ability classes in English are dominated by girls. As a mathematics teacher commented,

> I sometimes see the low ability [classes] to be badly behaved boys and very low-ability girls – that's not always the case but there is that tendency, and I think that's very difficult for the low-ability girls because they are putting up with a lot of unpleasantness.

Many researchers in the field of gender equity have warned of the dangers of seeing boys and girls as distinct homogeneous groups (e.g. Murphy and Gipps, 1996) and making generalizations about 'all boys' or 'all girls'. Certainly not all girls are 'angels' and not all boys are 'devils' but it was often individual boys who seemed to cause teachers most behavioural problems and who were identified by them as the main problem in their classes. Other pupils in the interviews also recognized this to be the case:

> *Int*:   Do you think there's a difference between boys and girls in groups?
> *Girl 1*: I think, I think the boys sort of they phase out a lot more than the girls.
> *Girl 2*: Take the opportunity ...
> *Girl 1*: The girls concentrate more.
> *Girl 3*: I think the girls can concentrate for a lot longer than the boys can.
> *Int*:   Do you think that's a fair ...
> *Boy 1*: Yeah, well some boys will work but some boys will just mess around.
> *Boy 2*: Like me, I can't concentrate for more than like 15 minutes. Aaron can like, he can like carry on for a whole lesson really.

A common strategy in schools is to sit pupils in boy–girl pairs (often alphabetically so that they are actually always next to the same person in every lesson), this is often done for behaviour reasons. An alternative strategy of always seating the 'good' girl next to the troublesome boy to contain him is particularly unfair on the girl. Both these seating strategies take no account of any pupil's learning needs. Within groups however, where the emphasis is on communication and collaboration, mixed-gender groups containing very different personality types can work if teachers use their knowledge of the individuals in their class and plan around the groups and not around the activity.

In some classes pupils said that group work was good because it confined the behavioural issues to that group and so the class could get on – this may be better for most of the class but is unpleasant for other members of the group responsible for the containment. Some groups with strong individuals within them can organize a difficult individual but these pupils are unlikely to be the quiet hard-working girls. A few teachers did think carefully where to place some boys (e.g. Chris in the following below) and did recognize that there were groups of girls who can deal with them but these groups cannot be left alone and may need more support:

> *T*: Chris – he's actually quite immature. He's quite weak in the group. He's probably the weakest. I wouldn't say he's naughty. I mean he's a bit of a lad. He's a Year 9 boy and he is immature and he needs very clear instructions and very clear boundaries otherwise he can get silly and he will if he can get away with doing very little. He's the sort of kid that needs lots of chivvying.
>
> *Int*: Do you think his group could get him back on task? Or do you think he needs you to get him back on task?
>
> *T*: Yes. I think he needs me. He's got quite a lot of kudos with the other kids so he's more a leader than a follower with the other kids. I think they would find it difficult to get him back on track. And the boy who was the one who was the mover and shaker in that group in terms of the work is actually a very quiet boy. And that's why when they choose their own groups those dynamics operate don't they? Sometimes I put Chris with girls because if anyone is going to they will. Because they'll be very direct and they'll give him a lot to do. You know that kind of thing. But he tends to need me to intervene really to make sure he's on track. I mean he's not horrible or desperately bad or anything and he actually quite wants to please but he's a boy. You know he's a Year 9 boy. Fairly typical.

Gender groupings within the classroom also need careful consideration – in the main few single girls or single boys want to be isolated in the other sex group. However, pupils can be more positive towards mixed-gender groups than teachers often think, especially if they have a friend alongside them. It is not possible to legislate about group composition in some cases and for some tasks single-sex groups work best whereas in others mixed-gender groups are better, for example in an English class where the issue of the 'rape sheds' in the 19th century American South could be more sensitively discussed in girl-only and boy-only groups whereas in a mathematics class exploring an investigation the girl-only group tended to 'play safe' and therefore did not really explore the problem in the depth it required (examples from lesson observations). Also for the Grace Nichol's poem discussed earlier (see box 5.3, Chapter 5) a boy remarked that 'I think like the boys probably wouldn't be as comfortable discussing it [in the class] whereas in a group you're more comfortable'.

Group composition can be contentious – the experience of our teachers was to use and develop the positive working relationships of pupils in the class. A successful initial strategy is to allow pupils to find a friend and to sit two boys in front of two girls (usually a pair they do not know) and then 'tweak' these groupings after getting to know the class. Friendship groups can be too 'close' – their members too similar to challenge each others' viewpoints whereas random groups were universally hated because some individuals could be completely isolated and therefore have no security within the group.

The attitude survey shows that there are real issues for girls in mathematics and particularly in science – that is, as they move up the school they become increasingly negative to these subjects (whereas English does not decline to the same extent and by Year 9 girls have remained on the positive side of neutral). Our own observations of groups in some classes, whether mixed gender or single sex, were also cause for concern. For example, in science we observed that one or two girls might run an experiment only to have the boys in their group copy their results at the end, having shared none of the work. The girls carried out this work on their own because 'it's easier to do it yourself' and to avoid being publicly blamed by boys – 'we haven't got any answers because "they" weren't helping us'. At other times a girl in the group was always allocated the role of 'scribe' because the boys did not like writing but were keen to generate the ideas. In these cases we would argue that teachers need to rearrange groups so that pupils assume different roles in different lessons and that girls gain too by working with other pupils who will collaborate and share. To encourage participation and 'saving face' it may be that similar types of boys (e.g. the shirkers) are sometimes made to work together so they cannot rely on others. In another case in a top Year 8 mathematics set a girl-only group appeared to take fewer 'risks' with an open investigation and therefore made little progress. It may be argued that this group of girls were more used to 'conforming' to get right answers and lacked the confidence to explore the problem (although an alternative view has been proposed (e.g. Boaler, 1997c), that it is the traditional approach to maths teaching that girls find particularly alienating). Again it also might be argued that the teacher could have stepped in to rearrange the groups.

Alternatively there do appear to be groups of girls who may benefit from girl-only groups in mathematics and science particularly to develop their confidence and to allow them to work in ways that they find more productive. In one case a mathematics teacher reflected on the changing attitudes and performance of a girl-only group in his classroom:

> It's grown with them. I mean you know at the beginning of the year Rachel and Alice were very much sort of top dogs and, you know, they were the best mathematicians and they tended to sit down there and so on and I've managed to get the other girls to be more confident and to sometimes challenge and to give their own views and so on and to tell people … there was an incident today where Harriet had got something wrong and they told her in a really nice way and actually moved her on and so on. So I think to me this group here is probably the one out of the whole class that has gelled the best and actually probably made the most progress – the two girls, Eleanor and Sally, who are probably weaker pupils or girls in the class have actually made more progress in terms of their understanding of mathematical concepts than they would have done had they been working on their own or just as a pair or something so I think yeah it's really benefited those two. And also, you know, it's … I don't think that it's held back the others. I think Harriet has really blossomed and I think these two as well, Rachel and Alice have just continued to push on really, really well. And they're motivated by working together as a group, they enjoy it.

The attitude questionnaire indicates that boys are less positive to English than girls. The excerpt in the section discussing English indicates that boys too can respond sensitively and thoughtfully to a variety of texts (even one about a woman giving birth in a field) if they feel secure. One English teacher talked about the positive outcomes of having mixed-sex groups to discuss the actions of Lord and Lady Macbeth in the Shakespeare play but this is a less controversial and less personal example.

Gabrielle Ivinson and Patricia Murphy (2006) have investigated a number of schools' seating and grouping policies aimed at raising boys' achievement. In one study they compare two English classes – one comprised of high- and middle-achieving boys, the other comprised of one-third low-achieving boys and two-thirds mixed-ability girls – the task for both classes was to write three novel openings. Group work was used in both classes and at the end individuals read out their work to the class. Not only did they find differences in the choices of genres of the two classes – in the first the boys wrote about horror, war, crime, adventure, science fiction and fantasy whereas in the second the high-achieving girls tended towards romance (when a few boys from this group also decided to experiment with the romance genre they were warned by the teacher against developing their writing into 'an X-rated sort of thing' or it was considered too pornographic to receive a mark) but also the atmosphere and talk were quite different. While discussion in the first class was encouraged, boys tended to 'play' to others and write for their approval whereas in the second group some girls and some boys were 'silenced' because they could not discuss with others they were unfamiliar with.

The researchers comment on their observations and interviews with students afterwards and conclude:

> Strategies that have been motivated by a heightened awareness of gender and are not backed up by research into how students learn are in danger of reproducing hegemonic social representations of gender. (Ivinson and Murphy, 2006: 178)

Clearly there are dangers associated with both same-ability grouping and same-sex grouping in English (and other subjects) if teachers' perceptions around both gender and ability do not change also. The issues in the classes mentioned earlier also point to the need for both these pupils and their teachers to be trained in group work and the need to be able to adapt their expertise within and for different classes (in particular within girl-only and boy-only classrooms if these are experimented with).

An often quoted adage is that 'girls like to collaborate whereas boys like to compete' – however, overall our results did not appear to support this (the ratios of girls to boys in the Type 2s – the *active collaborators'* and Type 4s – the *'quiet collaborators'* are within a few percentage points of each other); indeed we have some evidence that some boys in some classes are more favourable to group work and discussion than some girls. While we would advocate collaboration as a strategy for achieving more equitable and participatory classrooms we also recognize that there may be opportunities to build on the competitive streak that some boys have. By encouraging competition between groups some pupils will be encouraged while less competitive individuals will not be so disadvantaged because, as a strategy, it does not expose them in the ways that whole-class competitive approaches do (i.e. competition between groups may motivate some pupils and not demotivate others). However, when asked if 'competition' between groups was a useful strategy to use one teacher (still referring to Chris) said,

> I think that does help but I don't think it overcomes every problem. But I think it does help and I think the boys in particular like it. You know they do. Some of those groups have risen to that definitely. They are conscious that they're gonna be standing up in front of people and they just like the idea of competing don't they? Lots of boys do. It does spur them on a bit really. But I think probably with Chris not quite as much as you'd hope it would.

Exploring classroom relationships

While we have indicated that pupil–pupil relationships can be key to lesson success or failure, we have not explicitly discussed teacher–pupil relationships. In many cases teachers and pupils reported that these had improved as a result of group work, in particular pupils felt that teachers were interested in them and cared about them (i.e. that they were actually individuals in their own right). This different type of relationship between teacher and pupil could develop as teachers are less likely to be talking to the whole class and more to individuals or small groups and often at greater length. The following quote shows just how important the teacher–pupil relationship is:

> M: On parents' evening Mrs M asked me what I'd like to be when I'm older and I said a doctor 'cos that's what I've always wanted to be and she said, 'That's good, that means you'll always be one of my students'.
> S: But if we feel like ... oh I'm appreciated for my work.
> Int: Yeah that's brilliant. So is the teacher quite important? I mean we don't have to talk about different teachers, but is it important that you get on with the teacher in the classes?
> M: Yeah 'cos I think that if you don't really like your teacher then you're not going to ... like be as kind as you would be if there was like your favourite teacher.

Creating better relationships between teachers and pupils improves the learning environment and therefore better outcomes for all – in particular teachers reported that groups allowed them to know individuals much better and pupils were sometimes surprised by the freedom and therefore the trust afforded to them.

However, results from the pupil attitude survey showed that different classes, even those showing a similar attainment profile in the same subject, were composed of pupil types in very different ratios. It was clear that some teachers did have much more difficult classes, that is, those with a high proportion of Type 1 pupils – the *'dossers and shirkers'* and Type 3 pupils – the *'anxious introverts'*, which meant that in these classrooms group work was more challenging and that the climate could be tense (also discussed in Chapter 1). For a few classes with this difficult profile at the beginning of the year (from the first round of the survey) there was evidence that a substantial number of pupils shifted 'type', by the end of year (from the follow-up), which resulted in the majority of the class being positive towards collaborative learning (and therefore an easier class to teach). The role of the teacher in creating these 'converts' was not investigated in the course of our study as the results were analysed after the year's intervention. There could be a number of reasons for the 'conversion' of any class, for example we may have picked up pupils at the beginning of the year who were reflecting negative prior experiences of that subject, therefore we do not 'blame' teachers when their attempts at introducing more collaborative learning were not ultimately successful. The issue of a 'critical mass' of pupils either positive or negative towards any innovation may be the key as to what is possible and what is not. One teacher who, in his second year of the project did have a particularly difficult class, reflected on his role as a teacher and whether group work was possible with them:

> I think actually that comes down to experience. Because in my life as a teacher I think you are not aware of what you can achieve sometimes. The biggest learning curve for a teacher is to see how much pupils can achieve. And I think you don't really understand that until you have put them in a position to be able to achieve. [...]
>
> And you have to be confident in letting go. And when you first go into teaching you think teaching is all about control, order, organization and you as the gatekeeper. But sometimes you have to make sure that you are more of a shepherd. And you actually shepherd them through the gate. And I think that's kind of the thing that is most important, is having the confidence to realize that active learning makes your job easier. Because you can see them learning in front of you. And it stops all that kind of fear and worry of have they taken it in, are they learning da, da, da.

Conclusion

Within this chapter we have outlined some of the key challenges experienced by teachers in the SPRinG project, often coming from pupils themselves. These teachers did come to realize that not all pupils are or will ever be positive towards collaborative learning or even able to work with others. However, the key issue for successful teachers in tackling these challenges was changing the nature of the pupil–teacher and pupil–pupil relationships within the classroom:

> It's made me think far more about how students interact and the importance of that rather than me thinking about what I've got to mediate. So in other words I focus far more on the learning than maybe on the teaching.

Perhaps ironically for a project based on managing pupils in groups, the need to see and know students as individuals who can complement each others' strengths as well as supporting each others' weaknesses is also crucial. Therefore effective planning for group work should also include serious consideration as to how best to group pupils, that is, whether to develop stable and unchanging groups that can grow together or to regularly rearrange groups so as to introduce pupils to others different from themselves or to group pupils according to the nature of the task (e.g. same-sex groups for sensitive issues). We have recommended that teachers intervene and rearrange groups if they are not working rather than hope that, in the future, they will. Together with these strategies for grouping pupils teachers also need to consider their own role in any activity and their relationship with the class as well as with individuals within it. We argue that the role of the teacher in transforming the learning culture of the classroom is key – just as a conductor manages different players and their instruments within an orchestra so the teacher needs to 'orchestrate' learning in their classroom knowing the strengths and contributions that each pupil plays in a learning activity and how this comes together as a whole. As one of the teachers said at the end of the project,

'I used to think group work was a problem. Now I see it as a solution'.

 Questions

1. Can all pupils be 'included' in group work? Should all be included?
2. What do you consider the main reasons for pupil (and also teacher?) disaffection in our schools?
3. How much are classroom organization and student grouping the responsibility of the individual teacher and/or each subject department or is a whole-school approach needed?
4. Reflect on your own experiences as a learner – when did you 'learn' best (i.e. consider 'learning' rather than 'achieving')? How do these experiences influence your understanding of 'good teaching'? Are your experiences transferable to other learners?

7

One Big Family? Promoting Harmony and Resilience

Maurice Galton

In this final chapter we briefly review the evidence presented in the earlier part of the book. We then look at the implications for these findings for today's comprehensive schools, noting that one of the twin principles which led to their creation in the first place, the desire to maximize individual potential, has been somewhat forgotten amid the current emphasis on test outcomes and targets. Following on from this discussion we develop the argument that teachers, in coping with the negative aspects of the current 'performance' culture, need to foster a spirit of 'resilience' in their pupils. We illustrate how this might be accomplished by reference to the ways that artists who work in schools develop their relationships with pupils.

In the previous chapters we laid out evidence to suggest that there is a major crisis facing today's secondary schools. This crisis has in part been brought about by transformations in society, particularly in the post-Thatcher era, which has tended to emphasize the personal rights of individuals above community values. This has been disastrous for schools which, when they are at their best, operate as both social and learning communities. The crisis is also partly the result of the raft of reforms brought in by New Labour. Even when the motivation behind these initiatives has been the attempt to liberate the educational system and devolve greater responsibility to the profession, schools have continued to be overwhelmed by pressures emanating from the standards agenda with the emphasis on performance, targets and the like. In the first chapter we argued that such pressures, although designed to motivate teachers to improve attainment scores, have been largely counter-productive, since results, when placed in an international context have not been impressive. The government's reaction has been to introduce even more drastic reforms culminating now in the creation of the Academies, not all of whom appear to be successful (Curtis, 2008). For the rest, schools which still fail to reach the target of having 50 per cent of Year 11 gain five 'good' GCSEs will be faced with the prospect of closure and subsequent rebirth under the control of private entrepreneurs (New Vision Group, 2008). The result, as has been shown (Galton and Macbeath, 2008) is total disillusion among many practitioners coupled with resignation at the unlikely possibility of a change in direction. Many of today's teachers for the most part are compliant but unenthusiastic feeling that they are powerless to effect changes in government strategy.

But the chapter also pointed out a more serious and alarming trend in terms of pupils' motivation and attitudes. We have argued that what motivates children towards the end of their time in primary school and increasingly determines their behaviour at secondary level is the realization that school is something to be endured if one is to aspire to a decent future. The message, that education is about 'delivery' and is therefore primarily concerned with an end product, not processes, has been taken to heart by today's young adolescents so that if one is set a target of Grade 5 at Key Stage 3 that is the outcome one seeks to achieve. The consequence is that when teachers endeavour to push the boundaries of learning and to say to pupils, 'You've mastered this, now see if you can go a little further', a considerable number of pupils don't wish to know. 'Is it required for the examination?' they ask, and if the answer to this is 'No' then they show little interest in pursuing matters further. Perhaps most revealing of all was the answers given to the question in our survey, 'Do you ever find work so interesting at school that you continue with it when you get home?' to which a majority answered, 'Never'. Although there is no recent, similar research covering Higher Education, conversations with university admission tutors also suggest that the main concern of applicants appears to be what they need to do to get the required class of degree and that these potential undergraduates show little interest in the nature of the course, the strength of its teachers or the unique opportunities that study at a particular institution can provide. We appear to have created a generation of students who have lost interest in learning for its own sake.

We have sought throughout the book to argue that there is a way back from this rather depressing scenario and that this lies in a shift away from a target-driven curriculum, where the teacher largely controls what topics are selected and how they are to be taught, to an approach where teachers and pupils are regarded as co-learners and where pupils have some choice over the curriculum content so that it reflects both their interests and needs. In keeping with this shift it also involves greater use of cooperative approaches to learning. We have shown that attitudes improve when pupils have more control of the ways in which they learn. This is particularly true in groups of those children who have been referred to by the late Jean Rudduck as the 'dossers' and 'shirkers' (Demetriou et al., 2000). Furthermore, we have been able to show that in many cases pupils taught in groups do better and certainly no worse than those taught by whole-class methods. This is an important finding because allied to these academic gains are considerable social advantages. Most teachers reported in our study that developing group work, and importantly, making pupils aware of its functions through training and through briefing and debriefing, gradually changed the climate in the classroom. Pupils were more pleasant to each other, more tolerant of weaknesses, more keen to support and help their peers, and as we showed in the previous chapter, more understanding of the reasons why certain pupils sometimes behaved badly or refused to participate in the lesson. Working in groups gradually does transform a classroom so that it becomes more like a family arrangement where on occasions there are falling-outs, but such occurrences are usually resolved without major damage to the prevailing ethos.

The challenge for the comprehensive school in the 21st century

Comprehensive schools have had a bad press almost from the moment of their birth. In the earliest period, writers such as Pedley (1963) had to defend the new schools from the unfair comparisons that were frequently made between the comprehensive schools sitting side-by-side with local grammars; with the latter having creamed off the top ability range. Certain schools, such a Countersthorpe in Leicestershire, were a constant feature of newspaper articles and the target of the Black Paper writers (Watts, 1977). For a brief period in the 1980s there appeared to be a consensus across the political parties in favour of developing comprehensive schools but matters changed under Mrs. Thatcher and during New Labour's administration the term 'bog standard comprehensive' signalled a renewed contempt among our rulers, which now manifests itself in a decision to close many of those struggling with poor intakes in inner-city areas and to transform them into Academies under private partnerships. In all this acrimonious debate the rationale for comprehensive education and the attempts by teachers to give practical realization to its high-minded aims has perhaps been forgotten, particularly in an era where such emphasis is placed on test results.

As conceived by the earliest advocates for the system, the late Caroline Benn and Brian Simon (1970), the argument in favour of the change was driven by the evidence that the separation of pupils into two streams, the grammar and the secondary modern, by dint of intelligence tests was flawed; not only because intelligence tests were highly correlated with social class, did not measure intelligence, and were culturally dependent, but also because they made inefficient selections. In the Crowther (1959) Report, for example, a survey of National Service entrants who had attended secondary modern schools found that many, when subsequently tested, were above average in terms of their intelligence quotient. This was because selection to grammar school was something of a 'postal lottery' since the cut-off point on IQ in the selection for grammar school varied around the country according to the number of places available in each local authority. For all these educational reasons as well as social egalitarian ones, it was argued that pupils from a neighbourhood were better educated in one school. What was lost in this argument however, was that the switch away from a process of selection on the basis of ability required a different kind of thinking about pupils' intellectual development. This was largely because there were more pressing practical dilemmas, as for example, what should be the role of selection in a truly comprehensive school? Should pupils be included in mixed-ability groups or in broad bands or in narrow sets? How should the curriculum be organized? What principles should guide such choices?

In reality, the twin principles which underpin comprehensive education – providing equal opportunities while maximizing individual potential – were encapsulated in a theoretical model of intellectual development proposed by Caroll (1963) and extended by Bloom (1976). The latter, because of his work on the various taxonomies, has tended to be regarded as a hard-line behaviourist, although both he and Caroll shared the optimistic notions of education which were current in the 1960s. Both Caroll and Bloom rejected the idea that a pupil's capacity to learn was mainly determined by his inherited intelligence and instead proposed the concept of 'mastery'. For Caroll, any pupil, in principle, could be taught anything if allowed sufficient time. He expressed this proposition in a statement that the degree of learning was directly proportional to the ratio 'of time actually spent by a pupil on a task divided by the time needed by the pupil to master the demands of that task'. This radical proposition was directly opposed to the conventional view of ability. Psychometric approaches, as we have seen, regarded a pupil's IQ score as the best predictor of the child's capacity for learning and as such this capability was fixed and largely predetermined. It follows, therefore, from this line of reasoning that only some children were capable of learning certain things. At the time, even Piaget's developmental model as interpreted by many educationalists conceived of the notion of 'readiness' whereby some children who had not reached a certain stage were unable to undertake certain kinds of learning. Both of these approaches, as Simon (1981) observed, provided ready-made excuses on the part of schools and of teachers for explaining failure. If a pupil failed to master a certain task then he or she was either a 'slow learner' or 'was not at the right stage of intellectual development'. On this view it was more sensible and more efficient to stream pupils according to their abilities or their state of readiness so that the curriculum could be tailored to their specific needs. Caroll's proposition dispensed with the need to stream by ability in arguing that only time prevented a pupil from completing any task irrespective of their aptitude.

Of course in applying this model to everyday schooling there are practical limitations. Lessons occupy around 2000 hours annually so that time to learn is limited. In planning the curriculum there is therefore a clash between the two competing principles set out at the beginning of the previous paragraph. The first of these, associated with mastery, is to allow each pupil to maximize their potential. This implies that where a pupil needs more time to excel at a certain subject or activity then that should be provided. On the other hand, the second principle guiding comprehensive education – that of entitlement – seeks to maximize every child's opportunities by not deciding early in his or her school career that by reason of their ability they are not capable of taking certain subjects. This runs counter to the views of those who argued for parallel curricula, such as Bantock (1971) who proposed that pupils in the lower streams of comprehensive schools should be provided with a less rigorous 'folk' curriculum, which would largely be based on activities such as drama, dance and domestic studies.

Initially, comprehensive schools reacted against such arguments by overstressing the entitlement option. The work of Denis Lawton (1975) in advocating a common curriculum resisted the notion that there should be alternatives, for example for working-class pupils which reflected their culture (Ozolins, 1979). Lawton's view of a curriculum, based on the idea that all citizens had a right to share in a common culture, was well established in most schools during the 1980s so that pupils had to choose at least one subject from any of the five broad options (arts and design, science, humanities, languages together with English and mathematics). In practice this structural form often maintained social divisions because schools that permitted some more advanced pupils to do two languages or a double science found it was only possible to timetable such an arrangement if the same pupils were in the same group for Humanities, Art and Design, English and Mathematics. Pupils who required more time to master a subject to a particular level did so through the CSE (Certificate of Secondary Education) route whereby a top grade was equivalent to a 'C' grade at O Level (Ordinary Certificate Level). Pupils achieving a grade 1 CSE were then required to do an extra year in the sixth form taking the equivalent 'O' Level again before starting the 'A' Level course.

Although this latter example could be said to be partly in accord with Caroll's mastery principle – allowing children to fulfil their potential by arranging the curriculum so that they might have more time to study certain subjects – this has never been carried to its logical conclusion. The notion, for example, that a potential Wayne Rooney in football or an Andy Murray in tennis might be afforded extra curriculum time to hone their skills in the same way as the more academic pupils were given additional opportunities in science or languages has never been seen as a serious option. However, in some schools the creation of a modular curriculum allowed a more reasonable balance between the two competing principles to emerge. Pupils were required to do basic modules and then opt for others in particular subjects which reflected their talents, needs or interests. All this experimentation, however, ceased with the introduction of the National Curriculum with its statutory requirements and compulsory programmes of study.

The purpose of this slight digression in history is to argue that if trends identified in this book are to be reversed then some serious rethinking about the organization of comprehensive education in the 21st century is required. As David Hargreaves (1982) argued in his masterly analysis concerning the challenges facing the comprehensive school, the reform of the existing examination system was (and still is) an essential starting point for change. For Hargreaves, the abolition of public examinations at 16 would allow school curriculum to be reconstructed and more closely integrated with the needs of local communities. Since Hargreaves's book was first published, little has changed in the way that secondary schools are structured and, indeed, it can be argued that the schools of today are remarkably similar (in the way that certain subjects are prioritized, timetables constructed, pupils grouped etc.) to the schools that came into being as a result of the 1902 Act which created a national system of secondary education (Barnard, 1966). That this situation exists, despite the vast changes which have occurred in our society during the 20th century, should provide much food for thought.

But Hargreaves (1982) also observes that here and there schools can be found who have perhaps thought more deeply about these issues and began to develop change along the lines that he proposes. In our own work when investigating the relationship between school organization and classroom grouping (Kutnick et al., 2007) we came across two schools which were less than 20 miles apart with similar catchment areas. Both received good reports from Ofsted but in character and organization they were fundamentally different. The first school, we will call it *Marlbury*, had a fairly rigid banding system and by the end of the first half of the autumn term Year 7 pupils were set for maths, science and modern languages. Discipline was strictly enforced through a series of sanctions and rewards and covered most aspects of the pupils' lives. For example, classrooms were closed before and after lessons and pupils were expected to queue in an orderly manner on one side of the door so as not to block traffic down the corridors. There was a strict dress code which required pupils to wear ties with shirt collars buttoned up and to ensure that both blouses and shirts were tucked into skirts or trousers. Breaking these rules on several occasions warranted a detention.

In the second school, *Singlewell*, pupils were taught in mixed-ability sets up to GCSE with one exception, mathematics, where reluctantly the Head Teacher had allowed broad bands but not sets. Rules were kept to a minimum so that, for example, pupils could enter the classroom when they arrived at lessons without having to queue outside the door as at the other school. Singlewell did have a uniform but it was designed, in cooperation with the pupils, and consisted of a sweatshirt top which came just below the waist so that problems of tucking them into trousers and skirts were avoided. The contrast in behaviour in the two schools was very marked. In Marlbury it was quite common for teachers to have to shout at pupils first because they hadn't tucked their shirts in or because they hadn't done up their top collar button so that the tie knot was half-way down their chest. Outside the classroom it was usual to find teachers again shouting at pupils telling them to line up on the correct side of the door. Often this situation was exacerbated because the teacher taking the class was late arriving and another teacher going to another classroom found his or her way blocked. In Singlewell, it was rare during our visits, to find similar occurrences. Pupils entered the classroom and generally got on with something until the teacher came. When this didn't happen then the issue was dealt with at that point in time and such disturbances not anticipated as in the other school. The design of the uniform avoided continual arguments about whether shirts should be tucked in or out as at Marlbury, where it seemed to us that some pupils took an active delight in baiting the teachers by deliberately pulling their shirt out when they saw an adult member of staff approaching. In Singlewell, group work was in regular use in most subjects while in the other establishment it was generally retained for drama and music classes and in science when there was a need to share equipment. One frustrated teacher at Marlbury said to us,

> I've been trying to develop group activities and to give pupils more responsibility for their own learning and for the assessment of their work but this is very difficult when outside in the corridors they are treated as units rather than people and marched here and there or shouted at because they do not conform to the required dress code.

We would argue that the decision to emphasize mixed ability in the second school (and the Head Teacher's decision only to recruit staff who supported his approach) manifests a very different attitude to young adults which conforms with the ideal which Hargreaves (1982) was attempting to sustain in his challenge to the comprehensive school. The choice of mixed ability was designed to maximize the pupils' potential in accordance with the mastery principle and to see the school as a learning community where those who needed help were supported by those pupils who were more knowledgeable. This in turn bred an attitude of respect for the pupils' views which was reflected in the way that they were treated and the way in which rules were administered. In the first school, by the time lessons began, both teachers and pupils appeared to be exhausted by the battles that had gone on during breaks and lunchtime in the effort to get the students to line up outside classrooms or to dress in the required fashion. Collaboration under this latter system was in short supply and one suspected that a new teacher attempting to develop cooperative learning strategies would soon give up under the adverse effects of these organizational strategies.

Mixed ability or sets?

Certainly, there is mixed evidence to suggest that rigid banding and setting systems are a necessary requirement for improved attainment provided, of course, the teacher doesn't rely on a whole-class teaching approach for the majority of the lessons. The research evidence tends to support the view that providing suitable teaching approaches are used, ability grouping, particularly in the lower secondary school, tends to exacerbate the problems that we have discussed in the earlier chapters. Hamer (2001) found that most pupils were not aware of the basis for setting and tended to assume behaviour to be a key criterion. Lower sets also tend to have a disproportionate number of boys, pupils from ethnic groups and pupils from lower socio-economic groups and this affects both expectations and aspirations (Boaler, 1997a; Boaler et al., 2000). In the United States a review of ability grouping found no benefits overall in favour of setting (Slavin, 1990; Gamoran, 1992). It is suggested that one reason for these results is that even when ability grouping is used it does little to reduce the variability across the class because if the grouping is done on one particular aspect of attainment it usually leaves considerable variance on other criteria. Furthermore, as the earlier studies of streaming found (Hargreaves, 1967; Lacey, 1970) even when placed in ability sets, pupils initially make social comparisons in judging the standard of their work by comparing it with peers whom they judge to be of roughly equivalent ability. If during the course of the year these peers do better then a 'self-fulfilling prophecy' begins to operate and the gap between the more and less successful pupils widens.

In the United Kingdom Ireson et al. (2002) undertook a study of 45 mixed comprehensive schools which represented a range of different organizational grouping practices. In mathematics, pupils who did well at Key Stage 2 and were then grouped together made more progress at Key Stage 3 whereas those making less progress at Key Stage 2 tended to make more progress at Key Stage 3 when placed in a mixed-ability group. In English there was no relationship, partly because there were fewer attempts to set pupils in the lower secondary school according to their performance at Key Stage 2. But when the pupils were followed up to GCSE (Ireson et al., 2005) it was found that these differential effects in setting in English, mathematics or science were no longer consistent across the subjects. Other studies (Wiliam and Bartholomew, 2004) suggest that when mixed-ability groups and sets are compared the GCSE grades in the top sets are raised by half a grade in mathematics but lowered by half a grade in the bottom sets with little effects elsewhere.

Against these findings however the effects on pupils' behaviour and attitudes needs to be considered. Boaler (1997b) and Boaler et al. (2000) have noted that when set and mixed-ability mathematics classes are compared in secondary schools the former promotes not only underachievement among the less able but also polarization and anti-school attitudes in the lower-set classrooms. Ireson and Hallam (2001) tend to confirm these findings. As discussed briefly in the third chapter, Boaler's work also pointed to the detrimental effect that setting can have on high ability girls. She found that a third of the girls in the top sets in mathematics were underachieving. Boaler (1997c) rejects the notion that girls were somehow unable to cope with the demands of mathematics teaching and argues that the pupils themselves tend to attribute their failure to the specific style of teaching of these top sets which usually followed the form of high-paced interactive whole-class teaching with short sharp questioning. Girls reported that they found it difficult to think in this highly structured, competitive environment. Boaler argues that working in groups which allows more thinking time provides a means of overcoming this problem. Thus in summary, the effects of a shift in classroom practice (involving greater use of cooperative learning strategies through the use of pair and group work) is influenced by the forms of organization employed throughout the school and the various structures which govern the day-to-day behaviour and the relationships between teachers and pupils. This is not to say that group work cannot be undertaken in situations where the school organization consists of classes or sets based on initial ability, but in such situations we think it is more difficult to achieve collaboration in the classroom and that it is likely to be detrimental to the learning of many of the pupils who exhibit anti-school and anti-learning attitudes.

Creating a resilient classroom

When New Labour came to power one of the oft-repeated mantras was the phrase, 'tough on crime, tough on the causes of crime'. A similar philosophy prevailed in the field of education where the determination to name and shame failing schools and failing teachers was coupled with the aim of removing some of the causes of failure such as those associated with poverty, difficult family circumstances and so on. The various strategies beginning with 'action zones', the use of mentors to limit the effects of truancy and the implementation of the *Every Child Matters* agenda have all been designed to integrate the support work of various agencies within the world of school, and are indicative of the government's desire to remove the various factors which put pupils at risk so that the reform programmes can have a better chance of success.

The record of such initiatives is however, patchy. An earlier study by Alexander et al. (1989) which saw the City of Leeds institute its own version of an action zone to improve its weakest schools was judged only a limited success. As Alexander and his colleagues found, bringing so called 'expert' successful teachers from other schools to work with those schools deemed to be in difficulty tended to breed resentment on the part of those practitioners who had been struggling to teach their pupils under more difficult circumstances. The mentoring programme has helped to reduce truancy but the *Every Child Matters* agenda appears to have spawned a vast administrative additional burden for Special Needs Coordinators (SENCOs). As MacBeath et al. (2006) found SENCOs were now so often out of school attending conferences with other support services that they rarely had time either to improve their own knowledge or to support teachers in the classroom. In some cases, although this is now no longer permitted, Headteachers appointed untrained teaching support assistants as the SENCOs on the ground that the attendance at meetings and all that accompanied this activity was a waste of precious qualified teacher time.

In parallel to these various initiatives there has developed an alternative paradigm for tackling the development of the social, emotional and cognitive competence of pupils at risk. The starting point for this approach is to note that throughout history there have been societies where a marked resilience has enabled the community not only to survive but often to prosper. In an educational context the cause and effect of educational failure is what Cooper (2008: 12), quoting directly from Smith (2006), terms 'attachment to school'. This Cooper defines as the degree of commitment which pupils show towards schooling and includes the attachment that they feel for their teachers and also belief that success in school will signify rewards in the future. Weak attachment, as we have seen, leads to disaffection and the development of an anti-learning, anti-school attitude. As Cooper also argues, these problems are of a psychological rather than a social nature so that a policy which relies mainly on removing the social causes of failure and does not turn attention to the psychological needs associated with alienation is doomed to failure. A paradigm based on the notion of resilience is concerned with the psychological factors which help pupils to do well at school whereas the social approach attempts to avoid problems by eliminating the various factors which put children at risk of failure. Cefai (2008) suggests that an approach based on the resilience paradigm is therefore more concerned with promoting well-being while acknowledging the various dysfunctional elements in the pupils' life. The question these researchers working in this area ask is therefore, 'What makes children in difficult circumstances achieve and be successful?' rather than 'What prevents children in difficult circumstances from succeeding?' (Cefai, 2008: 22). Thus by studying pupils who manage to thrive and be successful at school despite the negative circumstances surrounding their lives it is possible to suggest a number of ways in which schools can encourage pupils to do better than personal circumstances would suggest. In this approach schools are required to focus on the strengths of these pupils rather than on the inherent weaknesses of their circumstances.

Resilience has been described 'as a set of protective mechanisms that give rise to successful adaptation, despite the presence of high-risk factors during the course of development' (Bernard, 1991). Early studies tended to concentrate on the various characteristics of individuals, particularly the manner in which they were able to resist stress so that they were able to survive in difficult environments (Anthony, 1974). With an increasing interest in the topic, however, it became clear that besides these personal characteristics an individual's capacity to achieve success in difficult circumstances is the result of 'dynamic interactions between the various systems impinging on a child's life' (Bronfenbrenner, 1979) so that it is the interaction between the individual and the individual's environment that is the key. An important contributing factor is the availability of alternative environments away from those causing the difficulties and stress, where in a calmer situation pupils could reflect on their circumstances and develop strategies for survival in the more hostile world which they normally occupy. Hence the importance of schools in providing these safe havens (Condly, 2006).

Later studies have identified a number of protective elements which allow pupils space and time to reflect on the individual circumstances and to devise ways of coping with them (Werner, 1990; Rutter, 1993; Werner and Smith, 1992). The three main elements concern the acquisition of what might be termed 'social competence'. This includes the development of problem-solving skills for dealing with difficult situations together with a growing sense of autonomy and the creation of a clear plan setting out future goals. The second element required, particularly in the early years, is family support and this needs to be supplemented at a later stage with continuation of such support in terms of relationships with the teacher once the individual enters school. In difficult home circumstances the teacher–pupil relationship obviously assumes even greater significance. These protective elements are strong indicators of success in the face of adversity (Dent and Cameron, 2003).

In summary therefore the paradigm based on a notion of resilience, seeks to help children cope with adversity rather than removing it by reducing its existence through various social interventions. According to Cefai (2008), quoting Rees and Bailey (2003), the literature suggests there are three aspects of schooling which can foster resilience in pupils and enable them to over-come social-economic disadvantage. The first of these is caring relationships between pupils and teachers, what Noddings (1992) terms, 'an ethic of caring'. This seeks to broaden the relationship beyond the classroom to include caring pupil–pupil, teacher–teacher and teacher–parent relationships. Second is the need to have high expectations for all pupils which maximize the pupils' own strengths and interests and attempt to motivate them to learn for intrinsic rather than extrinsic reasons. The third of these elements requires pupils to have some involvement and responsibility for their lives within school so that they are allowed to express opinions about the teaching.

These characteristics are not dissimilar from those which have been empha-sized throughout this book and will be open to the objection that teachers have to work in what Watkins (2003) has called a performance culture which makes the fostering of resilience difficult. We wish to argue that while it makes it difficult it does not make it an impossible task. To this end we con-clude with some examples, not in this instance of teachers, but of 'artists in residence' who are now under the current initiatives on creativity in schools referred to as 'creative practitioners'.

What artists can sometimes teach teachers

The Creative Partnership Programme came into being in April 2002. By 2006 around £75m has been spent setting up 40 partnerships in various areas of England. Funded through the Department of Culture, Media and Sport and the Department for Education and Skills it is administered through the Arts Council of England. The individual projects are located mainly in socially and economically deprived localities. Their aim is to create sustainable partner-ships between creative and cultural organizations and schools so that chil-dren are offered opportunities to develop their potential, their creativity and imagination. The term 'artist' was replaced by 'creative practitioner' in order to show that these interventions could involve a wide range of creative per-sons and not only those drawn from the commonly regarded art forms such as literature, music, drama and the visual arts. Creative Partnerships have employed photographers, film makers and horticulturalists. The initiative clearly differs from the earlier 'artist in residence' arrangements which have been common in schools for many years in that the key aim has been to develop 'sustainable practice' based upon the interaction of the teachers and the creative practitioners. Furthermore the secondary aim was that this practice should extend beyond the area of the particular creative practitioner's expertise so that it permeated other parts of the curriculum. The initiative reflects a tacit, if not an open acknowledgement by the Government of the kinds of motivational problems which have been the subject of this book. An Ofsted (2006) evaluation argued that in schools where there were clear aims the outcomes of the programme could be seen in changed attitudes and behaviours of the pupils and of teachers, particularly the latter of whom it was claimed, many lacked a belief in their own ability to inspire creativity in others.

For a small but significant number of pupils the Ofsted evaluation suggested that the Creative Partnership Programme had represented a fresh start. What the Ofsted evaluation does not do however is to discuss the pedagogy involved in sustaining this improvement in attitude and motivation among the pupils involved. For an initiative to become sustainable it is clearly necessary to identify the form of the teaching practices which have led to these improved attitudes. This was precisely the aim of a study carried out by Galton (2008). This research set out to identify what creative practitioners did that appeared to influence pupil dispositions. The latter were measured by means of questionnaires similar to those presented in Appendix A and also by using projective tests in which various pictures of classrooms during normal lessons or in Creative Partnership sessions were presented and the respondents had to write down an imagined conversation between two of the participating pupils. If it was thought that the teacher (or the creative practitioner) was speaking respondents also had to imagine what s/he was saying. The questionnaire results showed that over the period of involvement with the creative practitioner which was never less than six weeks and often extended over the whole year, self-esteem improved, most markedly in Year 7 and while school and learning dispositions did not improve significantly they did not decline as in the case of the studies presented in the first chapter. In the analysis of the projective tests there were very positive outcomes in favour of the creative practitioners compared to normal lessons, although these did not extend into the analysis of the secondary schools because pupils there found it very difficult to write an imaginary conversation around the pictures. This compared with the response from primary pupils who appeared to find the task a relatively simple one. For example a girl from a Year 5 class in response to a picture showing children in a mathematics lesson wrote the following:

First pupil:	Seven times eight, what does that equal?
Second pupil:	What time's lunch?
First pupil:	Soon I hope. This is boring.
Second pupil:	I don't get this question.
Teacher:	Stop talking. Get on with your work.

The responses to mathematics and English lessons often carried negative connotations of this kind.

The first noticeable difference between the creative practitioners and teachers concerned the way they introduced themselves when they first met the pupils. Whereas a teacher facing a new class as in the transfer studies would generally say something of the kind, 'I'm Mr Smith, I'm going to teach you mathematics this year', which seemed designed to establish the respective roles of the participants, and to a certain extent reinforce the power of the relationship between the teacher and the class, those of the creative practitioners appeared to take the form of an opening conversation gambit signifying an attempt to establish a more equal relationship. For example in one secondary school Glynn, a film maker, arrived late for his first morning. His opening remarks to a group of pupils (a mixture of Years 8 and 10) were as follows:

> My name's Glynn and I'm a film maker. I'm sorry I'm late, blame it on the trains, but it's made me anxious because I wasn't here to set up before you came. I've been doing this kind of work for some years now and I got into it by helping out with groups of pupils who were excluded from school – so I've had to learn the hard way.

The latter part of the introduction is also interesting in that by telling the pupils about his work in a referral unit he would seem to be sending a message to the pupils that he has seen and coped with most manifestations of disengagement.

The second feature which distinguishes these practitioners follows on immediately from the introduction and seems aimed at stimulating pupils' interest as a means of increasing intrinsic motivation. Although the actual means of doing this varied from one creative practitioner to another and also across different disciplines, what each approach had in common was that all the creative partners sought to increase motivation by first exploring pupils' own ideas, even where that meant departing from the main purpose of the activity. Teachers, on the other hand, because they are more constrained by the curriculum, tend to avoid wide-ranging discussions which don't stick to the topic. Thus Simon, a photographer, used PowerPoint to display a picture of a baby and then asks the following series of questions:

Simon:	What is it?
Pupil:	It's a picture of a baby.
Simon:	Yes, but it's a special picture.
Pupils (chorus):	It's you.
Pupil:	It's a picture which makes you happy.
Pupil:	It's a memory.
Simon:	Yes it's one of the things my mother particularly remembers about me as a young child. There isn't anything else that can give you a memory except a drawing or a film. So how do films differ from photographs?
Pupil:	It's time.
Pupil:	It's place.
Simon:	(after a pause when no more answers are forthcoming): OK. Where do we see photographs?
Pupil:	In a museum.

Pupil:	In a photo album.
Pupil:	The living room.
Pupil:	The bedroom.
Pupil:	In a scrapbook.
Pupil:	In books.
Simon:	And something else? What about something your parents read that comes through the door each day?
Pupils (chorus):	Oh! Newspapers.
Simon:	OK then, why don't we go and take some pictures outside. But before we do we need to think about what makes a good photograph. (He then goes on to explore ideas about line, shapes, patterns and emotions using a sequence of his own pictures.)

Here Simon's main purpose was to teach pupils to consider line, shape and patterns before they went out to take some films but he started with a digression by showing the class pictures of himself as a baby. In an even clearer use of this approach Glynn began by showing the new pupils a film made by another group during the previous term. At the end of the film he asked for comments but received none. Two girls, in particular, appeared totally disinterested (one played continuously with her hair) and when Glynn called for a volunteer who will act as a model for others to photograph nobody offered. Faced with this negative reaction, Glynn just smiled and said, 'OK I'll have to volunteer myself again'. He then asked pupils to take different shots (his head, a half portrait, followed by a full length profile) and then displayed the results on a computer. There's laughter when one shot showed a light above Glynn's head:

Girl:	(the one playing with her hair) It's like you've got a halo.
Glynn:	Anything else you noticed? (prolonged silence) OK, I read that you guys spend all your time downloading videos illegally. So tell me something about the movement that goes with music on these videos. (Again there is silence) I can't believe this. You spend your time downloading videos and you can't tell me one thing about them. (Another long pause) OK, think about an Oasis video and someone like Justin Timberlake, can you think of any difference?
Girl:	One's a story and one's a movement. (Again more silence)
Glynn:	Is there an MTV style?
Boy:	It features unusual places like standing on a volcano.
Glynn:	Would a video for a rap look the same as an indie?
The two disinterested girls:	No.
Glynn:	Why not?
Girls:	Different dress and movement.
Glynn:	OK I'm going to take you back to those pictures. Which tells you most about whether I'm happy or sad?
Pupils (chorus):	The full one.
Glynn:	I'm going to disagree with you there. Look at my feet. Are they sad?
Pupils:	No.
Glynn:	OK, what about my face, does that show sad?
Pupils:	Yes.
Glynn:	So it's got to be the face that shows most emotions.

The purpose of the lesson as it emerged later on was to get pupils to understand that although a film tells the story it's the camera angle, the particular features displayed, which shape the structure and narrative in the eyes of the viewer. Glynn had wanted to use pictures taken by pupils to draw out these conclusions but getting little response he looks for something to gain their interest and picks on music videos before returning to the pictures once he'd gained their attention.

Typically, as discussed in earlier chapters, in such situations teachers will use what Edwards and Mercer (1987) called 'cued elicitations' in which the teacher asks questions while providing heavy clues as to the answers required. Such exchanges are dominated by what Tharp and Gallimore (1988) call the *recitation script* whereby the teacher asks the question and the pupil, having responded, the teacher repeats the answer coupled with another question by way of a prompt for the response he or she was seeking in the first place. During such sequences according to Tharp and Gallimore there are both explicit and tacit rules governing such classroom discourse and these give rise to the kind of situation described by Flanders (1970) where two-thirds of the classroom activity consists of talk and two-thirds of this talking is done by the teacher. This in part explains the reluctance of Glynn's group of pupils to respond initially to his questions since instead of giving them a clue when they remained silent he asked for comments on pictures they had taken and then appears to go off at a tangent by introducing the topic of videos. In a similar situation a teacher following the recitation script might have prompted with a series of questions such as 'What about my face? What does it look like? Is it happy, sad?' and so forth until the required response was forthcoming. It is noticeable in the earlier sequence involving the photographer, Simon, that 13 out of the 19 utterances come from children and in one case there is a sequence of six replies by pupils before Simon intervenes. In one sequence involving a conceptual artist, Andy, admittedly in a primary classroom, the question and answer session extended for a whole lesson. When Andy was questioned about the purpose in having these extended conversations he replied,

> To me being here in this school is about several things. One important thing is to look at a different model of working of the way that artists can work with schools and teachers in a much more collaborative way rather than expect to come in and deliver and then go away. Another important thing is the children. What we are trying to do here is to be a person who responds to ideas that children are coming up with and then to bring our own practice for them to share.

In the same way Glynn appears to place a high priority on getting pupils to think for themselves because at the end of the lesson in which he first tries to stimulate the students' interest by getting them to talk about music videos he concludes by saying,

> What have we learnt today, anything? Nothing? Loads? (most pupils nod in agreement). Well it's been about raising questions rather than just making decisions. Films don't happen by accident, we're going to have to make lots of decisions about the kinds of ways we want to produce the juice bar and that's what we've been starting to do here.

These creative practitioners seem to be attempting to promote a notion of creativity which might be described as aesthetic intelligence (Raney, 2003) designed to encourage flexibility of the mind. To these creative practitioners the process is everything whereas for policy makers, as one might have expected, it is the outcomes which are key in recognizing a creative mind, in that the Government's main justification for funding the Creative Partnership Programme is to produce students who will eventually become entrepreneurs. Hence in all official publications there is the insistence that creative act not only has to be original but to have value. Creative practitioners, on the other hand, appear to take the view that if pupils can learn to think flexibly they will naturally come up with imaginative solutions to problems. Elsewhere Pringle (2008) argues that creative practitioners' approach to dealing with their pupils stems from their own experiences of working in small artistic communities where the emphasis is on 'participatory arts practice, wherein creativity is developed and meanings emerge through collaborative processes and facilitated dialogue and making activities'. When creative practitioners work in schools they tend therefore to regard both the teacher and the pupils as co-learners in the same way as they view their colleagues in their cooperatives and this goes some way to explaining the introductory phrases of school projects when the practitioners strive to establish relationships with the pupils as fellow workers rather than as teacher and taught.

All this is not to claim that creative practitioners were averse to periods where it was necessary to instruct rather than explore. In another secondary school, for example, where the PE curriculum was being extended to include contemporary dance, pupils were instructed in the differences between *unison, mirrors* and *canons* by Maggie who demonstrated each movement and then got pairs of pupils to copy her actions. Following on from this, however, pupils were set in pairs to design their own sequence of dances incorporating these moves. Generally, however, whenever the situation allowed, creative practitioners preferred to begin lessons by getting pupils to explore their own ideas before going on to decide the task to be undertaken. Only when new knowledge or skills were required in order to perform these tasks did creative practitioners begin with direct instruction.

Risk taking and the management of time or space

There is a long history of research showing that many students are averse to risk taking. Among this evidence is that of Holt (1984) and Pollard (1985), who argues that pupils cope with the risk by quickly developing 'knife-edging strategies' in which they steer a course between responding to teachers' questions so as not to be thought stupid while at the same time not showing too much interest in case their peers label them as swots. The concerns that Pollard identified in primary school also appear to dominate secondary (Rudduck et al., 1996) particularly in the period after transfer when pupils are seeking to establish their positions within the year group. These feelings appear to develop right from the start of formal schooling (Barrett, 1986) and although some at the time argued that these feelings were particular to children starting school for the first time Barrett's results were replicated by Galton with older pupils, using pictures similar to those in the study of pupils' dispositions towards the creative practitioners which were described earlier. In Galton's (1989) case one pupil in response to the picture said,

> There's no teacher [*in the picture*]. You're worried in case you get things wrong. The children in the picture are trying to learn how to do sums. They feel nervous and scared in case they get it wrong.

The avoidance of risk mainly because of fear of failure has therefore long been a typical part of school life. The feelings expressed by pupils also help to explain why the cued elicitation discourse described by Edwards and Mercer (1987) has dominated classroom discourse for so long. Pupils develop ways of encouraging teachers to respond and to give more clues through a form of guided discovery until the point is reached where they are certain of the kinds of answers that are required and therefore are no longer uncertain about whether they can provide an answer to satisfy the teacher.

With this in mind, perhaps the most notable difference between the teachers and the creative practitioners was the limited use the latter made of guided discovery. Whereas teachers tended to rush to pupils to help and make suggestions, creative practitioners more often stood back and watched in silence. In a Year 10 class for example Maggie was focusing on the use of arms during the dance. The edited fieldnote describes what took place:

> 'You do jazz with long arms, ballet with curved but contemporary dance because the Africans were quite short, is in between' (demonstrating). The students then practised the movements Maggie demonstrated. When one student complains she can't manage all of them she's told, 'Don't worry just do as much as you can'. The class then form groups of three and are asked to build a sequence using the arm movement demonstrated and also incorporating both mirrors and canons.
>
> For the next ten minutes Maggie just watches unless a group of students approach her for advice. For example one group wish to do a roll on the floor but the floor's hard and one of the girls hits her head. Maggie suggests they try going backwards instead of going forwards so the head is not exposed. Meanwhile the teacher who is present immediately joins a group. She does most of the talking. Although I'm not near enough to hear what's said, the talk is accompanied by frequent gestures as the teacher demonstrates possible dance combinations.

This approach is not confined to secondary school teachers but seems characteristic of most classroom practitioners. In one primary school, for example, Pam, a playwright and producer, was creating a short play with a Year 5 class. Because she wished everyone to be involved, and there were only a limited number of acting parts, she told the class there was no money for scenery so they needed to use mime. The first requirement was for a row of houses. Whereas the practitioner, Pam, left the pupils to their own devices (as did Maggie in the previous example) the class teacher immediately went to one group and began to arrange them into a position, gripping the pupils by the shoulders and propelling them into their various stations while explaining, 'You can be a pair of semi-detached houses, you can be the garage on one side'. However, on a later occasion, when the task was to mime a river with a bridge, this teacher was called away for a telephone call and in his absence the children created their own mime without any difficulty and their performance was then evaluated best by the rest of the class.

Careful scaffolding is one way of managing risk taking. Maggie, the dancer, supplied various pictures of professional dancing not, as she told the pupils, for you 'to copy but for you to take ideas and make your own'. But creative practitioners also seem to appreciate that many of the reasons which determine pupils' dependency are emotional rather than cerebral. Teachers on the other hand rarely tend to attribute pupil behaviour to feelings. A recent study by Ravet (2007) looked at teachers' and parents' explanations of pupil disengagement. Most of the teachers' explanations involved deficit theories either of ability or personality or attributed disengagement to contexts outside the control of the school such as the home situation and the family background. Parents on the other hand tended to attribute lack of interest to feelings of boredom, shyness or fatigue. Creative practitioners therefore tend to work at the emotional level, particularly where fear of failure often determines pupils' response to challenges. Thus in the following episode Glynn confronted a pupil, Chris, with his tendency to be dependent on others for ideas. Having made their film the pupils were asked to include a little signature piece that would describe them as a person. They could do this by filming some object, cutting out a picture from a magazine or doing their own drawing. One pupil for example filmed himself in a football kit. Chris however chooses to copy a picture drawn by another boy. The following exchange then took place:

> *Glynn*:   This is about yourself. What does it say about you that it's a copy?
> *Chris*:   I don't know.
> *Glynn*:   Have a little think about that.

Creative practitioners appeared quick to recognize such situations where the pupils were reluctant to expose their feelings. Another boy in Year 10, Gavin, drew a picture which showed a person with half the torso submerged in smoke. He explained to Glynn that it represented his character; the visible part was the way that others saw him. Around the edge of the visible part of the picture Gavin had written words such as 'superior, scornful' while on the other side (the part that other people don't see) were the words, 'vulnerable, sensitive, and uncertain'. When the teacher arrived and is shown the picture she reacted by saying, 'That could be an eye, you could draw another eye,' whereas Glynn's response was to say, 'I think it's quite challenging to be so open about yourself. It's very courageous, well done'.

One very frequently used approach was for creative practitioners to express their own feelings as if conveying a message to pupils that talk of this kind was acceptable currency among the group. We saw earlier that in the initial encounters creative practitioners often included emotional statements about who they were. They also referred to emotions to explain reasons for their decision making. This was particularly true in situations where there was a possibility of disruption. For example in another class, admittedly a primary one but it illustrates the point, children designed a dance sequence in which they had to make a spiral. After completing the spiral they then had to undo it and move to the next sequence which was to be done in groups of four. On this particular day one girl, Melissa, left the spiral too early and ran to her next position. Realizing her error she put her hand to her mouth in horror. The teacher (shouting above the music) called out, 'Melissa, concentrate and pay attention'. But the dance teacher, this time called Alex, waited until the music was finished. There had been a lot of pushing and shoving because when the children came out of the spiral they didn't always end up on the exact spot where they were supposed to stand waiting for the next move to begin. The consequence was that when more pupils arrived they tried to take over the occupied space. This was Alex's response:

> *Alex* (turning to Melissa): I want to congratulate you. You did exactly the right thing. You went to the next spot and didn't run back into the spiral. I did something like that when I was your age and I was embarrassed so I did what you did and put my hand over my mouth. But afterwards I realized that nobody in the audience realized it was a mistake, that is until I put my hand to my mouth. They thought I was doing a solo and now then, you others (turning to address the rest of the class) Melissa has taught us something. Mistakes are going to happen. It doesn't matter. What matters is how you cope with them. So when you come out of the spiral and you find someone is in your position don't try to move him away but go to his place instead. So well done Melissa for teaching us all such an important lesson.

In this episode Alex made it clear by her own example that she understood how Melissa felt but she turned the incident to advantage by stopping the pushing and shoving which was going on when the pupils moved out of the spiral and this is a very different approach from the teacher simply telling Melissa that she was not paying attention. When these pupils were interviewed and asked, 'Is Alex like a teacher?' they all gave negative responses and said this was mainly because she didn't shout like teachers. When asked to explain further most pupils talked about this incident with Melissa. Whether it left a similar impression on the class teacher we shall never know since in a subsequent interview with Alex it was established that neither of them ever referred to the matter afterwards.

Yet another strategy to increase pupils' self-confidence and thus the capacity to cope with risk taking is to allocate responsibility while displaying great confidence that the pupils will be able to cope without mishap. For example, pupils in Glynn's group were given the task of taking the video camera around the school and filming any subject which interested them. Rather than warning the pupils directly about the cost of the equipment and how they needed to act carefully Glynn had the following conversation:

Glynn: How much do you think this particular camera cost (various guesstimates).
         Who's highest?
Chris: Me, I said £850.
Glynn: Double it.
Chris: What happens if it breaks?
Glynn: I'd cry. Now who's going to carry the camera? OK Jack's hand is up first.
         What's the most expensive part?
Jack: The camera.
Glynn: OK then hold it there (pointing to the handle) and not the tripod.

In all these episodes it's clear that creative practitioners to a greater degree than teachers foster those characteristics which go towards creating resilience. In their relationships they show care and understanding, particularly in demonstrating to pupils that they recognize the motives which sometimes cause pupils to behave badly or to refuse to cope with challenge. They show high expectations for pupils as illustrated for example in Glynn's confidence that they will be able to take the camera and do the filming or as demonstrated by the dancer, Maggie, who stood silent for 10 minutes and let the pupils create their own dance routine without interference. Creative practitioners strived hard also to build their activities around the pupils' own strengths and interests in order to increase their intrinsic motivation, as illustrated by the sequence of Glynn and the two disinterested girls. It could be argued however that the creative practitioners enjoy a privileged position. They do not need to conform to the requirements of the National Curriculum nor to the demands of the testing and targeting regime. They are, in one teacher's words, 'free to go with the flow'. Pringle (2008) acknowledges that there exists a clash of cultures. In describing the creative practitioners' mode of operation she argues that

> artists tend to define themselves in opposition to teachers or to school scenarios. They resist describing their practice as teaching. Although respecting the teaching profession, the constraints of the curriculum and the need to transmit a specific body of knowledge are seen by them as counter to their mode of pedagogy. Instead artists seek to engage the participants primarily through discussion and in exchange of ideas and experiences. In line with the co-construction learning model these artists typically identify themselves as co-learners who question and recognise their knowledge rather than as infallible experts transmitting information.

This clash between these two pedagogies, that of teacher and creative practitioner, has also been identified in the work of Thomson et al. (2006). They introduce Bernstein's (1966) notions of competence and performance pedagogies to distinguish between the different approaches of the teachers and the creative practitioners. Competence pedagogies tend to focus on the learner and what the learner has achieved so they tend to be active, creative and self-regulating. Control is usually implicit in that it tends to inhere in personalized forms of communication so that learners have a greater degree of control over what they learn and the pace and sequencing of the lessons (Hall et al., 2007). Performance models of pedagogy place the emphasis upon clearly defined outputs so that learners are expected to acquire certain skills or to construct specific texts or products in fulfilment of required outcomes. For Bernstein this requires visible practice where the sequence and pace of the lessons are controlled by the teacher and the criteria for success are made explicit. As a result there is a clear hierarchical relationship between the teacher and the pupil in contrast to the approach adopted by these successful creative practitioners where the relationship is seen as one of co-learning. Hall et al. (2007) argue that one of the reasons that creative practitioners and teachers are not able to resolve these differences is that there are few opportunities to engage in detailed discussions about what they term 'the pedagogic text'. For teachers the evaluation is primarily about whether the pupils have achieved the set criteria while for the creative practitioner its main purpose is to create possibilities for the learner's future development (Hall et al., 2007).

Even in cases where attempts were made to integrate creative practice within standard lessons rather than in the examples cited previously where most of the activities consisted of special projects outside the normal school curriculum the separation between the teacher's and the creative practitioner's role was maintained. In another secondary school for example two ecological artists, Sue and Phil, were asked to work with science teachers. In one Year 7 class the topic, Food Chains, was being investigated. The teacher chose two examples of the shift from a plant to an herbivore to carnivore and then to a predator, one on land and one on sea. For the sea example the shift was from the plankton to the seahorse and then the fish and then the shark and finally the killer whale. The creative practitioners produced a large piece of decorated hardboard and at various points cut out holes so that pupils could insert their heads. Their task consisted of face-painting various children to represent the different creatures and then recording the enactment of a particular food chain using a video camera. The teacher acted for the most part as the provider of information. She wrote down for each child several lines of dialogue of the form, 'I am the mouse; I get my energy from eating juicy caterpillars'. These descriptive food chains were then filmed with pupils reciting the teacher's chosen words. Although both the creative practitioners were ardent ecologists as well as visual artists, and might have therefore been expected to have had something to contribute to the exploration of the different parts played by these animals in the food chains, their roles remained primarily those of technicians with expertise in painting and filming.

The main purpose of describing these incidents with creative practitioners however is not to explore this clash of pedagogies and the way in which dialogue between the two groups might be better established, although this is an important issue. Rather is it to suggest that in using the principles established earlier in support of the resilient classroom these creative practitioners did no more than accomplish those things which have been identified in a group of so called expert teachers (Berliner, 2002). Like the experts identified in Berliner's expertise research these creative practitioners created a classroom where pupil exploration usually preceded formal presentation; where the pupils' questions and comments often determined the focus of classroom discourse, where there was a high proportion of pupil–pupil talk and where pupils were required to reflect critically on the procedures and methods used.

Whenever possible the creative practitioners, like expert teachers, attempted to ensure that what was to be learned was related to pupils' lives outside school. Pupils were encouraged to use a variety of means and media to communicate their ideas and tasks were structured in ways which limited the complexity involved. Furthermore higher-order thinking or flexibility of the mind was developed within the context of the whole curriculum and not taught as a discrete set of skills as part of PHSE. Finally like expert teachers these creative partners were able to develop a classroom ethos which encouraged pupils to offer speculative answers to challenging questions without being too concerned about failure.

In most schools up and down the country there exist teachers who are able to create these kinds of resilient classroom. Although limited by the pressures exerted by government reform and by the emphasis on the performance culture, they are not strangled by them. In the same way, the creative practitioners, who were not so limited by these constraints when given the opportunity to work in classrooms adopted similar practices to those which have been chronicled for expert teachers and in doing so were able to increase the motivation and the enjoyment of their students. Thus the problem confronting schools in the present political climate although difficult is not insurmountable. As recorded in other studies (Jeffrey and Woods, 2003; Galton and Macbeath, 2008) many teachers' response to the government reforms has been to become compliant while remaining unconvinced of their effectiveness. If the present increasing patterns of disenchantment exhibited by pupils are to be overcome then it requires more teachers to take more risks and follow their expert colleagues in becoming more like these creative practitioners.

Much is currently made of the importance of school leadership in fostering a successful school. But the resilience literature suggests that it is possible for groups of like-minded teachers to band together to enact reform, even when the pervading ethos of the school is unhelpful, as for example in the case of Marlbury where the rules worked against the notion of pupils taking responsibility for their behaviour as well as their learning. The 'communities of practice' described by Chris Watkins (2005) and by Stoll and Louis (2007) here in the UK and Louis and Marks (1998) in America are examples of possible ways forward. An important result of these developments is that it regenerates teachers' sense of their own professionality.

Writing recently on the Government's current preoccupation with school leadership Eric Hoyle (2008) argues that the effect of the current reforms has been to replace professionalism by managerialism. He quotes Freidson (2001), a strong advocate of the view that the idea of a profession is vital to the health of our democracies. According to Hoyle, teachers' professionality, like complementary forms in other occupations, must be strongly defended. This defence, according to Freidson should be

> aggressive in joining the attack on the pathologies that stem from material self-interests in the market place, and from the reduction of work and its products to formal procedures in bureaucracy. But it can be no less aggressive in joining the

attack on practices or professionals that compromise the integrity of the model. Only by maintaining its own integrity can it leave no doubt of its superiority over the atomistic play of self-interest or the iron cage of formal rationality.

If Freidson is correct in his analysis then it is surely time for the teaching profession to begin the fight back.

Questions for discussion

1. Do you think the original purpose of the comprehensive school – to maximize individual potential while seeking to maintain equality of opportunity – is now an outdated concept?
2. What position do you take on the issue of mixed ability versus grouping by ability?
3. How far is it possible to develop a degree of resilience in young adolescents in the current educational climate? Where would you start?

Appendix A
Details of the attitude and motivation inventories used in the study

Motivation items
Motivation questionnaires used a 5-point response scale ranging from *strongly agree* to *strongly disagree*.

Pre-test motivation items
1. I am doing well in most subjects.
2. I work hard to please my parents.
3. I am pretty confident about doing the tasks I am set.
4. I do my best to get the highest level in the SATs.
5. I try to learn as much as I can.
6. I can write really well in English.
7. I need to work hard to get to university.
8. I like to start new, more difficult work.
9. I would say that I am a really hard worker.
10. I feel proud when I get good marks.

Achievement mastery motivation: 1, 3, 5, 6, 9
Academic satisfaction motivation: 2, 4, 7, 8, 10

Post-test motivation items
1. I am doing well in most subjects.
2. I would say I mess-about a lot at school.
3. I work hard to please my parents.
4. I am pretty confident about doing the tasks I am set.

5.   Learning in school is a bit of a bore.
6.   I do my best to get the highest level in the SATs.
7.   I try to learn as much as I can.
8.   I can write really well in English.
9.   I need to work hard to get to university.
10.   I like to start new, more difficult work.
11.   I am often in trouble at school.
12.   I would say that I am a really hard worker.
13.   I don't do much homework.
14.   I feel proud when I get good marks.
15.   I don't write any more than I have to.
16.   No matter what, I always do my best.

Achievement mastery motivation: 1, 4, 7, 8, 12
Academic satisfaction motivation: 3, 6, 9, 10, 14
'Anti'-school motivation: 2, 5, 11, 13, 15, 16 (Reverse the scoring for the first five items to get 'pro'-school motivation)

Subject attitudes
Subject attitude questionnaires used a 5-point response scale ranging from *strongly agree* to *strongly disagree*.

Liking English items
1.   I like English more than any other school subject.
2.   I hate spelling tests.
3.   English is a good subject for everybody to learn.
4.   I like talking rather than writing.
5.   We are finding out new things all the time in English lessons.
6.   We should have fewer English lessons.
7.   I like trying to spell out new words.
8.   I like writing my own stories.

(Continued)

(Continued)

9.	Sometimes, English is boring.
10.	I like to listen to people who speak really well.
11.	I always look forward to English lessons.
12.	I should like to be given a dictionary as a present.
13.	Learning English makes me think better.
14.	Writing long sentences is very hard.
15.	I seem to get tired easily in English lessons.
16.	I should like to get a job where I can use all I know about English.

Reversed scoring is used for items 2, 4, 6, 9, 14 and 15.

Liking mathematics items	
1.	I like maths more than any other school subject.
2.	Now we have computers, we don't need so much maths.
3.	I like doing maths projects.
4.	We should have fewer maths lessons.
5.	I would rather work out a sum myself than use a calculator.
6.	Sometimes, maths is boring.
7.	I like to watch maths programmes on TV.
8.	I should like to get a job where I can use all I know about maths.

Reversed scoring is used for items 2, 4 and 6.

Liking science items	
1.	I like science more than any other school subject.
2.	Science is good for everybody.
3.	Too much money is spent on science.

4.   I don't like doing experiments.
5.   It is easy to find out new things in science lessons.
6.   I often do science experiments at home.
7.   In an experiment, I like finding out what happens myself.
8.   Sometimes, science is boring.
9.   School science clubs are a good idea.
10.   I like telling my teacher what I have done.
11.   I like to watch science programmes on TV.
12.   I like finding out why an experiment works.
13.   We should have fewer science lessons.
14.   Science makes me think.
15.   I am always reading science stories.
16.   I should like to be given a science kit as a present.
17.   I should like to be a scientist.

Reversed scoring is used for items 4, 8 and 13.
Item 3 is not used in computing an aggregate total.

Peer relationship items
The questionnaire used a 5-point response scale ranging from *strongly agree* to *strongly disagree*.

Peer relationship items
1.   If I don't like someone, I won't work with them.
2.   I like working with friends all the time.
3.   I like to make my point of view.
4.   I have lots of ideas to share with others.
5.   Its 'cool' not to be too smart.
6.   Others are always winding me up.

(Continued)

(Continued)

7. I keep quiet about my own ideas.
8. I have some really close friends.
9. I usually follow the others and do what they do.
10. I would say I am a popular person.

Active participation: 3, 4, 7 (reversed)
Anti-boffin sub-culture: 1, 2, 5, 9

Personality items
The questionnaire used a two point response scale of *Yes/No.*

Personality items
1. Do you like team games?
2. Do you always feel under pressure?
3. Do you like going to parties?
4. Do lots of things annoy you?
5. Would you like parachute jumping?
6. Do you find it hard to get to sleep at night because you are worrying about things?
7. Do you often feel life is very dull?
8. Can you let yourself go and enjoy yourself a lot at a lively party?
9. Do you ever feel 'just miserable' for no good reason?
10. Do you think others often say nasty things about you?
11. Do you have lots of friends to go with at school?
12. Are tour feelings rather easily hurt?
13. Do you often feel 'fed-up'?
14. Would you call yourself happy-go-lucky?

Anxiety items: 2, 4, 6, 7, 9, 10, 12, 13
Extraversion items: 1, 3, 8, 11

Working in groups items

The questionnaire used a 5-point response scale ranging from *strongly agree* to *strongly disagree*.

Working in groups items
1.   I like to share what I know with others in the group.
2.   Learning is more interesting in groups.
3.   We should help others in the group if there is a problem.
4.   If we don't all agree, we should look for common ground.
5.   Groups encourage you to work hard.
6.   I get more work done when in a group.
7.   We should all have a say in the decisions made.
8.   Group work is fun.
9.   To get a job done in the group you have to work together.
10.   You get to think more in groups.

Attitudes to co-operative working: 1, 3, 4, 7, 9
Liking group-work: items 2, 5, 6, 8, 10

Quality of group working items

The questionnaire used a 5-point response scale ranging from *always, nearly always, sometimes, only now and again,* to *never* in reply to the question *'Does this happen in your class?'*.

Quality of group working environment items
1.   We take turns when talking.
2.   There is interrupting or cutting off.
3.   We are sensitive to the needs of others.
4.   We discuss things and do not argue.
5.   We get on well together.
6.   We are well organised.

Appendix B

NFER (National Foundation of Educational Research) Conversion from Levels to Points

A typical pupil at the end of primary, Year 6 should reach Level 4 and at the end of lower secondary, Year 9, Level 5. A year's progress therefore equals 2 NFER points.

Level 3 = 21	Level 5 = 33
Level 3+ = 23	Level 5+ = 35
Level 4– = 25	Level 6– = 37
Level 4 = 27	Level 6 = 39
Level 4+ = 29	Level 6+ = 41
Level 5– = 31	

Bibliography

Adhami, M., Johnson, D. and Shayer, M. (1997) Does CAME Work? Summary report on Phase 2 of the Cognitive Acceleration in Mathematics Education, CAME, Project. In *Proceedings of the British Society for Research into Learning Mathematics Day Conference, Bristol*, 15 Nov. 1997. London: BSRLM, 26–31.

Ajegbo, K. (2007) *Diversity and Citizenship: Curriculum Review*. London: DfES.

Alexander, R. (2008) *Towards Dialogic Teaching: rethinking classroom talk* (4th edn.). Thirsk, North Yorkshine: Dialogos.

Alexander, R. (2001) *Culture and Pedagogy: International Comparisons in Primary Education*. Oxford: Blackwell.

Alexander, R. (2004) Still no pedagogy? Principle, pragmatism and compliance in primary education. *Cambridge Journal of Education*, 34(1): 7–33.

Alexander, R. (2006) *Towards Dialogic Teaching: Rethinking Classroom Talk*. York: Dialogos.

Alexander, R., Doddington, C., Gray, J., Hargreaves, L. and Kershner, R. (Eds.) (2009) The Cambridge Primary Review Research Surveys. London: Routledge.

Alexander, R., Willcocks, J. and Kinder, K. (1989) *Changing Primary Practice*. London: Falmer Press.

Anderson, L. and Burns, R. (1989) *Research in Classrooms*: The Study of teachers, teaching and instruction. Oxford: Pergamon Press.

Antony, E. (1974) The Syndrome of the Psychologically Invulnerable Child, in Anthony, E. and Koupernick, C. [Eds] *The Child in His Family: Children at Psychiatric Risk*. New York: Wiley.

Association for Science Education (ASE) (1979) *Alternatives for Science Education*. Hatfield: ASE.

Audit Commission (2002) *Getting in on the Act: Provision for Pupils with Special Educational Needs – The Natural Picture*. London: HMSO.

Baines, E., Blatchford, P. and Kutnick, P. (2003) Changes in grouping practices over primary and secondary school, *International Journal of Educational Research*, 39, 9–34.

Baker, K. (1993) *The Turbulent Years: My Life in Politics*. London: Faber & Faber.

Bantock, J. (1971) 'Towards a popular theory of education', in R. Hooper (ed.), *The Curriculum: Context, Design and Development*. London: Oliver & Boyd.

Barnard, H. (1966) *A History of English Education*. London: University of London Press.

Barnes, D. and Todd, F. (1977) *Communication and Learning in Small Groups*. London: Routledge and Kegan Paul.

Barnes, M. (2000) 'Effects of dominant and subordinate masculinities on interactions in a collaborative learning classroom', in J. Boaler (ed.), *Multiple Perspectives on Mathematics Teaching and Learning*. London: Ablex.

Barrett, G. (1986) *Starting School: An Evaluation of the Experience*. Final Report to the AMMA, CARE. Norwich: University of East Anglia.

Benn, C. and Simon, B. (1970) *Halfway-There*. Harmondsworth: Penguin.

Berliner, D. (2002) 'Learning about learning from expert teachers', *International Journal of Educational Research*, 37 (6): 1–37.

Berliner, W. (2004) 'Heaven knows why they are miserable now', *The Guardian*, April.

Bernard, B. (1991) *Fostering Resilience in Kids: Protective Factors in Family, School and Community*. San Francisco, CA: Far West Laboratory for Educational Research and Development.

Bernstein, B. (1996) Pedagogy, symbolic control and identity. New York: Rowman & Littlefield.

Blatchford, P., Kutnick, P., Macintyre, H. and Baines, E. (2001) *The Nature and Use of within-class Groupings in Secondary Schools*. Final Report to Economic and Social Research Council (ESRC). London: ESRC.

Bloom, B. (1976) *Human Characteristics and School Learning*. New York: McGraw-Hill.

Boaler, J. (2008) Promoting 'relational equity' and high mathematics achievement through an innovative mixed ability approach. *British Educational Research Journal*, 34 (2): 167–94.

Boaler, J. (1997a) When even the winners are losers: evaluating the experiences of top set students, *Journal of Curriculum Studies*, 29 (2): 165–82.

Boaler, J. (1997b) 'Setting, social class and the survival of the quickest', *British Educational Research Journal*, 23 (4): 575–95.

Boaler, J. (1997c) 'Reclaiming school mathematics: the girls fight back', *Gender and Education*, 9 (3): 285–306.

Boaler, J. (2008) 'Promoting "relational equity" and high mathematics achievement through an innovative mixed-ability approach', *British Educational Research Journal*, 34(2) 167–94.

Boaler, J., Wiliam, D. and Brown, M. (2000) 'Students' experience of ability grouping: disaffection, polarisation and the construction of failure', *British Educational Research Journal*, 26 (5): 631–48.

Bradshaw, J., Sturman, L., Vappula, V., Ager, R. and Wheater, R. (2007) *Achievement of 15-year Olds in England: PISA 2006 National Report*. Slough: NFER.

Brinton, B., Fujiki, M. and Higbee, J. (1998) 'Participation in cooperative learning activities by children with specific language impairment', *Journal of Speech, Language and Hearing Research*, 41, 1193–206.

Brofenbrenner, U. (1979) *The Ecology of Human Development*. Cambridge, MA: Harvard University Press.

Brophy, J. (1999) 'Research on motivation in education: past, present and future', in T.C. Urdan (ed.), *Advances in Motivation and Achievement, Volume 11: The Role of Context*. Stamford, CT: Jai Press.

Brown, A. (1997) 'Transforming schools into communities of thinking and learning about serious matters', *American Psychologist*, 52 (4): 399–413.

Carroll, J. (1963) 'A model for school learning', *Teachers College Record*, 64: 723–33.

Cefai, C. (2008) *Promoting Resilience in the Classroom: A Guide to Developing Pupils' Emotional and Cognitive Skills*. London: Jessica Kingsley.

Cockcroft, W.H. (1982) *Mathematics Counts*. Report of the Committee of Inquiry into the Teaching of Mathematics in Schools under the Chairmanship of Dr. W.H. Cockcroft. London: HMSO.

Cohen, E. (1994) 'Restructuring the classroom: conditions for productive small groups', *Review of Educational Research*, 64 (1) 1–35.

Cohen, J. (1988) *Power Analysis for the Behavioral Sciences*. New Jersey: Lawrence Applebaum Associates.

Cole, M., John-Steiner, V., Scribner, S. and Souberman, E. (Eds.) (1978) *Mind in Society: The Development of Higher Psychological Processes*. Cambridge, Mass: Harvard University Press.

Condly, S. (2006) 'Resilience in Children: a review of the literature with implications for education', *Urban Education*, 41 (3): 211–36.

Cooper, P. (2008) 'Series editor's foreword', in C. Cefai (ed.), *Promoting Resilience in the Classroom: A Guide to Developing Pupils' Emotional and Cognitive Skills*. London: Jessica Kingsley.

Coopersmith, S. (1967) *The Antecedents of Self-esteem*. San Francisco, CA: W.H. Freeman & Co.

Covington, M.V. (1992) *Making the Grade*. Cambridge: Cambridge University Press.

Cowie, H. and Rudduck, J. (1988) *School and Classroom Studies*. London: BP Educational Service.

Cowie, H., Smith, P., Boulton, M. and Laver, R. (1994) *Cooperation in the Multi-ethnic Classroom*. London: David Fulton.

Crowther (1959) *15 to 18: The Report of the Central Advisory Council for Education (England)*. London: HMSO.

Currie, C., Gabhainn, S.N., Godeau, E., Roberts, C., Smith, R., Currie, D., Pickett, W., Richter, M., Morgan, A. and Barnekow, V. (eds) (2008) *Inequalities in Young People's Health*. HSBC International Report from the 2005/2006 survey. World Health Organization (online). Available at: http://www.euro.who.int/assets/InformationSources/Publications/Catalogue/20080616_1

Curtis, P. (2008) 'Academies criticised for expelling 10,000', *The Guardian*, 25 June.

Dainton Report (1968) *Enquiry into the Flow of Candidates in Science and Technology into Higher Education*. London: HMSO.

Damon, W. and Phelps, E. (1989) 'Critical distinctions among three approaches to peer education', *International Journal of Educational Research*, 13 (1): 9–19.

Dawes, L., Mercer, N. and Wegerif, R. (2000) *Thinking Together: a programme of activities for developing thinking skills at Key Stage 2*. Birmingham: Questions Publishing.

Delamont, S. and Galton, M. (1986) *Inside the Secondary Classroom*. London: Routledge Kegan Paul.

Demetriou, H., Goalen, P. and Rudduck, J. (2000) 'Academic performance, transfer, transition and friendship: listening to the student voice, *International Journal of Educational Research*, 33 (4): 425–41.

Dent, R. and Cameron, R. (2003) 'Developing resilience in children who are in public care: the educational psychology perspective', *Educational Psychology in Practice*, 19 (1): 3–19.

Department for Children, Schools and Families (DCSF) (2007) *Getting Back on Track: Pupils Who Make Slow Progress in English, Mathematics and Science in Key Stage 3*. London: DCSF.

Department for Children, Schools and Families (DCSF) (2008a) *Truancy Sweeps*. Available at: http://dcsf.gov.uk/schoolattendance/truancysweeps/index.cfm.

Department for Children, Schools and Families (DCSF) (2008b) Major Reforms to School Accountability Including an End to Compulsory National Tests for Fourteen Year Olds. Available at http://dcsf.gov.uk/pns/DisplayPN.cgi?pn_id=2008.

DfEE (1998) The National Literacy Strategy: A Framework for Teaching. London: DfEE.

DfEE (2001a) Key Stage 3 National Strategy. Framework for teaching mathematics: Years 7, 8 and 9. London: DfEE publications.

DfEE (2001b) Key Stage 3 National Strategy. Framework for teaching English: Years 7, 8 and 9. London: DfEE publications.

DfEE (2001c) Key Stage 3 National Strategy. Framework for teaching science: Years 7, 8 and 9. London: DfEE publications.

Department for Education and Skills (DfES) (2003) *Raising Standards and Tackling Workload: A National Agreement*. London: DfES.

Department for Education and Skills (DfES) (2004a) *Removing the Barriers to Achievement*. London: DfES.

Department for Education and Skills (DfES) (2004b) *A National Conversation About Personalised Learning*. Nottingham: DfES.

Department for Education and Skills (DfES) (2004c) *Pedagogy and Practice: Teaching and Learning in Secondary Schools*. London: DfES.

Department for Education and Skills (DfES) (2006) *Science and Innovation Investment Framework 2004–2014: Next Steps*. London: HMSO.

Dewey, J. (1916) *Democracy and Education*. New York: Macmillan.

Doyle, W. (1983) 'Academic work', *Review of Educational Research*, 53: 159–99.

Dutch, R. and McCall, J. (1974) 'Transition to secondary: an experiment in a Scottish comprehensive school', *British Journal of Educational Psychology*, 44 (3): 282–9.

Dweck, C. (1986) 'Motivational Approaches Effecting Learning', *American Psychologist*, 41: 1040–8.

Eccles, J., Alder, T. and Meece, J. (1984) Sex differences in achievement: A test of alternate theories, *Journal of Personality and Social Psychology*, 46 (1): 26–43.

Eccles, J. and Midgley, C. (1989) 'Stage/environment fit: Developmentally appropriate classrooms for young adolescents', in R. Ames and C. Ames (eds), *Research on Motivation and Education: Goals and Cognition*. New York: Academic Press.

Edwards, A.D. (1987) 'Patterns of power and authority in classroom talk', in B. M. Mayor and A. K. Pugh, (eds) *Language, Communication and Education*. London: Routledge.

Edwards, A.D. (1980) 'Patterns of power and authority in classroom talk', in P. Woods (ed.), *Teacher Strategies: Explorations in the Sociology of the School*. London: Croom Helm.

Edwards, D. and Mercer, N. (1987) *Common Knowledge and the Development of Understanding in the Classroom*. London: Routledge.

English, E., Hargreaves, L. and Hislam, J. (2002) 'Pedagogical dilemmas in the National Literacy Strategy: primary teachers' perceptions, reflections and classroom behaviour', *Cambridge Journal of Education*, 32 (2): 276.

Entwistle, N.J. (1973) 'Personality and academic attainment', in H.J. Butcher and H.B. Pont (eds), *Educational Research in Britain, 3*. London: University of London Press.

Entwistle, N.J. (1977) 'Strategies of learning and studying: recent research findings', *British Journal of Educational Studies*, 25: 225–38.

Entwistle, N.J. and Wilson, J.D. (1977) *Degrees of Excellence: The Academic Achievement Game*. London: Hodder & Stoughton.

Eysenck, H.J. (1972) 'Personality and attainment: an application of psychological principles to educational objectives', *Higher Education*, 1: 39–52.

Eysenck, H.J. and Eysenck, S.B.G. (1969) *Personality Structure and Measurement*. London: Routledge & Kegan Paul.

Eysenck, H.J. and Eysenck, S.B.G. (1975) *Manual of the Eysenck Personality Questionnaire (Junior and Adult)*. London: Hodder & Stoughton.

Fairbrother, R. (2008) 'The validity of the Key Stage 3 science tests', *School Science Review*, 89: 107–13.

Farivar, S. and Webb, N. (1991) *Helping Behavior Activities Handbook: Cooperative Group Problem Solving in Middle School Mathematics*. Los Angeles, CA: UCLA.

Flanders, N. (1970) *Analysing Teacher Behaviour*. Reading, MA: Addison-Wesley.

Fontana, D. (1977) *Teaching and Personality*. Oxford: Basil Blackwell.

Frean, A. (2007) 'Less than half of teachers have degree in subject', *The Times*, 19 July.

Freidson, E. (2001) *Professionalism: The Third Logic*. Chicago, IL: Chicago University Press.

Gage, N. (1978) *The Scientific Basis for the Art of Teaching*. New York: Teachers College Press.

Galton, M. (1989) *Teaching in the Primary School*. London: David Fulton.

Galton, M. (2007) *Learning and Teaching in the Primary Classroom*. London: SAGE.

Galton, M. (2008) *Creative Practitioners in Schools and Classrooms*. Final Report of the Project: The Pedagogy of Creative Practitioners in Schools, University of Cambridge: Faculty of Education.

Galton, M. and MacBeath, J. (2008) *Teachers under Pressure*. London: Sage.

Galton, M. and Patrick, H. (1990) *Curriculum Provision in the Small Primary School*. London: Routledge & Kegan Paul.

Galton, M. and Willcocks, J. (eds) (1983) *Moving from the Primary School*. London: Routledge & Kegan Paul.

Galton, M. and Williamson, J. (1992) *Group work in the Primary Classroom*. London: Routledge.

Galton, M., Gray, J. and Rudduck, J. (2003) *Transfer and Transitions in the Middle Years of Schooling (7–14) Continuities and Discontinuities in Learning*. Research Report RR443. Nottingham: DfEE Publications.

Galton, M., Simon, B. and Croll, P. (1980) *Inside the Primary Classroom*. London: Routledge & Kegan Paul.

Gamoran, A. (1992) 'Is ability grouping equitable? Synthesis of research', *Educational Leadership*, 50 (1): 11–17.

Gill, B., Dunn, M. and Goddard, E. (2002) *Student Achievement in England: Results in Reading, Mathematics and Scientific Literacy among 15-year-olds from OECD PISA 2000 Study*. London: The Stationery Office.

Gillies, R. (2003) 'Structuring cooperative group work in classrooms', *International Journal of Educational Research*, 39, 35–49.

Gillies, R. (2004) 'The effects of cooperative learning on junior high school students during small group learning', *Learning and Instruction*, 14: 197–213.

Gillies, R. and Ashman, A. (eds) (2003) *Cooperative Learning: The Social and Intellectual Outcomes of Learning in Groups*. London: Routledge Falmer.

Good, T. and Brophy, J. (2002) *Looking in Classroom*. Boston, MA: Allyn & Bacon.

Gorwood, B. (1986) *School Transfer and Curriculum Continuity*. London: Croom Helm.

Goswami, U. and Bryant, P. (2007) *Children's Cognitive Development and Learning* (Primary Review Research Survey 2/1a), Cambridge: University of Cambridge Faculty of Education. Retrieved December 12, 2008 at www.primaryreview.org.uk

Hamer, J. (2001) *Key Stage 3 Grouping and Statutory Assessment*. London: QCA.

Hall, C., Thomson, P. and Russell, L. (2007) 'Teaching like artists: the pedagogic identities and practices of artists in schools', *British Journal of Sociology of Education*, 28 (5): 605–19.

Hargreaves, A. and Tickle, L. (eds) (1980) *Middle Schools: Origins, Ideology and Practice*. London: Harper & Row.

Hargreaves, D.H. (1967) *Social Relations in the Secondary School*. London: Routledge & Kegan Paul.

Hargreaves, D.H. (1982) *The Challenge for the Comprehensive School*. London: Routledge & Kegan Paul.

Hargreaves, L. and Galton, M. (2002) *Transfer from the Primary Classroom: 20 years on*. London: Routledge Falmer.

Hargreaves, L., Cunningham, M., Everton, T., Hansen, A., Hopper, B., McIntyre, D., Oliver, C., Pell, T., Rouse, M. and Turner, P. (2007) *The Status of Teachers and the Teaching Profession: Views from Inside and Outside the Profession.* Evidence Base for the Final Report of the Teacher Status Project. Research Report 831B. London: DfES.

Hattie, J. (2005) 'The paradox of reducing class size and improving learning outcomes', *International Journal of Educational Research,* 43 (6): 387–425.

Haylock, D. (2001) *Mathematics Explained for Primary Teachers,* 2nd edn. London: Paul Chapman Publishing.

Hirst, P.H. (1968) 'The Contribution of Philosophy to the Study of the Curriculum', in J.F. Kerr (ed.), *Changing the Curriculum.* London: University of London Press, pp. 39–62.

Holt, J. (1984) *How Children Fail.* London: Penguin.

Hope, C. (2008) 'Metropolitan police chief calls for an end to targets imposed by the government', *Daily Telegraph,* 19 June.

House of Commons (2008a) *Testing and Assessment. Volume I.* Report together with formal minutes of the House of Commons Children, Schools and Families Committee. HC Paper 169-I. London: The Stationery Office.

House of Commons (2008b) *Testing and Assessment. Volume II.* Oral and written evidence to the House of Commons Children, Schools and Families Committee. HC Paper 169-II. London: The Stationery Office.

House of Lords (2006) *Science Teaching in Schools.* Report with evidence of the House of Lords Science and Technology Committee. HL Paper 257. London: The Stationery Office.

House of Lords (2007) *Science Teaching in Schools: Follow-up.* A Report with evidence of the House of Lords Science and Technology Committee. HL Paper 167. London: The Stationery Office.

Howe, C. and Mercer, N. (2007) *Children's Society Development Peer Interaction and Classroom Learning* (Primary Review Research Survey 2/1b), Cambridge: University of Cambridge, Faculty of Education. Retrieved December 12, 2008 at www.primaryreview.org.uk

Hoyle, E. (2008) 'Changing perceptions of teaching as a profession: personal reflection', in D. Johnson and R. Maclean (eds) *Teaching, Professionalization, Development and Leadership.* Berlin: Springer.

Ireson, J. and Hallam, S. (2001) *Ability Grouping in Education,* London: Sage Publications.

Ireson, J., Hallam, S., Hack, S., Clark, H. and Plewis, I. (2002) 'Ability grouping in English secondary schools: Effects on attainment in English, mathematics and science', *Educational Research and Evaluation,* 8 (2): 299 318.

Ireson, J., Hallam, S. and Hurley, C. (2005) 'What are the effects of ability grouping on GCSE attainment?', *British Educational Research Journal,* 31 (3): 443–58.

Ivinson, G. and Murphy, P. (2006) 'Boys don't write romance', in M. Arnot and M. Mac an Ghaill (eds), *The Routledge Falmer Reader in Gender and Education.* London: Routledge Falmer.

Jeffrey, B. and Woods, P. (2003) *The Creative School: A Framework for Success, Quality and Effectiveness.* London: Routledge Falmer.

Johnson, D. and Johnson, F. (2000) *Joining Together: Group Theory and Group Skills.* Boston, MA: Allyn & Bacon.

Joncas, M. (2008) 'TIMMS 2007 sampling weights and participation rates', in J.F. Olson, M.O. Martin and I.V. Mullis (eds), *TIMMS 2007 Technical Report.* Boston, MA: Boston College.

Kagan, S. (1988) *Cooperative Learning: Resources for teachers.* Riverside, CA: University of California Press.

Kelly, A. (ed.) (1981) *The Missing Half-girls and Science Education.* Manchester: Manchester University Press.

Kelly, A. (ed.) (1987) *Science for Girls?* Milton Keynes: Open University Press.

Kelly, A., Whyte, J. and Smail, B. (1987) 'Girls into science and technology: Final Report', in A. Kelly (ed.) *Science for Girls?* Milton Keynes: Open University Press. pp. 100–12.

Kinchin, I. (2004) 'Is teacher innovation on the verge of extinction?', *School Science Review,* 86: 315.

Kingsley-Mills, C., McNamara, S. and Woodward, L. (1992) *Out from Behind the Desk: A Practical Guide to Group Work Skills and Processes.* Glenfield: Leicestershire County Council Publications.

Kulik, J. and Kulik, C. (1992) 'Meta-analytic findings on grouping programs', *Gifted Child Quarterly*, 36: 73–7.

Kutnick, P., Hodgkinson, S., Sebba, J., Humphreys, S., Galton, M. Steward, S., Blatchford, P. and Bains, E. (2007) *Pupil Grouping Strategies and Practice at Key Stage 2 and 3*. Research Report 796, Nottingham: DfES Publications.

Kutnick, P. and Mason, I. (1998) 'Social life in classrooms: towards a relational concept of social skills for use in classrooms', in A. Campbell and S. Muncer (eds), *The Social Child*. Hove: The Psychology Press.

Kutnick, P., Blatchford, P. and Baines, E. (2002) 'Pupil groupings in primary school classrooms: sites for learning and social pedagogy?', *British Educational Research Journal*, 28 (2): 189–208.

Kutnick, P., Blatchford, P., Clark, H., MacIntyre, H. and Baines, E. (2005a) 'Teachers' understandings of the relationship between within-class (pupil) grouping and learning in secondary schools', *Educational Research*, 47 (1): 1–24.

Kutnick, P., Hodgkinson, S., Sebba, J., Humphreys, S., Galton, M., Steward, S., Blatchford, P. and Baines, E. (2006) *Pupil Grouping Strategies and Practices at Key Stage 2 and 3: Case studies of 24 Schools in England*. London: DfES.

Kutnick, P., Sebba, J., Blatchford, P., Galton, M. and Thorp, J. with MacIntyre, H. and Berdondini, L. (2005b) *The Effects of Pupil Grouping: Literature Review*. Research Report 688. Nottingham: DfES Publications.

Lacey, C. (1970) *Hightown Grammar School*. Manchester: Manchester University Press.

Lahelma, E. and Gordon, T. (1997) 'First day in secondary school: learning to be a "professional pupil"', *Educational Research and Evaluation*, 3 (2):119–39.

Lawrence, D. (1981) 'The development of self-esteem questionnaire', *British Journal of Educational Psychology*, 51: 245–51.

Lawton, D. (1975) *Class, Culture and the Curriculum*. London: Routledge & Kegan Paul.

Light, P., Buckingham, N. and Robbins, A. H. (1979) The conservation task as an interactional setting. *British Journal of Educational Psychology*, 49, 304–310.

Lou, Y., Abrami, P., Spence, J., Poulsen, C., Chambers, B. and d'Apollonia, S. (1996) 'Within class groupings: a meta analysis', *Review of Educational Research*, 66 (4): 423–58.

Louis, K. and Marks, H. (1998) 'Does professional community affect the classroom? Teachers' work and student experiences in restructured schools', *American Journal of Education*, 106 (40): 532–75.

MacBeath, J. and Galton, M., with Steward, S., MacBeath, A. and Page, C. (2006) *The Cost of Inclusion: A Report Commissioned by the National Union of Teachers Concerning Inclusion in Schools*. London: NUT and Cambridge: Faculty of Education.

MacBeath, J. and Galton, M. with Steward, S., Page, C. and Edwards, J. (2004) *A Life in Secondary Teaching: Finding Time for Learning*. Report for the National Union of Teachers. Cambridge: Faculty of Education, University of Cambridge.

MacBeath, J., Gray, J., Cullen, J., Frost, D., Steward, S. and Swaffield, S. (2007) *Schools on the Edge: Responding to Challenging Circumstances*. London: Paul Chapman.

Mansell, W. (2008a) 'Pass mark for GCSE is forced down', *Times Educational Supplement*, 24 October.

Mansell, W. (2008b) 'England joins the elite for maths and science', *Times Educational Supplement*, 12 December.

Marsh, H. (1989) 'Age and Sex Effects in Mutiple Dimensions of Self-concept: Pre-adolescence to early adulthood', *Journal of Educational Psychology*, 81: 417–30.

Martin, M.O., Mullis, I.V.S., Gonzalez, E.J. and Chrostowski, M.J. (2004) *TIMSS 2003 International Science Report*. Boston, MA: TIMSS and PIRLS International Study Centre, Lynch School of Education, Boston College.

Martin, M.O., Mullis, I.V.S. and Foy, P. (2008) *TIMMS 2007 International Science Report*. Boston, MA: Boston College.

Matthews, B. (2004) 'Promoting emotional literacy, equity and interest in KS3 science lessons for 11–14 year olds: the "Improving Science and Emotional Development Project"', *Journal of Science Education, 26* (3): 281–308.

Mayall, B. (2007) *Children's Lives Outside School and their Educational Impact*. Primary Review Research Survey 8/1. Cambridge: Primary Review. Also available at www.primaryreview.org.uk.

Mayer, C. (2008) 'Britain's mean streets', *Time*, 26 March.

Measor, L. and Woods, P. (1984) *Changing Schools: Pupils Perspectives on Transfer to a Comprehensive*. Milton Keynes: Open University Press.

Mercer, N. (1995) *The Guided Construction of Knowlegde: Talk Amongst Teachers and Learners*. Clevedon: Multilingual Matters.

Mercer, N. (2000) *Words and Minds: How We Use Language to Think Together*. London: Routledge.

Mercer, N., Dawes, L., Wegerif, R. and Sams, C. (2004) Reasoning as a scientist: ways of helping children to use language to learn science. *British Educational Research Journal*, 30(3), 359–377.

Mercer, N. and Littleton, K. (2007) *Dialogue and the Development of Children's Thinking: A Sociocultural Approach*. London & New York: Routledge.

Millar, R., Leach, J., Osborne, J. and Ratcliffe, M. (2003) 'Towards evidence-based practice: using diagnostic assessment to enhance learning', *Teaching and Learning Research Briefing*, 1 (June). Available at: http://www.tlrp.org.

Miller, C. (1986) 'Puberty and person-environment fit in the classroom', in P. Lee [Chair] *Decision Making Fit at Early Adolescence: A Developmental Perspective*. An American Educational Research Association (AERA) Symposium, San Francisco, April.

Morrison, L. and Matthews, B. (2006) How Pupils Can be Helped to Develop Socially and Emotionally in Science Lessons. Pastoral Care, March 2006.

Mortimore, P., Sammons, P., Stoll, L.D. and Ecob, R. (1988) *School Matters: The Junior Years*. Wells: Open Books.

Mroz, M., Smith, F. and Hardman, F. (2000) 'The discourse of the literacy hour', *Cambridge Journal of Education*, 30 (3) 379–90.

Mullis, I.V.S., Martin, M.O. and Foy, P. (2005) *TIMSS 2003 International Report on Achievement in the Mathematical Cognitive Domains*. Boston, MA: TIMSS and PIRLS International Study Centre, Lynch School of Education, Boston College.

Mullis, I.V.S., Martin, M.O. and Foy, P. (2008) *TIMSS 2008 International Mathematics Report*. Boston, MA: TIMSS and PIRLS International Study Centre, Lynch School of Education, Boston College.

Mullis, I.V.S., Martin, M.O., Gonzalez, E.J. and Chrostowski, M.J. (2004) *TIMSS 2007 International Mathematics Report*. Boston, MA: TIMSS and PIRLS International Study Centre, Lynch School of Education, Boston College.

Mullis, I.V.S., Martin, M.O., Kennedy, A.M. and Foy, P. (2007) *PIRLS 2007 International Report, IEA'S Progress in International Reading Literacy in Primary Schools in 40 Countries*. Boston, MA: TIMSS and PIRLS International Study Centre, Lynch School of Education, Boston College.

Murphy, P. and Gipps, C. (1996) *Equity in the Classroom: Towards Effective Pedagogy for Girls and Boys*. London, The Falmer Press in association with UNESCO Publishing.

Musgrove, P.H. (1968) 'The contribution of sociology to the study of the curriculum', in J.F. Kerr (ed.), *Changing the Curriculum*. London: University of London Press. pp. 79–95.

Nardi, E. and Steward, S. (2003) 'Is mathematics T.I.R.E.D.? A profile of quiet disaffection in the secondary mathematics classroom', *British Educational Research Journal*, 29 (3): 345–68.

National Union of Teachers (NUT) (2006) Memorandum by the National Union of Teachers. In *Science Teaching in Schools. Report with Evidence of the House of Lords Science and Technology Committee*. HLPaper 257 (Written evidence pp. 81–3). London: The Stationery Office.

New Vision Group (2008) *Combating disadvantage and the academies programme,* London: The New Vision Group.

Noddings, N. (1992) *The Challenge to Schools,* New York: Teachers' College Press.

Noddings, N. (2005) 'What does it mean to educate the whole child?', *Educational Leadership* (September): 8–13.

North Yorkshire County Council in conjunction with Dialogos (2006) *Talk for Learning: Teaching and Learning through Dialogue* (DVD/CD pack).

Ofsted (1998) *Secondary Education 1993–7: A Review of Secondary Schools in England*. London: The Stationery Office.

Ofsted (2004) *Special Educational Needs and Disability: Towards Inclusive Schools*. London: Ofsted.

Ofsted (2005) *Managing Pupil Behaviour*. London: Ofsted.

Ofsted (2006) *Creative Partnerships: Initiative and Impact*. London: Ofsted.

Ofsted (2008) *Success in Science* Available at: http://www.ofsted.gov.uk/assets/Internet_Content/Shared_Content/Files/2008/june/sucini.doc.

Opportunity '2000' (1996) *How Employers Can Attract Girls into Science Education.* Available at: http://www.lboro.ac.uk/orgs/opp2000/chap3.htm.

Organization for Economic Cooperation and Development (OECD) (2004a) *Messages from PISA 2000.* Paris: OECD.

Organization for Economic Cooperation and Development (OECD) (2004b) *Learning for Tomorrow's World: First Results from PISA 2000.* Paris: OECD.

Organization for Economic Cooperation and Development (OECD) (2007) *PISA 2006. Science Competencies for Tomorrow's World Volume 1: Analysis.* Paris: OECD.

Osborne, J., Erduran, S., Simon, S. and Monk, M. (2001) 'Enhancing the quality of argument in school science', *School Science Review,* 82 (301): 63–70.

Osler, A. and Starkey H. (2005) *Changing Citizenship: Democracy and Inclusion in Education.* Maidenhead: Open University Press.

Oversby, J. (2006) Memorandum by Dr. John Oversby. In *Science Teaching in Schools, Report with Evidence of the House of Lords Science and Technology Committee.* HL Paper 257 (Written evidence, pp. 188–91). London: The Stationery Office.

Ozolins, U. (1979) Lawton's refutation of a working class curriculum', *Melbourne Working Papers,* University of Melbourne.

Palincsar, A. and Herrenkohl, L. (1999) 'Designing collaborative contexts: lessons from three research programs', in A. O'Donnell and A. King (eds), *Cognitive Perspectives on Peer Learning.* Mahwah, NJ: Lawrence Erlbaum Associates.

Paton, G. (2008) 'Four-year degrees for weak students', *Daily Telegraph,* 12 June.

Pedley, R. (1963) *The Comprehensive School.* Hamondsworth: Penguin.

Pell, T., Galton, M., Steward, S., Page, C. and Hargreaves, L. (2007) 'Group work at Key Stage 3: solving an attitudinal crisis among young adolescents?', *Research Papers in Education,* 22 (3): 309–32.

Pollard, A. (1985) *The Social World of the Primary Classroom.* London: Holt, Rinehart & Winston.

Pringle, E. (2008) *Artists' Perspectives.* Provocation stimulus papers for Implementing Creative Learning. An Investigative Seminar for Creative Partnerships, 13 February, London.

Putnam, J., Markovchick, K., Johnson, D. and Johnson, R. (1996) 'Cooperative learning and peer acceptance of pupils with learning disabilities', *Journal of Social Psychology,* 136: 741–52.

Raney, K. (2003) *Art in Question.* London: Continuum.

Ravet, J. (2007) 'Making sense of disengagement in the primary classroom: a study of pupil, teacher and parent perceptions', *Research Papers in Education,* 22 (3): 333–62.

Rees, P. and Bailey, K. (2003) 'Positive exceptions: learning from students who beat the odds', *Educational and Child Psychology,* 20 (4): 21–49.

Resolution (2008) *High Court Judge Warning on Family Breakdown,* News Release 5 April. Available at: http://www.familyand parenting.org/inthePress.

Reznitskaya, A., Kuo, L., Clark, A., Miller, B., Jadallah, M., Anderson, R. and Nguyen-Jahiel, K. (2009) Collabrative reasoning: a dialogic approach to group discussions. *Cambridge Journal of Education,* 39(1), 29–48.

Rogers, C. (1994) 'A common basis for success', in P. Kutnick and C. Rogers (eds), *Groups in Schools.* London: Cassell. pp.144–64.

Rosenshine, B. (1979) 'Content, Time and Direct Instruction', in P. Peterson and H. Walberg (eds), *Research on Teaching Concepts: Findings and Implications.* Berkeley, CA: McCutchan.

Rosenshine, B., Meister, C. and Chapman, S. (1996) 'Teaching students to generate questions: a review of intervention studies', *Review of Educational Research,* 66 (2): 181–221.

Royal Society (RS) (2007) *The UK's Science and Mathematics Teaching Workforce: A 'State of the Nation' Report, 2007.* London: RS.

Royal Society of Chemistry (RSC) (2008a) *The Five-decade Challenge: A Wake Up Call for UK Science Education?* London: RSC.

Royal Society of Chemistry (RSC) (2008b) Downing Street Demands Reversal of Catastrophic Decline in School Science Exam Standards. Press Release, 27 November, Available at: http://www.rsc.org/AboutUs/News/PressReleases/2008/November10Petition.asp.

Rudduck, J. (2003) 'Managing institutional and personal transitions: developing the work in schools', In M. Galton, J. Gray and J. Rudduck (eds), *Transfer and Transitions in the Middle Years of Schooling (7–14): Continuities and Discontinuities in Learning*. London: DfES. (pp. 75–102).

Rudduck, J. and Flutter, J. (2004) *How to Improve Your School: Giving Pupils a Voice*. London: Continuum.

Rudduck, J. Chaplin, R. and Wallace, G. (1996) *School Improvement: What Can Pupils Tell Us?* London: David Fulton.

Ruddock, G., Sturman, I., Schagen, I., Styles, B., Gnaldi, M. and Vappula, H. (2004) *Where England stands in the trends in international science and mathematics study (TIMSS) 2003*. National Report for England for the DfES. Slough: National Foundation for Educational Research.

Rutter, M. (1993) 'Psychosocial resilience and protective mechanisms', in J. Rolf, A. Masten, D. Cicchetti, K. Nüchterlein and S. Weintraub (eds), *Risk and Protective Factors in Development of Psychopathology*. New York: Cambridge University Press.

Schools Council (1972) *Education in the Middle Years*. Working paper No 2. London: Evans-Methuen.

Sharan, Y. and Sharan, S. (1992) *Expanding Cooperative Learning through Group Investigation*. New York: Teachers' College Press.

Shayer, M. (2008) Teenagers' Learning 'dumbed down'. *BBC News* (online). Available at: http://news.bbc.co.uk/l/hi/education/7692843.stm.

Shayer, M. (2006) Children are falling behind in maths and science. *ESRC The Edge*. 21 (March), 28.

Shayer, M. and Adey, P. (1981) *Towards a Science of Science Teaching*. London: Heinemann.

Simon, B. (1981) 'Why no pedagogy in England?', in B. Simon and W. Taylor (eds), *Education in the Eighties: The Central Issues*. London: Batsford. pp. 124–45.

Sinclair, J. and Coulthard, J. (1975) *Towards an Analysis of Discourse: The English Used by Teachers and Pupils*. London: Oxford University Press.

Slavin, R. (1983) 'When does cooperative learning increase student motivation?', *Psychological Bulletin*, 94 (3): 429–45.

Slavin, R. (1987) 'Ability grouping and student achievement in elementary schools: a best evidence synthesis', *Review of Educational Research*, 57: 293–336.

Slavin, R. (1990) 'Achievement effects of ability grouping in secondary schools: a best evidence synthesis', *Review of Educational Research*, 60 (3): 471–99.

Slavin, R. (1995) *Cooperative Learning*. Boston, MA: Allyn & Bacon.

Smith, D. (2006) *School Experience and Delinquency at Ages 13 to 16*. University of Edinburgh.

Smith, F., Hardman, F., Wall, K. and Mroz, M. (2004) 'Interactive whole-class teaching in the national literacy and numeracy strategies', *British Educational Research Journal*, 30 (3): 395–412.

Smith, L. (1996) 'The social construction of rational understanding', in A. Tryphon and J. Vonèche (eds), *Piaget-Vygotsky: The Social Genesis of Thought*. Psychology Press.

Spelman, B. (1979) *Pupil Adaptation to Secondary School*. Belfast: Northern Ireland Council for Educational Research.

Stoll, L. and Louis, K. (eds) (2007) *Professional Learning Communities: Divergence, Depth and Difficulties*. Maidenhead: Open University Press.

Stoll, L., Stobart, G., Martin, S., Freeman, S., Freedman, E., Sammons, P. and Smees, R. (2003) *Preparing for Change: Evaluation of the Implementation of the Key Stage 3 Pilot Strategy*. London: DfES.

Talk for Learning: teaching and learning through dialogue (DVD/CD pack), North Yorkshire County Council in conjunction with Dialogos, July 2006, ISBN 978-0-9546943-4-0 http: www.robin alexander.org.uk/dialogos.htm#TDT mike.smit@northyorks.gov.uk.

Terwel, J. (2003) 'Cooperative learning in secondary education: a curriculum perspective', in R. Gilles and A. Ashman (eds), *Cooperative Learning: The Social and Intellectual Outcomes of Learn in Groups*. London: Routledge Falmer.

Tharp, R. and Gallimore, R. (1988) *Rousing Young Minds to Life: Teaching, Learning and Schooling in Social Context*. Cambridge: Cambridge University Press.

Thompson, P., Hall, C. and Russell, L. (2006) An arts project failed, censored or …? A critical incident approach to artist-school partnerships, *Changing English*, 13(1): 29–44.

Tomlinson, S. (2005) *Education in a Post-welfare Society*. Maidenhead: Open University Press.

Vygotsky, L.S. (1934/1986) 'An experimental study of the development of concepts', in A. Kozulin (ed.), *Thought and Language*. Cambridge, MA: MIT Press.

Vygotsky, L. (1935/1978) 'Interaction between learning and development', in M. Cole, V. John-Steiner, S. Scribner and E. Souberman (eds), *Vygotsky, Mind in Society: The Development of Higher Mental Processes*. Cambridge, MA: Harvard University Press.

Warrington, M. and Younger, M. (2006) *Raising Boys' Achievement in Primary Schools: Towards an Holistic Approach*. Maidenhead: Open University Press.

Watkins, C. (2003) *Learning: A Sense-makers Guide*. London: Institute of Education for Association of Teachers and Lecturers (ATL).

Watkins, C. (2005) *Classrooms as Learning Communities: What's in It for Schools?* London: Routledge.

Watts, J. (ed.) (1977) *The Countesthorpe Experience*. London: Allen & Unwin.

Webb, N. (1985) 'Student interaction and learning in small groups: A research summary', in R. Slavin, S. Sharan, S. Kagan, S. Hertz-Lazarowitz, N. Webb, and R. Schmuck (eds), *Learning to Cooperate, Cooperating to Learn*. New York: Plenum Press. 147–72.

Webb, N. (1989) 'Peer interaction and learning in small groups', *International Journal of Educational Research*, 13: 21–39.

Webb, N. and Farivar, S. (1994) 'Promoting helping behavior in cooperative small groups in middle school mathematics', *American Educational Research Journal*, 31: 369–95.

Webb, R. and Vulliamy, G. (2006) *Coming Full Circle? The Impact of New Labour's Education Policies on Primary School Teachers' Work*. London: Association of Teachers and Lecturers (ATL).

Webb, N. and Mastergeorge, A. (2003) 'Promoting effective helping behaviour in peer directed groups', *International Journal of Educational Research*, 39 (1–2): 79–97.

Webb, N., Baxter, G. and Thompson, L. (1997) 'Teachers' grouping practices in 5th grade science classrooms', *The Elementary School Journal*, 98 (2): 91–113.

Webb, N., Franke, M.L., Ing, M., Chan, A., Tondra, D., Freund, D. and Battey, D. (2008) 'The role of teacher instructional practices in student collaboration', *Contemporary Educational Psychology*, 33: 360–81.

Wedell, K. (2005) 'Dilemmas in the quest for inclusion', *British Journal of Special Education*, 32 (1): 3–11.

Werner, E. (1990) 'Protective factors and individual resilience', in S. Meisels (ed.), *Handbook of Early Childhood Intervention*. Cambridge: Cambridge University Press.

Werner, E. and Smith, R. (1992) *Overcoming the Odds: High-risk Children from Birth to Adulthood*. New York: Cornell University Press.

Wikipedia (2008) *Ernest Rutherford* (online). Available at: http://en.wikipedia.org/wiki/Ernest_Rutherford (accessed 16 April 2008).

Wilkinson, J. and Canter, S. (1982) *Social Skills Training Manual: Assessment, Programme, Design and Management of Training*. Chichester: John Wiley & Sons.

Wiliam, D. and Bartholomew, H. (2004) 'It's not the school but which set you're in that matters: the influence of ability grouping practices on student progress in mathematics', *British Educational Research Journal*, 30 (2): 279–94.

Willms, J.D. (2003) *Student engagement at school: A sense of belonging and participation. Results from PISA 2000*. Paris: OECD Publishing.

Wood, D. (1998) *How Children Think and Learn*. Oxford: Blackwell.

Youngman, M. (1978) 'Six reactions to school transfer', *British Journal of Educational Psychology*, 48: 280–89.

Youngman, M. and Lunzer, E. (1977) *Adjustment to Secondary School*. Nottingham: School of Education.

Index